Rara!

*The publisher gratefully acknowledges
the generous contribution to this book
provided by the General Endowment
Fund of the Associates of the
University of California Press.*

Elizabeth McAlister

Rara!

Vodou, Power, and Performance in Haiti and Its Diaspora

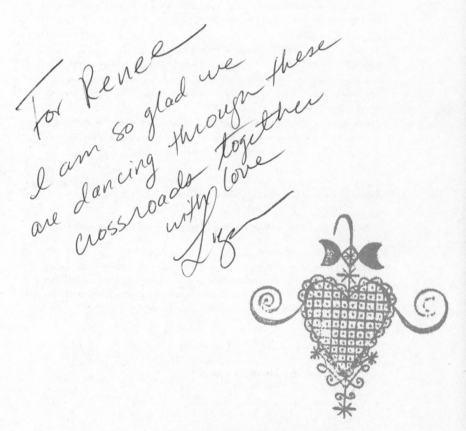

For Renee
I am so glad we
are dancing through these
crossroads together
with love
Liz

University of California Press
Berkeley   Los Angeles   London

University of California Press
Berkeley and Los Angeles, California

University of California Press, Ltd.
London, England

Grateful acknowledgment is made for permission to reuse material from the author's essay
" 'The Jew' in the Haitian Imagination: Premodern Anti-Judaism in the Postmodern
Caribbean," in *Black Zion: African American Religious Encounters with Judaism*, edited by
Yvonne Chireau and Nathaniel Deutsch, copyright © 2000 by Oxford University Press, Inc.
Used by permission of Oxford University Press, Inc.

Thanks also for use of the following CD recordings:
"Notre Dame de 7 Douleurs," "Cemetery at Bizoton," and "Carrefour de Fort" ["Kalfou"]
from the recording entitled *Caribbean Revels: Haitian Rara and Dominican Gaga,*
Smithsonian Folkways 40402, provided courtesy of Smithsonian Folkways Recordings.
© 1991. Used by Permission.
"Grosè Bagay sa, Mwen Pa Kapab Ankò" and "Guantanamo M'Rive" from the recording
entitled *Rhythms of Rapture: Sacred Musics of Haitian Vodou,* Smithsonian Folkways
40464, provided courtesy of Smithsonian Folkways Recordings. © 1995. Used by
Permission.

Library of Congress Cataloging-in-Publication Data

McAlister, Elizabeth A.
    Rara! : vodou, power, and performance in Haiti and its diaspora / Elizabeth McAlister.
    p. cm.
    Includes bibliographical references, discography, and index.
    ISBN 0-520-22822-7 (cloth : alk. paper)—ISBN 0-520-22823-5 (paper : alk. paper)
    1. Rara Festival—Songs and music—History and criticism. 2. Voodoo music—Haiti—
History and criticism. 3. Folk music—Haiti—History and criticism. 4. Folk songs, Creole—
Haiti—History and criticism. 5. Haiti—Social life and customs—20th century. 6. Haiti—
Social conditions—1971–   . I. Title.
    ML3565 .M384 2002
    394.265'96897294—dc21   2001005016

Manufactured in the United States of America

11 10 09 08 07 06 05 04 03 02
10 9 8 7 6 5 4 3 2 1

The paper used in this publication meets the minimum requirements of ANSI/NISO Z39.48–1992
(R 1997) (*Permanence of Paper*).

*For **Lovely** and **Julien**. This is where Mama was dancing, getting ready for you.*

*And for **Phenel**, wherever you are. You saved me in the streets of Port-au-Prince. I wish I could have saved you from the streets of East Saint Louis.*

To get anywhere in life you have
to follow a road. . . . To make
anything happen, you have to walk
through the crossroads.

Moris Moriset,
president of Rara Ti-Malis Kache

Contents

List of Illustrations **xi**

Acknowledgments **xiii**

Guide to the Compact Disc Rara! **xv**

Introducing Rara **1**

1 Work and Play, Pleasure and
  Performance **25**

2 Vulgarity and the Politics of the Small
  Man **59**

3 Mystical Work: Spirits on Parade **85**

4 Rara and "the Jew": Premodern Anti-
  Judaism in Postmodern Haiti **113**

5 Rara as Popular Army: Hierarchy,
  Militarism, and Warfare **135**

6 Voices under Domination: Rara and
  the Politics of Insecurity **159**

7 Rara in New York City: Transnational
  Popular Culture **183**

*Appendix: Chronology of Political
Events, 1990–1995, Annotated with
Transnational Rara Band Activity* **209**

Glossary **213**

Notes **217**

Sources **237**

Index **249**

Illustrations

1   Rara *kolonèl* in the Artibonite set off with whips in hand *xx*

2   A Rara queen sings into a swoon *24*

3   Rara musicians play *banbou*, plastic *vaksin,* and metal *konè* *38*

4   *Majò jon* pose in sequined costumes *53*

5   Queens hitch up their skirts and dance *58*

6   Young Rara kings and a queen dance for the ancestors at a tomb *84*

7   Rara *kolonèl* use a bonfire to mystically heat up the band *94*

8   A country Rara in full swing *112*

9   A stuffed "Jew" sits waiting to be burned *115*

10   Rara officers pose with batons *134*

11   Raraman poses in distinct costume from the Artibonite *149*

12   An old-style *makout* and a coup-era military police *158*

13   A pro-Duvalier Rara demonstration *164*

14   Rara feels like home in Prospect Park, Brooklyn *182*

15   Rara *kolonèl* directs the band with whip and whistle *197*

Acknowledgments

Many Rara bands received us and played for us. I thank these bands who took us in and invited us to "walk through the crossroads" with them, especially Ti-Malis in Léogâne, Rara Brilliant Soleil in Léogâne, Rara Nou Vodoule in Port-au-Prince, La Belle Fraîcheur de l'Anglade in Fermathe, Mande Gran Moun in Darbonne, Rara La Fleur Ginen in Bel Air, Rara Inorab Kapab in Cité Soleil, and Rara Ya Seizi in Verettes. I also thank the New York City Rara bands Rara Djakout and Neg Gran Bwa, and all their regular members.

There is no way I could have gotten along in Haiti without the help and support of a great many people whose generosity surpassed even the warm hospitality Haiti is known for. I thank Jacques Bartoli, Boukman Eksperyans, Joelle Destouches, Nori and Tom at the Hôpital St. Croix, Ira Lowenthal, Richard A. Morse, Jean-Paul Poirier and Djimi at Pi Rèd, Dieupè Peristyl, Papa Mondy Jean, Eleanor Snair at the Haitian-American Institute, and Fathers Antoine Adrien and Jean-Yves Urfie. My research team, which makes its presence felt throughout these pages, made the work possible: I am indebted to Blanc Bazlair, Phenel Colastin, and Chantal Regnault.

It was my colleague at Yale, David Hilary Brown, who first suggested that I choose the Rara celebrations in Prospect Park as a research topic; he remained a valuable advisor throughout. I must also thank Bob Lamothe, who taught me to speak Haitian Kreyòl at Yale University. Gage Averill enabled me to go to Haiti for the first season of research when he shared a travel grant and encouraged me to join him in the Raras in Léogâne. Jon Butler led a stimulating research seminar at Yale, during which I outlined the topic for the first time. John F. Szwed, who knew of Rara long before I did, steered me through the West Indian literature. Hazel V. Carby helped me to link the anthropological literature to contemporary cultural studies and deepened my understanding of race and racisms. James C. Scott, himself once deported from Duvalier's Haiti, brainstormed with me about the problems of expressive performance under repressive conditions.

I am grateful to a number of other scholars who have helped me to think about Rara in conversation or correspondence: Rachel Beauvoir-Dominique, Judith Bettelheim, Karen McCarthy Brown, Carolle Charles, Rénald Clerismé,

Donald Cosentino, Henrietta Cosentino, Harold Courlander, Leslie Desmangles, Georges Fouron, Bunseiki Fu-Kiau, Verna Gillis, Paul Gilroy, Henry Goldschmidt, Leon-François Hoffmann, Laennec Hurbon, George Lipsitz, Larry Mamiya, Cathy Maternowska, Daisann McLane, Patricia Pessar, Bernice Johnson Reagon, Karen Richman, Tricia Rose, Thérèsè Roumer, Nina Glick Schiller, Nina Schnall, Robert Farris Thompson, Betsy Traube, Rolph Trouillot, David Yih, Dolores Yonker, Jeremy Zwelling, and also Deborah Dash Moore and my fellow "Creoles" at the Pew Program for Young Scholars in American Religion: Ava Chamberlain, Tracy Fessenden, Kate Joyce, Laura Levitt, Leonard Norman Primiano, and Jennifer Rycenga. I am very grateful to Bob Corbett and the many members of the Corbett listserv on Haiti. The constant exchange of information and conversation for the past seven years in this virtual Haitian diaspora—with people whom I know and people I do not know—has been invaluable. Thanks also to my student assistants, especially Mathew Mulvey and Brandon Dotson, and to Cynthia Eller and Carolyn Hill for help in editing. As always, honor and respect to Papa Mano and La Societé La Fleur d'Or. I am grateful to have entered Haitian culture along with a talented set of friends, who have become like family: Steve and Emilia White, Steve and Rose Deats, Paul Uhry Newman and Valerie Feuer. I especially thank Toshi Reagon for all of her support through my time at Yale. My family, Mommie Beebe, Pete, Lovely, Sacha, Juju, and especially Koukou Holly, offered love and a healthy perspective on work and play.

This study benefited from a great deal of support from both individuals and institutions. Research was funded by the Yale Center for International and Area Studies. Writing support was provided by a dissertation grant from the Henry S. NcNeil Fellowship at Yale and by a dissertation fellowship from the New Ethnic and Immigrant Congregations Project at the University of Illinois at Chicago. I wrote the manuscript as a resident at The Writer's Room in New York City. My colleagues in the Department of Religion at Wesleyan generously gave both critique and time off for revisions. I revised the work as a grateful fellow at the Center for the Humanities at Wesleyan University and with funding from a faculty fellowship from the Pew Program in American Religious History at Yale.

Guide to the
Compact Disc *Rara!*

TRACK 1. "Jan, Men Kouto" (Jean, Here Is Your Knife). 52 sec. A Rara colonel sang this a cappella song that speaks of militarism and preparedness. It is recorded here without chorus.

TRACK 2. "Instrumental from Rara Se Malè." 2 min. The Rara was playing on the side of the road in Beaufort, in the Artibonite Valley, on Good Friday 1993. This track shows the "heat" of the drums and horns (*vaksin, konè,* and *kès*) in full swing. See discussion on pages 19–21.

TRACK 3. "Kay Ile" (The House of Ile). 2 min., 5 sec. This is an *ochan* (salute song) sung in Fermathe on Easter weekend 1992. The Rara had stopped in front of a Vodou temple in order to collect money. See discussion on pages 26–30 and 50–52.

TRACK 4. "Instrumental Isolations." 3 min., 29 sec. Rara La Belle Fraîcheur de l'Anglade. After the Rara saluted the Vodou temple recorded in track 3, they stopped to play in place. I made the recording by moving among the musicians, capturing first one group and then another. You can clearly hear the various instruments: *kès* (drum), *graj* (scraper), high and bass *vaksin* (bamboo tube), and finally a bit of chorus. The whistle is directing the dancers, who are performing for the Vodou priest. See discussion on pages 19–21 and 26–30.

TRACK 5. "Notre Dame de 7 Doleurs."* 3 min., 45 sec. This ceremony was recorded in Bourg Champagne in 1978 at 9:30 A.M., inside a Vodou temple before the drawing of the *vèvè* (ritual designs made on the floor). A Vodou priest leads the singing, and you can hear many religious songs: "Ouve Baye Pou Djab-La" (Open the way for the spirit), and "Gwo Lwa, Gwo Pwen, Simbi

---

All tracks recorded by Elizabeth McAlister with assistance from Phenel Colastin except those indicated. Used by permission. This CD was recorded in Haiti by Elizabeth McAlister and produced at Wesleyan University by Holly Nicolas, who had been present at some of the recording in Haiti in 1993. Mixing and mastering was carried out by Peter Hadley of the music department at Wesleyan University using a Macintosh computer and Soundedit computer software.
*Recorded by Verna Gillis and released on *Caribbean Revels: Haitian Rara and Dominican Gaga* (Smithsonian Folkways). Used by permission.

Nan Dlo" (Great spirit, great "point," Simbi-of-the-water). See discussion of religion in Rara in chapters 3 and 4.

TRACK 6. "Kwiy Nan Men, M'ap Mande . . . al Roule Tete." 1 min., 55 sec. This Vodou song says, "Bowl in my hand, I am begging, but it's a spirit I am seeking." Then the chorus launches into the vulgar ditty, "Go roll your mother's titties." You can hear how tired the voices are; it is late in the day. See discussion in chapter 2, especially page 62.

TRACK 7. "Tripotay Fanm Pi Rèd Pase Wanga" (Women's Gossip Is Worse Than Magic). 1 min., 27 sec. The chorus is well balanced with the instruments in this recording.

TRACK 8. "Fre Dieuvè Pa'p Mande Prete" (Brother Dieuve Will Not Be Asking to Borrow This Year). 54 sec. This is an original song by Rara La Belle Fraîcheur de l'Anglade that boasts about the good fortunes of their president, Fre Dieuve. The chorus sang the song for me without instruments. See discussion in chapter 5, especially pages 142–45.

TRACK 9. "Fre Dieuvè Pa'p Mande Prete." 1 min., 44 sec. Easter Sunday 1992. This is the same song as on track 8, with the addition of the full Rara orchestra, out on parade. You can hear the *graj* particularly well.

TRACK 10. "M'ap Antre ak Tout Kò Divisyon Mwe, Osay O" (I Am Arriving With My Regiment, Ossagne Oh). 2 min., 4 sec. Easter Sunday 1992. This *ochan* is probably derived from European signal corps drumming style. See pages 50–52 and 135 and the discussion of militarism in chapter 5.

TRACK 11. "Grosè Bagay sa, Mwen Pa Kapab Ankò" (The Size of That Thing—I Can't Deal with It).* 2 min., 15 sec. Rara Ya Seizi, Verettes, Holy Saturday 1993. The ostinato (melody tag) of this Rara had words that were not sung here. See page 46, chapter 2, and page 145.

TRACK 12. "Pa Gen Fanm Konfyans" (There Are No Trustworthy Women). 2 min., 47 sec. Rara Bann Bourgeois de la Lwa, Pont Sonde, Good Friday 1993. This *charyio-pye* (foot-stomping) Rara creates rhythm by their stomping feet. You can hear cars passing on the roadway. See discussion on pages 45, 64–66, and 145–46.

TRACK 13. "Pa Vle Zenglendo" (We Don't Want Criminals). 3 min., 44 sec. Rara Modèl, Port-au-Prince, Easter Monday 1993. The words to this melody were commonly known but were not sung in times of repression. Instead, the *banbou* (bamboo tube) stood in for the lyrics. The Rara recorded here was returning to the Vodou temple from the season; you can hear the whip cracking. See discussion of *zenglendo* on pages 176–77 and whips on page 108. The chorus is singing "Sodo m'prale" (I'm leaving for Sodo), a song that became politicized during the coup; see discussion on pages 175–77.

---

*Recorded by Elizabeth McAlister and featured on *Rhythms of Rapture: Sacred Musics of Haitian Vodou* (Smithsonian Folkways). Used by permission.

TRACK 14. "Cemetery at Bizoton."* 6 min., 53 sec. This track was recorded in 1978 in the cemetery at Bizoton, one of the neighborhoods just outside downtown Port-au-Prince. You can hear four *vaksin,* a whistle, and the distinct sound of a flute, as well as three *konè* and drum. The group was leaving the cemetery after a midnight ceremony. Finished with their important religious work, the Rara sang the "vulgar" and sexualized *betiz* songs that are the discursive domain of the Gede spirits. Working the cemetery is discussed in chapter 3, and *betiz* are discussed in chapter 2.

TRACK 15. "M'Pap Mache a Tè" (I Don't Walk on the Ground). 1 min., 13 sec. La Belle Fraîcheur de l'Anglade sang this boasting song about one of their leaders, Dieuvè, whose Rara was like a plane and allowed them to fly above the ground. The second song on the track talks about barring "whores" from the area; see discussion on page 66.

TRACK 16. "Jan Dantò Ki Voye Yon Lèt Pou Mwen Pou'm Al O Zaye" (Jean Dantor Sent a Letter for Me to Go to Zaire). 2 min., 21 sec. This is a Petwo song used in Rara that may reference Zaire.

TRACK 17: "Guantanamo M'Rive" (I Ended Up in Guantanamo).** 1 min., 49 sec. Rara Inorab Kapab, Citè Soleil, March 1993. This Rara music is in the style of Jérémie; its members moved from that southern coastal town to Port-au-Prince. When they arrived in the capital, they found that making a living was still impossible. This song tells how they sold everything they had and left the country by boat but were returned from Guantanamo to Haiti to starve. Note that in the southern Rara style, typically there are about six *vaksin* but no drums. As usual in Rara, a sustainer rhythm is played on the side of the *banbou* with sticks, but here the only other percussion is a *graj*. See discussion on pages 40–42.

TRACK 18. "Kalfou."* 5 min., 17 sec. This Rara from Léogâne features the distinct sound of that region, which often includes brass such as trumpets and trombones. The *vaksin* are played here by humming into them, producing a sound distinct from that in other regions, where they are hocketed (alternated) in blown tones.

TRACK 19. "Instrumental by Rara Se Malè." 2 min., 35 sec. Beaufort, Good Friday 1993. This track features a "hot" performance by the high-pitched *vaksin*.

TRACK 20. "Bann Sanpwèl-la nan Lari-a" (The Chanpwèl Band Is in the Streets). 1 min., 31 sec. Rara Delin, Tomasin, 1992. This Rara was also a Chanpwèl (secret society) band; the lyrics say, "The Chanpwèl band is in the streets— What will I give them?" See discussion of Chanpwèl in chapter 3 and on pages 140–45.

---

*Recorded by Verna Gillis and released on *Caribbean Revels*. Used by permission.
**Recorded by Elizabeth McAlister and featured on *Rhythms of Rapture*. Used by permission.

TRACK 21. "Mwen Antre Nan Lakou-a; Kote yo?" (I'm Entering the Compound; Where Are They?). 2 min., 5 sec. Rara La Belle Fraîcheur de l'Anglade, Fermathe, Easter 1992. The Rara band was entering a Vodou temple and preparing to ask for a contribution. See related discussion on pages 166–67.

TRACK 22. "Yo Vin Gade'm Pou Yo Pote'm Ale" (They're Coming To Watch Me and Take Me Away). 3 min., 32 sec. Rara La Belle Fraîcheur de l'Anglade, Fermathe, Easter 1992. The call and response singing of this Rara's original song is easy to hear on the track. The song displays the fearfulness and paranoia of some Vodou songs. See discussion on pages 171–74.

TRACK 23. "Instrumental from Rara Se Malè." 1 min., 14 sec. Artibonite, Good Friday 1993. The melody of the *vaksin* almost sounds like a slow bolero. You can hear the band "break" almost like a Brazilian samba band.

TRACK 24. "Mama'm Sere Zozo'm" (My Mother Hid My Dick). 2 min. Rara Modèl, Port-au-Prince, Easter Monday 1993. This Rara was slowly heading toward home, finishing up the season by singing vulgarities: "My mother put away my dick so I won't screw whores. If I screw I'll get AIDS—go fuck your mother." The band's lyrics combined absurdity, vulgarity, and AIDS awareness. See discussion of sex and politics in chapter 2.

Rara *kolonèl* in the Artibonite set off with whips in hand (photo © Chantal Regnault)

Introducing Rara

Ogou Badagri, what are you doing?
    On watch, they put me on watch
Ogou Badagri, what are you doing?
    On guard, they put me on guard
    I won't sleep, Feray, I won't sleep
    I'm already a warrior, I couldn't
        sleep
    I won't sleep, Feray, I won't sleep
    I'm already a warrior, I couldn't
        sleep
Feray, Oh!
    I was at war, they put me on watch
Ogou Feray, Oh!
    I was in the war, they put me on
        guard

Ogou Badagri sa w ap fè la-a?
    Se veye, yo mete m veye
Ogou Badagri sa w ap fè la-a?
    Se veye, yo mete m veye
    M' pap dòmi Feray m' pap dòmi
    M' deja gason lagè m' pa sa dòmi
    M' pap dòmi Feray m' pap dòmi
    M' deja gason lagè m' pa sa dòmi
Feray O!
    Nan lagè m te ye yo mete m veye
Ogou Feray O!
    Nan lagè m te ye yo mete m veye

1

We stood a small distance away from a huge mapou *tree and watched one Rara procession after another advance along the dusty road, playing drums and bamboo horns and singing. Small armies led by men called colonels, whose command included queens, captains, and majors, would approach the* mapou *tree, encircle it with music, and pour cane liquor libations among the high gray roots sticking up from the ground. It was Good Friday 1993, and we were outside the Lakou Souvenance, a religious compound in central Haiti dedicated to the Dahomean deities in the Afro-Haitian religious system. The* mapou *tree was a powerful natural repository of several mystical spirits. One band was singing a song to the Haitian warrior spirit: "Ogou Badagri, what are you doing? I was in the war, they put me on guard." It was a melody I had heard at Vodou ceremonies about being prepared for battle, one of the many songs of struggle within the religion of Vodou. Band after band came in the swirling dust that afternoon to the* mapou, *performing the mystical "work" Rara required of them—asking for a plentiful harvest in the fall, bidding for good health, hoping for the return of President Aristide, who had been overthrown two years before in a coup d'état.*

A few months earlier I had been invited to a recording studio in Port-au-Prince to hear the new Carnival tune by Boukman Eksperyans, a band that plays mizik rasin, *"roots music," mixing the African-based rhythms of Vodou and Rara with American rock. When I got to the studio, the lights were all out because of the* blakawout *(blackout) in most of the city. A generator was pumping energy only to the console, and candles lit the recording booth. I heard the unmistakable harmonic tones of Rara* banbou *trumpets underneath the rock guitar. The voice of the female lead singer cut through the music, proclaiming, "Ogou Feray, Oh! I was at war, they put me on watch." The band members looked up through the candlelight from their sprawled postures on the studio sofa. "We have to watch the politicians," one member said. "They are plunging our country into misery."*[1]

The song, which this band had borrowed from the traditional repertoire of Vodou and arranged with their own music, would be played constantly on the radio in Haiti during Carnival.[2] *The coup government declined to invite the band to play at the festivities, the Carnival of Fraternity, which featured one army truck after another loaded with soldiers waving beer in one hand and an Uzi in the other.*

On a bright summer Sunday in 1994, in New York City, hundreds of Haitians have gathered in Brooklyn's Prospect Park for an informal afternoon. A core group of young men is walking down the park road, playing drums and blowing bamboo tubes, and hundreds of people are dancing after them, singing, drinking, and trying to have a good time. On everyone's mind is the political violence in Haiti. Poor neighborhoods are targeted for brutal beatings, and everyone here has a family member who is missing, hungry, or sick. A song goes up in the crowd: "Ogou Badagri, what are you doing? I'm already a warrior, I couldn't sleep."

Some of the people singing and dancing here are stuck in New York on unplanned extensions of vacation or business trips because a multinational embargo has sealed off Haiti to passenger travel. They are waiting out "the situation" as best they can, mingling with people at a sort of gathering they might have seen only years ago in Haiti. Some wear dreadlocks, sport Malcolm X t-shirts, or carry straw djakout bags over their shoulders, peasant style. "We have to be on watch," someone says. "If Bill Clinton wants Aristide to return, he will return. If not, we have to be ready for the fight."

Rara is the yearly festival in Haiti that, even more than Carnival, belongs to the so-called peasant classes and the urban poor. Beginning the moment Carnival ends, on the eve of Lent, and building for six weeks until Easter Week, Rara processions walk for miles through local territory, attracting fans and singing new and old songs. Bands stop traffic for hours to play music and perform rituals for Afro-Haitian deities at crossroads, bridges, and cemeteries. They are conducting the spiritual work that becomes necessary when the angels and saints, along with Jesus, disappear into the underworld on Good Friday. The cast of characters who have a hand in the six weeks' events includes the captains, priests, queens, sorcerers, musicians, and armies of Rara members, as well as the spirits of Afro-Haitian religion, the *zonbi* (recently dead), Jesus, Judas, and "the Jews." At times the cast has drawn the unwelcome attention of the Haitian military, known to violently repress Rara bands. The season's ritual events combine the symbols and tropes of Afro-Haitian religion with the plots and personae of the Christian narrative and rehash them in local ritual dramas. Their content is generated from various moments in the history of the Atlantic world, from the European

Middle Ages to the contemporary condition of global capitalism in the Americas.

The Haitian Lenten Rara season remembers a history of the Americas that is usually silenced.[3] Said by residents of the town of Léogâne to be an "Indian festival," Rara provides a fleeting yearly remembrance of the 250,000 Tainos who died in the first two years after Columbus's fateful 1492 arrival in Haiti, known then as Aiyti-Kiskeya, the "mountainous land."[4] But this is only the first of many fragmented historical memories. Harnessing the spiritual power of the deities in the Petwo, Lemba, and Kongo branches of Afro-Haitian religion, Rara also recalls and activates religious principles from the African kingdom of Kongo that flourished in the fourteenth and fifteenth centuries.

The festival carries Creole memories too, layers of American-side history.[5] Rara parades come to their climactic finish during Easter Week precisely because Holy Week was mandated (in 1685, under the Code Noir) to provide a respite from labor for enslaved Africans of the colony. Rara is a fine example of what Joseph Roach calls the "circum-Atlantic interculture" of indigenous, African, and European blendings, a continuing product of what Paul Gilroy describes as the intercultural and transnational "Black Atlantic."[6] Rara festivals are Creole performances par excellence, imbued with historical memories so terrible and profound that they are transmitted not in everyday speech, but through the dancing body and in the cryptic texts of songs and rituals.

Yet Rara is not only about historical memory. More immediate is what Rara has to say about the present realities of Haiti's disenfranchised poor majority. Rara season is one of the few times that the poor assemble freely, en masse, relatively unharmed, in bands from around thirty people to several thousand. A drastic disparity of wealth divides Haiti, and the appearance of thousands of poor people in public space is a deeply charged moment, considered "dangerous" both culturally and politically by the wealthy. For members of the educated enfranchised classes, hundreds of noisy people celebrating in the streets conjure up nightmares about mass uprising. So the monied groups avoid traveling at night during Holy Week, uneasily giving the Rara kings and colonels reign over the streets. During Rara season the religious and political tensions in Haitian society rise to the surface as religious ritual is brought into public space, the popular classes confront the powerholders, and Rara bands confront one another.

Rara activity has also recently emerged in New York, after thirty years of heavy Haitian immigration. The summers of 1990 through the present have seen several Rara bands in both Central Park and in Brook-lyn's Prospect Park, competing musically for attention and followers, singing songs in favor of democracy in Haiti, and denouncing racism and police brutality in the United States. As a form of cultural expression, these Raras help Haitians adapt to life as transnational migrants—those who go back and forth from home to host countries.[7] They create entirely new songs that speak of the diaspora experience, and lyrics are carried to families and circulated through neighborhoods after the festivities are over. Rara in New York has come to express a point of view about the Haitian diasporic predicament.

This book is the first ethnography of Rara festivals and Rara performance. For various reasons—partly having to do with researchers' anxieties about the poor assembling en masse—few scholars have treated Rara seriously. Thus there is much ground to cover here. I explore the practices and meanings of Rara, suggesting its possible history, its religious foundation, its role in cultural politics as well as national politics, and its gendered, sexualized, and transnational dimensions. In particular, I focus on the recent uses Haitians are making of Rara performance, first in Haiti and then in the United States. In turn, I use Rara to make various arguments about Caribbean history and popular culture.

Things have been changing rapidly in Haiti since the fall of the infamous Duvalier dictatorship in 1986. Even now, as I write, the political landscape is quite different from what it was during the period of this study. The years during which I conducted field research—1990 through 1995—were volatile in Haitian politics. As the United States developed a contradictory neoliberal plan for Haiti as part of its New World Order, a fledgling democratic process in Haiti underwent numerous changes. This period saw the "free and fair" election of President Jean-Bertrand Aristide, his ousting in a coup d'état, the return of repressive military rule, an international embargo on Haiti, a resulting refugee crisis, and finally, the return of Aristide after a U.S.-led "inter-vasion."[8] Rara bands, in their turn, marched loudly across the political stage, both during the Lenten season and throughout the year in Rara-style protest demonstrations. This study reads the popular cultural wind through the lyrics and messages of these community-produced musical groups.

Rara festivals are unusual because, unlike contemporary popular culture that is received through the media, Rara parades are grassroots performance events that typically go unrecorded and unbroadcast. There is no Rara audience per se, since the parades' movements through local territory—often at night—can take the bands miles away from their starting point. The people passing by on the roads, or the households that line the roads to view the procession, become momentary audiences who stop and watch or join in and *pran yon roulib* (take a ride) in the Rara.[9] In this way the distinction between audience and performer is erased as soon as it is constructed. A moving community festival, Rara is a popular performance that invites its audience to become part of the group and move away with it. Ideally, those present at a Rara are not watching passively but are singing and dancing along.

As I researched Rara, I became aware of an irony in the publicity that Rara affords. The Haitian poor are "the poorest in the Western Hemisphere," and their Rara festivals usually go unreported in local newspapers or scholarly literature. Yet the festival is nevertheless a boisterous performance event that has loudly marched through the streets for centuries, now landing squarely in the public parks of New York City. I was struck by this tension between the sheer volume of the festival and its silence in official Haitian—and United States—discourses. As Haiti's most popular public festival, Rara produces and displays key values of the culture of the Haitian majority—a culture historically considered illegitimate by the country's leaders and foreign chroniclers. In both political and religious ways, the poor are rendered invisible yet simultaneously use invisibility to their own advantage. Because they are officially ignored, they can express opinions and perform religious rituals in public that would be quite impossible to do if those in power were paying closer attention. The expressive communities Rara bands create, and the religious works they perform, serve to strengthen community, mystically empower the bands and their followers, and consolidate public opinion around political players and international events. They also operate through, and reinforce, the political structures of patronage at work in the larger society.

I am trying to work against tropes that cast poor neighborhoods as sites of suffering that are in turn transcended through Carnival. Rather, I am interested in understanding the Rara festivals in terms of larger historical and political events. I view Rara as a public ritual through which poor Haitians in a range of locations remember history, create publicity, and negotiate power under conditions of insecurity. Living in insecurity means being unable to trust the permanence of political structures, social ties, or financial institutions that would give life its stability.[10] Much of the research for this book took place during a particularly violent period in Haiti, including the three long years of the coup. The military repression toward the poor was severe, and Rara activity was deeply affected by the political upheaval and violence. One of the points the book argues is that in forming Rara bands under the patronage of both Vodou deities and local "big men," members of Haiti's disenfranchised classes deployed the only two forms of speech that are not repressed in the public arena: Vodou songs and obscene, carnivalesque songs. These songs are polyvalent, coded expressions that speak to disempowered Haitians. Using the power harnessed from the spirits of Vodou and from collective performance, Rara participants broadcast coded points of view that had local, national, and transnational dimensions. This study reads the religious and cultural expressions of Haitian disempowered communities through the lyrics of these grassroots-produced musical groups.

Rara has both historical and contemporary lessons to teach. It is a festival that shares a history with other Afro-Atlantic performance traditions. And Haitians at home and in diaspora are currently making interesting uses of Rara. Rara is about a certain kind of performative orality. It is part of a cultural complex that includes public verbal wordsmithing, displays of masculinity, and competitive performance of dance and music, all growing out of a religious core. Although it is made invisible by the postcolonial elites of the nation, Rara and its performative orality sustain possibilities and postures of survival for the long-suffering, disenfranchised majority classes.

In its orality, performative competition, and masculinity, as well as in its oppositional stance, Rara shares similar characteristics with other Black Atlantic performance traditions like Carnival, Jonkonnu, capoeira, calypso, blues, jazz, New Orleans' second-line parades and Black Indians' parades, reggae, dance-hall, hip-hop and numerous other forms. Unlike many Afro-Creole masculinist forms, however, Rara is explicitly religious. What I learned by walking and dancing with the Rara bands is that at its deepest level, Rara is concerned with performing religious work in the unseen Afro-Creole spirit world. Under the patronage of the Vodou spirits, Rara bands fulfill mystical contracts, salute sacred places, and pay tribute to the recently dead. In this sense, Rara shares characteristics with the many African-based religions of the Americas, like the Vodou it grows from in Haiti and the Orisha traditions of Cuba and Brazil. But Rara's religious work is largely secret and is purposely kept hidden. Surrounding and hiding Rara's religious core is an outer layer of carnivalesque play.

This combination of religious seriousness and public play enables certain kinds of speech and assembly in the face of the political insecurity that characterizes Haiti's history. A Rara band may salute the spirits in the crossroads at one moment, then sing in favor or disapproval of particular politicians. The very next instant the band can launch into the absurd ditties of Carnival. The two registers of seriousness and play can happen simultaneously, or the band can move swiftly between them as a protective technique.

The Afro-Haitian performance techniques at work in Rara comprise an indigenous theory of dialogic communication spanning religion, magic, and politics. Within this expressive politics, the significance and connotations of words and phrases are manipulated in a constant process of figurative change. This means that, like the national climate of insecurity, meanings and their referents can shift quickly and unpredictably. This politics can be a sophisticated way to circulate sentiment through a community and to critique those in power while minimizing the risk of repercussion.

One Rara band that I often followed in downtown Port-au-Prince started the evening with a religious ritual that activated the spirits and asked them to work on behalf of the band. The band members gathered around a small bonfire outside the Vodou temple that was their base. They knelt over a rope and a rock, using techniques of travay maji *(magical work) to "tie up" the other neighborhood Rara bands who were their competitors. As they sang songs to the spirits, the band members one by one bathed their torsos and heads in a special infusion of medicinal leaves. This instructed the spirits to afford them protection against spirits working for other bands, as well as against any physical violence.*

After the ceremony, we danced into the streets as the band played a song for Ogou, the lwa *(spirit) of militarism and discipline. The song was a common one, straight out of the Port-au-Prince Vodou repertoire and easily recognizable. We were having a good time, moving quickly, and I felt the exhilaration of taking over the streets of the capital with sound and bodies in motion. Dancing a lively two-step down the middle of the street, I felt that we owned the air itself. The bamboo horns electrified the black night of the unlit city with sparks of sound. The band was moving through one of the most central, most crowded areas of the city, an area that was a stronghold of support for President Aristide, who had been ousted in the coup d'état. "Ogou Badagri, what are you doing?" roared the crowd's song.*

*Then several things happened at once. The tune changed abruptly:
"Marie, where did you go? I have nowhere to put my big dick."
All of a sudden the Rara band was singing a* betiz *song, a vulgar
ditty out of last month's Carnival. Phenel, my field assistant, yelled
to me, "Liza, Babylon is here," using the term that the downtown
street culture had picked up from the Rastafari movement to signify
the military or their* atache *agents. Sure enough, a military* atache
*stepped from behind a pillar to confront the revelers. As Phenel
grabbed me by the shoulders and took us both down to the pavement, the* atache *open-fired on the entire Rara band with a semiautomatic
rifle. Either the protective baths were working, or the* atache
*intended simply to frighten us, because nobody was hit. After a brief
panic, the band was up and streaming down a side street away from
"Babylon."*

Moments later, everyone paused to rest and drink kleren *(cane
liquor). "What was that?" I panted to Phenel as we swigged liberally
from the liquor bottle that passed our way. The cold heat of the
raw, fermented cane helped calm our nerves. As he lit a cigarette,
Phenel's eyes met mine in the brief glow of match-light. "That militaire
didn't like us singing for Ogou," he replied in a low voice. "Ogou
stands for the army, you know, so to them, any song for Ogou could
be talking bad about the military. The songleader tried to switch to*
betiz, *but it was too late." My mind raced with questions, but the
music started up again. Despite having a close call with a spray of
bullets, the band set off down the narrow streets of Port-au-Prince,
merrily singing the vulgar songs of Carnival.*

Like the darting feints of boxing, or of Brazilian capoeira, where one
player moves left only to end up right, Rara bands are in constant lyrical
movement. Meaning, too, shifts quickly according to the circumstances
at hand. The Rara festival moves back and forth from the most intense
religious work to the silliest Carnival, from painful memories (of the
period of slavery) to innovation, from powerful political possibilities
(such as mass mobilization) to shouting misogynist vulgarities. One minute a Rara band can invoke the supernatural and gear up for a fight,
and the next minute it can sing silly songs, recalling the lighthearted
celebrations of Carnival.

This work explores the feints and starts of Rara activity. The book
follows Rara bands as they dance back and forth between private and

public spaces, as well as between sacred and secular protocols, between Caribbean male and female value systems, between the spheres of the living community and its recently deceased (when Rara bands capture the spirits of the recently dead and mystically carry them in the parade), between royal-priestly and military social hierarchies, and between popular laughter and engaged politics. The final chapter examines how Rara music and performance have danced from Haiti into the Haitian United States, emerging as signifiers of progressive politics in the transnational arena of the Haitian diaspora.

The book is organized into sections along thematic lines, each section using distinct theoretical tools to explore central questions. While no sequence of chapters can maintain a perfect logical progression when trying to deal simultaneously with topics, regions, and periods, there is a movement within the work from early forces to late, from Haiti to New York, and from rural-agrarian themes to urban-industrial ones.

DEEP BACKGROUND: RELIGIOUS CULTURE
AND THE HISTORY OF HAITI

The modern history of the Americas begins in Haiti, when Columbus "invaded," "discovered," or "encountered" the island on his famous voyage of 1492. In 1698 the western part of the island was transferred from the Spanish to the French, to become their colony of Saint-Domingue. To work their sugar and coffee plantations, the French imported thousands of enslaved Africans, and Haiti became the site of brutal torture as the plantation system generated immense wealth for planters and utter misery for slaves.

Enslaved African peoples, versed in various African religions, met with the conversion practices of the French Catholic Church. What was (and is) called Vodou is a variety of practices from diverse nations in Africa (including the Dahomean, the Yoruba, and the Kongo) in forced conversation with the Catholicism of the colonial masters. Their god is the same—a high god who created the world. But Vodou's Gran Mèt-la (God) is remote and uninvolved, while the spirits are immediate and responsive to their *sèvitè* (human "servants"). Vodou is a religious system, but it is more than that. Throughout the whole of their nation's difficult history, the majority of Haitians have been agriculturalists, and as in other agricultural societies, philosophy, cosmology, medicine, religion, and justice systems are rolled into one worldview.

In 1804, barely three decades after the American Revolution, Haiti freed itself simultaneously from French rule and from slavery. Punished by the rest of the hemisphere for this radical uprising, the nation went into a sixty-year period of isolation during which neither the Vatican nor other world powers gave Haiti diplomatic recognition. Historians argue that during this time the Afro-Creole religion crystallized as Haiti's dominant worldview. The nation came into being as a self-consciously Black nation, the overwhelming majority of its people of African descent. A tiny elite, the descendants of the colonial mulattoes, enfranchised itself with full economic and political power, and these families continue to hold power in Haiti. They look to France—and now the United States—for language, religion, culture, education and trade.[11]

The rich history of Haiti is far too complex to capture here and has been the subject of much prejudiced treatment. But the general statement can be made that the Haitian poor majority has been *peze souse* (squeezed and sucked) by the economic elite through inequitable trade practices and tax burdens, without benefit of political enfranchisement. The United States government, in turn, has consistently developed policies toward Haiti that benefit American trade and political and military supremacy. Over time, the military ethos that enabled Haiti's revolutionary victory in 1804 was refined and centralized with the help of the United States. Historian Michel-Rolph Trouillot demonstrates that the extremism of "Papa Doc" Duvalier's dictatorship was simply the logical culmination of these processes in Haitian history.[12] For what I term the disenfranchised majority, life has revolved around agricultural work, militarism, an ethos of independence in the context of extreme exploitation, political disenfranchisement, insecurity, oral culture, and an Afro-Creole religious imagination enveloped inside a Roman Catholic one.

In a country with a literacy rate of 15 percent or less, Vodou has grown into a creolized blend of African and (to a lesser extent) European knowledge, focused not on texts but on embodied forms of spirit work. Rather than speak about "a religion called Vodou," practitioners will more likely explain that they *sèvi lwa* (serve the spirit). Haitians work with a complex pantheon of divinities who both shape and reflect the world for their spiritual "children." Above all, Vodou is a religion of survival, which produces meaning and protective strategies for the poor who cope, on a daily basis, with the traumas of poverty and insecurity.

Haiti during the Coup: 1990 to 1995

This book is, in part, a case study of popular expression during times of drastic political upheaval and violence. The five years that the book examines were in turn exhilarating and hopeful, and then brutally repressive, for the Haitian majority. My research began in 1990, when Father Jean-Bertrand Aristide entered the Haitian presidential race. This Salesian priest and philosopher of liberation theology was an unequivocal supporter of Haiti's poor majority. He advocated land reform, human rights, and literacy, and was staunchly anti-American and anticapitalist. When he won the country's first-ever free elections with 67 percent of the vote, the hegemony previously enjoyed by the French-speaking enfranchised groups was seriously challenged. His inauguration on 7 February 1991 launched Carnival season. By the time I arrived to do research for two weeks at Eastertime, the mood in the country was hopeful. The Raras were announcing their entrance into political enfranchisement with a common refrain: "The People Are Here!" I divided fieldwork between Léogâne and Port-au-Prince, while dodging the *zenglendo,* the new breed of former *tonton makout* criminals that had sprung up during the Aristide government.

The next research trip I made was for Rara season in March 1992. Aristide had been ousted in a coup in September 1991, and his military commander, General Raoul Cedras, was the de facto chief executive. The political reality, however, was that various military strongmen were vying for unregulated commodity markets and engaging small armies of retired *tonton makout* as enforcers; the scenario was close to anarchy. The army viewed any assembled group as a threat and targeted Rara bands for repression. The group Human Rights Watch/Americas reported that:

> The range of organizations targeted by the army's campaign of repression is exceedingly broad. Since hostility to the military dictatorship is widespread among Haitians, the army views virtually any popular association as a potential conduit for organized opposition. As a result, all gatherings not controlled by pro-military forces are suspect. Any sign of public protest or dissent is swiftly and violently repressed. The tools of this repression have been intimidation, arrests, beatings, rape and murder. . . . Fear grips the population across all social groupings.[13]

On the advice of friends, I moved from Port-au-Prince to the mountains in Fermathe and walked with a small Rara band that consisted of a large extended family.

I returned again to Haiti in January 1993, planning to stay for a year. My research on Haiti had always focused on religion, and I had begun to understand how Rara festivals are, in part, religious rituals. But the political realities of Haiti and in the Raras forced me to extend my view to hemispheric politics. The repression of the Cedras regime took on a brutality that many reported was worse than the Duvalier dictatorship. The United States imposed economic sanctions. Haitian people fled the country in unseaworthy boats by the thousands, to be picked up by U.S. coastal patrols and interned at the U.S. naval base at Guantanamo Bay. During Lent, the Rara bands became vocal critics of the military. "The People Are Here" became "Where Are the People?" as bands repeatedly asked about compatriots who had disappeared, been killed or gone to sea. I left Haiti in late September 1993, soon after Antoine Izmery, a businessman critical of the military, was assassinated by *makoutes* during a Catholic mass.[14]

The political economy of violence that I witnessed and became part of in Haiti was devastating to that country. Although the climate of terror has been documented by groups such as Amnesty International, Human Rights Watch/Americas, and the National Coalition for Haitian Refugees, there has been relatively little documentation of everyday life under the repression of the coup, or of the cultural changes that accompanied it. This work looks beyond the strict politics of coups, sanctions, and troops and considers the religion and expressive politics of the poor: what it was possible to say in public, and how it was possible to say it.[15]

When I returned to Haiti briefly in March 1995, Aristide was back in power behind the Plexiglas shields provided by United Nations peacekeeping forces. The country and the people were trying to recover from years of embargo, brutality, and despair. Many people whom I knew were sick and malnourished. The Raras were still out, broadcasting public opinion—some opposing the new World Bank "structural readjustment" plan to privatize state-owned services like the electricity and telephone companies.

Now things have changed again. Aristide is consolidating power. This time, reports from various quarters insist that he has changed since his days as a firebrand liberation theology priest and first-time president. Allegations of corruption, monopolizing, and repressive use of force plague him. Cocaine trafficking, which took hold during the coup years, has exploded, and Haiti has become a major narcotics transshipment point. Nobody knows how all of this will affect Haiti's efforts at democratization. While the poor majority in Haiti still appears to support Aristide, he has been condemned by many important supporters, and diasporic communities are now divided. Nothing is clear about Haiti's future, except that a long struggle remains to end the drug trade, to raise the majority above the poverty level, and to attain health care, basic literacy, and access to justice for all.

SOME WORDS ON THEORY

Rara festivals are a number of things at once: they are musical bands, carnivalesque crowds, religious rituals, armies on maneuvers, mass political demonstrations, and performances of national pride. Although I did not wish to write this book in a theoretically heavy-handed way, I needed a *djakout* bag of various analytical tools to keep up with the twists and turns of Rara's meanings. This work relies on methods and theory from cultural anthropology, history, and religious studies, and it ventures into ethnomusicology and performance studies in order to understand Afro-Creole expressive politics. My analysis of Rara derives from the conviction that rituals are primary documents that can be "read" just as well as books in a library and that can reveal as much about culture as any written text.[16] In placing intensive and stylized performance rituals at the center of inquiry, one can discern a number of things: history remembered and embodied, power negotiated, and meaning created in community.

Along these same lines, this work pays close attention to the songs composed, recycled, and circulated through the Raras. There is evidence that many Rara songs are drawn from a long-standing national repertoire that has been archived in the minds and voices of generations of Haitian people. I take these songs seriously as texts that people actively remember and re-create, pass along, and leave to their children. Their enduring circulation gives them a weightier significance as key popular texts than, say, a long-forgotten song written down. I treat older Rara songs as historical and social texts that people have used for generations to reveal truths about the moment at hand. Because Rara music and song is so central to this festival, I made recordings whenever I was permitted in Haiti and compiled some songs onto the compact disc that accompanies this book.[17]

I therefore understand Rara festivals to be essentially dialogic in character. Mikhail Bakhtin uses this term to describe how the meaning of language always recalls past uses of the language and depends on its use in specific times and places. Language will always contain competing definitions, and in situations where there is overlapping and multiple dialogue, there are always many meanings at once. Rara bands masterfully draw on a national repertoire of traditional songs to sing quite specific messages at certain occasions. But even within one band during the singing of one song, individuals within the band may intend various meanings, at multiple levels of interpretation. Seen in the context of the complexity and insecurity of life in Haiti, dialogism enables us to attend to the contradictions in both Rara songs and Rara bands' activities as well as the inconsistencies in Rara's politics of opposition. This is also the reason that I include the Kreyòl translations of the songs in the text: other readers may well discern interpretations that I myself have missed.

I make use of the scholarship on the carnivalesque, also following Bakhtin, that investigates the uses of the grotesque body, the vulgar, and the ways that "high" culture and "low" culture depend upon and structure one another in certain political moments.[18] Much of the reason that elites disdain Rara and render it invisible is because they consider it a "base" celebration of "les classes dangereuses." But I found that Rara members subversively embrace the idea of what Stallybrass and White call "the low-Other."[19] In some cases they perform the very vulgarity expected of them, by singing obscenities. At other times Rara members take on the identity of *djyab* (devils) or "Jews," to oppose the classes of Catholic, French-speaking elites who would give them these labels. Exploring the ways that Rara members view the cultural divide in Haiti offers insight into the self-constructed identities of repressed, subaltern peoples and how these identities are shaped by the power of class and of religion.

Also underlying my analysis is the realization that Rara is controlled not by the entire community but mostly by men. I work with gender theory less for what it says about women and more for what Rara reveals about Haitian masculinity. Although women participate in Raras as queens in the chorus, Rara is dominated by talented and skilled "men-of-words," who compete to enhance their reputations. Reputation is paramount in a political system where charisma and personal ties determine who becomes a powerful local *gwo nèg* (big man).[20] But Rara's "big men" presidents and colonels are far outnumbered by its singing followers. I use the Kreyòl phrase *ti nèg* (small man), seeking to understand how the "small man" positions himself in the political patronage system that anthropology calls "big man-ism." Although "small man" may sound belittling, I certainly do not intend it to be. Rather, I am interested in the kind of publicity Rara affords "singing followers" and under what conditions the average, disenfranchised Haitian male can participate in the public sphere.

In order to understand the "small man" in a situation where power is so drastically uneven and where political insecurity is so intense, this study borrows from James C. Scott the performative concepts of stage and script. During Rara season the song texts of the "hidden transcript"—discourse that takes place offstage, outside the purview of powerholders—are brought into the "public transcript," the site of "the open interaction between subordinates and those who dominate."[21] The popular classes in Haiti emerged into the public transcript in new ways with the entrance into politics of Jean-Bertrand Aristide, only to be pushed brutally into subordination during the coup that ousted him from office. The "small men" in the Raras used the expressive publicity of Rara for political effect.

Last but not least, I view the Raras as a performance form that has both a transnational past and present. Rara is a by-product of the Atlantic slave trade and the creolized "interculture" that colonialism produced. At present, Rara retraditionalizes itself as a transnational Black Atlantic popular culture. The movements and political expressions of Rara actors mirror the more complex realities of Haitian immigrants whom social scientists are now defining as "transmigrants." Transmigrants live, operate, and "develop subjectivities and identities embedded in networks of relationships that connect them simultaneously to two or more nation-states."[22] Indeed, when I began to walk in the Raras of Port-au-Prince, Léogâne, and even the more remote Artibonite Valley, I encountered young men from Brooklyn or Miami who were home for vacation, or who had returned to walk in pilgrimage in a family Rara. A song created in Léogâne can be sung in Brooklyn a week later, creating a diasporic popular Haitian discourse that allows for knowledge rooted in rural culture, now inflected with the diaspora experience, to circulate internationally through many Haitian social spheres.

As Rara songs circulate, they pick up layers of meaning and throw other meanings off to take on new ones for novel circumstances. Even as I write, I have the unsettling sense that this study may walk down one interpretive path, while the Raras veer suddenly in quite another direction. This is to be expected, I suppose, because intrinsic to the talents of the man-of-words in the Rara—and popular culture generally—is the ability to innovate rapidly.

Power and politics in Haiti are once again in flux. And so the Haitian political terrain remains uncertain, and the poor still live under the exhausting conditions of insecurity. Until major and lasting change takes hold in Haiti, the Rara festival will be a way that people remember with their bodies and their voices and a tactic for expressing and sometimes resisting the forces conspiring against their survival. Embedded in the rituals, songs, and dances of Rara is an entire history of ideas transmitted through the performances themselves, through the orality and verbal dexterity of the songwriters, the movements of the dancers, and the spirit work of the Rara priests and sorcerers.

Anthropologist Initiate—Outsider Insider

The first time I went to Haiti, I traveled with a group of friends accompanying Frisner Augustin, a master drummer in Afro-Haitian religious music who had settled in New York and was returning to Haiti for a visit. The trip was in 1984, two years before the fall of Papa Doc Duvalier's son, Jean-Claude. I was majoring in anthropology in college and interested in religious ritual. I was interested in Haiti because my father had founded a Haitian community center in our town, where he continued his Civil Rights Movement activism through pro-immigrant and antiracist work. But mostly I went because I loved Afro-Haitian music and I wanted to hear, learn, and play more. This entry into "the field" was a revision of the classic anthropology script. I was not traveling alone to a chosen country to pursue a predetermined research agenda. Instead, mirroring patterns of transnational migration, I was one of a group of friends "going home" with an immigrant who had settled in our neighborhood.

Since we were traveling in July, Frisner insisted that we go on Sodo, the mountain pilgrimage for Our Lady of Mount Carmel, to receive good luck from the spirits. Much has happened between us as a result of that trip launched under the auspices of the Virgin—long stories too complex to tell here. Some of us created families with Haitians. Six wonderful children have been born, along with two doctoral dissertations on Haitian culture.[23] Three of us were initiated together, to become *marasa* (twins) in the Afro-Haitian spiritual system.

Music has remained central to all of our lives. We joined Augustin's folkloric performance group, La Troupe Makandal (although I left to go to graduate school), and performed on bills with David Byrne, Puntilla Rios, Kip Hanrahan, and the Fugces. Augustin himself opened the Rolling Stones "Voodoo Lounge" tour and in 1999 became the first Haitian citizen to win the National Heritage Fellowship from the National Endowment for the Arts. Lois Wilcken wrote a book with a CD featuring Frisner Augustin. I produced two albums on sacred musics of Haitian Vodou, as well as the CD that accompanies this book.[24] Best of all have been the performances in Haiti and the United States with our children's dance company, Ti Aiyti (Little Haiti).

Anthropologists are supposed to go off to the field by themselves (or with a spouse who is rarely mentioned in final academic work) and to conduct fieldwork and interviews alone. This has rarely been the case for me working in Haiti or in Haitian New York. Starting with that first visit to Haiti with a group of friends, I have always traveled with others. During research for this book, I was part of what Haitians call an *"ekip solid"* (solid team). There were two reasons for this. First, Raras can be dangerous. They are small armies of people walking late at night, sometimes conducting warfare and sometimes doing mystical work. After 1991 some Raras were targeted by the army for repression. Second, people of consequence in Haiti move with an entourage. Traveling with others gave me a measure of protection and at the same time conveyed to the Rara *gwo nèg* that I too was a person who "had people." To convey the proper respect and to be taken seriously, it was best to arrive with one's own small "battalion." I had the good fortune to be joined by Chantal Regnault, a veteran photographer and videographer. I also had the great luck of meeting Phenel Colastin, a young man who had been informally adopted as a child by Katherine Dunham, the great American choreographer who lived in Haiti. Phenel became my field assistant, as well as a solid friend and good sport. To leave them out of the account would seem duplicitous.

Doing fieldwork in another society means being as conscious as possible of one's relationship to that culture and to the individuals one meets. Much of my knowledge of Afro-Haitian religion comes from being a partial "insider" as a daughter of the spirits in Vodou—and as a mother raising Haitian children—although I recognize myself fundamentally as an "outsider" to Haitian culture. The commitments of sustained research, religious involvement, and family ties gave me a taste of the experience of transnational migration, as I went back and forth to Haiti seven times in five years.

Still, any participant-observer who is a (white) American working in Haitian culture is in a position of extreme privilege, because of the workings of power and systems of racialization both in Haiti and in the United States. I know that this privilege gave me a sort of immunity against the political and economic violence many Haitians face in everyday life, which in turn facilitated my research. Studying Haiti from the time of Jean-Claude Duvalier through the coup against Jean-Bertrand Aristide until the present, I have watched the country go through countless political regimes that administered untold violence against the poor majority. I have learned firsthand lessons about what Paul Farmer terms "the political economy of brutality" in Haiti and how it mirrors other parts of Latin America.[25] Although I was able to return to the United States and eventually bring to this country my new partner and new daughter—whom I met during fieldwork—the majority of Haitians who wish to leave their country are barred by racialized migration policies from entering other nations. Our family has been privileged, but we are still haunted by the aftereffects of the violence and insecurity we experienced in the early 1990s.[26]

A side effect of the privileges of foreign status was that I had to be extremely careful not to endanger those Haitians with whom I worked. Too often researchers enter a volatile situation and place their local colleagues in danger through ignorance or selfishness. More than one colleague recounted horror stories of assistants or informants being jailed or tortured because of their association with the anthropologist. I was fortunate not to cause any such problems. Though the events recounted in this book are over, I am still mindful of others' vulnerability, and for this reason I use pseudonyms in many instances, although for the historical record most names of Rara bands, localities, and public figures are rendered accurately.

RECORDING THE COMPACT DISC OF RARA

Rara is above all a musical parade, and the songs the choruses sing are both old, historic songs and new expressions of present realities. The music, hocketed on the distinctive *banbou* horns, produces a sound unlike any other. (Hocketing is the technique where each player blows a single sound, and together all the players create a rhythmic melody.) When I was preparing to go to Haiti to study Rara, I had the good fortune to be mentored by Bernice Johnson Reagon, the distinguished

Smithsonian Institution historian who is also a composer, vocalist, and producer. Professor Reagon advocates that communities document their own histories and their own traditions whenever possible. Although I am not Haitian, Reagon advised me to record and videotape the Rara when it was appropriate. We also spoke about my training and facilitating Haitian recordists themselves.

Digital audiotape (DAT) recorders had just come on the mass market in the early 1990s, but they were too expensive for my research budget. Reagon recommended that I purchase a portable Marantz cassette recorder and a good stereo microphone. That I did, and I made analog recordings of most of the Rara bands I studied.[27] There turned out to be a distinct advantage in using cassettes: Rara members had cassette players, so I could distribute copies of my recordings to them. Often this was unnecessary, however, because the vast majority of bands I worked with also made their own recordings on their own *boum boks* (boom boxes).

Recording in the field is always difficult, but for Rara in Haiti there were serious challenges. First of all, Rara is a moving parade, so equipment has to be easily portable and relatively unobtrusive to avoid disrupting the ritual atmosphere. Recording while walking for miles, sometimes on uneven mountain paths, is a feat of focus and coordination. Moreover, electricity is not regularly available for the majority of the population, so all equipment has to be battery operated. To reduce expense, I used rechargeable batteries, which meant I had to keep vigilant track of what battery power was left and where the next possible electrical recharge would be. To accomplish this, our team had to forge alliances with "big men" who had inverters, generators, or electric power. Wealthy Vodou societies, hotels, and, ironically, supportive Catholic missions became pit-stops as we walked and danced with the Raras.

Another challenge of recording Rara has to do with its constant movement and its parading form. While the colonel is in front leading with whistle and whip, the drums, *banbou*, metal horns, and percussion (scrapers, bells, and so on) walk in battalion-like waves, one group after the other, followed by the chorus. Because of this spatial configuration it is almost impossible to capture all of the music being produced in any one moment of performance. It is particularly hard to record the instruments and chorus in a balanced fashion. In the best moments, I was able to enter a Rara and focus the microphone on groups of musicians from the inside. Track 4 is an example of this sort of recording. Other good times to record are when Rara bands stand together to warm up before they set off on parade. But the most realistic way to hear Rara music is from afar, as it comes closer and then passes by, one wave at a time, until it slowly fades into the distance.

A related challenge is that the Rara band is accompanied by an ebullient community of followers. There is always commotion. People move around and jostle the microphone. Just when you perfect your recording levels and the performance reaches its height, a man in front of you shouts loudly to his friend for a cigarette. When you shift through the recordings to see what to publish, you must reject wonderful performances because of interruptions by one thing or another.

The recordings have had two related uses. First, I could play and replay them to make sense of aspects of the festival that went unnoticed in the moment. Working with Haitian colleagues, I transcribed each tape in order to analyze the lyrics and the music. I was able to have conversations with other Haitian associates about the possible meanings of these songs and to take them seriously as texts with both historical and contemporary valence. Second, the tapes have been used in teaching. Mixed down in the recording studio to discrete tracks, I produced several albums—including the one presented here—so that others can better understand the music.

Throughout this book I have noted when you can listen on the CD to something that I discuss. I recommend that you read with the CD on hand, pausing to listen here and there to the musical examples. Alternatively, readers who wish to let the music guide them can begin by listening to the CD and looking at the track notes at the front of the book. As you listen, you can read the brief discussion of each track and refer when you wish to the more elaborate analysis within the book. Another way to better understand Rara festivals is to view the music, dance, and religious ceremonies on film. I recommend the short documentary called *Rara,* produced by Verna Gillis.[28]

Notes on Language

My fieldwork on Haitian Rara all happened in a specific time-frame, one which has already passed. So I have written this in the past tense, using mostly real names and places, to treat events seriously as a recent history of Rara. Yet by describing the Raras as operating in the past, I am troubled by the implication that they are not still doing magic at the crossroads, capturing *zonbi* in the cemetery, and burning "Jews" in effigy. And in fact the practices I describe are still going on—right this very minute if you happen to be reading this on an early spring day during Lent. I was relieved to read Anna Lowenhaupt Tsing's thoughts on this subject. She too feels a strange discomfort, noting the political implications of each tense. The use of the "ethnographic present" has been criticized for creating an ahistorical picture of remote peoples who are outside of civilized history. Yet a historical tone implies the peoples "are" history. I like Lowenhaupt Tsing's answer: "I cannot escape these dilemmas," she says. "I can only maneuver within them. In this book, I find uses for both the historical past and the ethnographic present. I am inconsistent."[29]

I too use both tenses. If my points are historical, I use a historical voice; if the subject at hand is surely still happening I use the present. The chapters are organized by theme—religion, militarism, sexuality, transnationalism, and so forth—and yet they deal with events that took place during four different governments in Haiti and two presidential administrations in the United States. The reader is advised to make use of the chronology provided in the appendix, to keep track of the events that the Raras are reacting to, participating in, or marching through.

Haitian Creole—Kreyòl—became an official language of Haiti, along with French, in 1987 when a new constitution was ratified. I use the codified orthography instituted by the Institut Pédagogique National d'Haiti (I.P.N.). Kreyòl is essentially a phonetic language; the reader is encouraged to sound out words and will find that many are derived from French.

In Kreyòl, the plural form is indicated by adding -*yo* to the word. *Gato* (cake, from the French *gateau*) would be *gato-yo* in the plural. Some English writers on Haiti indicate the plural by adding an -*s* so that gato becomes *gato-s*. I have chosen to leave the word in its singular form, so that the sentences read the way they would if I were speaking English salted with Kreyòl words. I would say, for example, "Then we sat and ate a few *gato*." This choice is simply a matter of style.

I have provided both the English and the Kreyòl song lyrics because I recognize that my translations of the Kreyòl may only be partial. Kreyòl is a rich, metaphorical language that is sophisticated in its use by the men-of-words in Haitian Raras.[30] It is quite possible that I have misunderstood meaning, misinterpreted it, or heard a double entendre where in fact there was a triple or quadruple entendre. By including the original language, I offer future researchers fluent in Kreyòl access to the original meanings.

Rara is about play, religion, and politics and also about remembering a bloody history and persevering in its face. But at its most bare philosophical level, Rara is a ritual enactment of life itself and an affirmation of life's difficulties. The 1991 president of Rara Ti-Malis Kache, in the southern town of Léogâne, explained that historically Rara was performed after the *corvée,* the forced system of labor used against the Haitian peasants first by the French colonists, later by Haitian rulers, and still later by the Americans during the marine occupation. The president knew this directly from his band's own history: Ti-Malis was founded in 1916 during the U.S. occupation (and is still going strong as arguably the most famous Rara band in Haiti). After a hard day or a grueling week of labor, road-builders would relax body and soul by singing and dancing in a Rara. "To get anywhere in life you have to follow a road. To make anything happen, you have to move through the crossroads." Taking long routes toward the end of Holy Week, covering miles of territory at night, Rara is a stylized ordeal. Rara Ti-Malis's president characterized it as a struggle. A man who spent two years in Duvalier's jail, he is conscious of the political implications of the word. "Because life is something hard. In order to have something tomorrow, you have to struggle and if you don't struggle you haven't got anything."[31]

I hope this book will serve as a documentary of the Rara festivals that have been so loud and yet so disdainfully ignored. The festival and its attendant rituals, performances, and violence are a production of the popular classes—the poor, the disenfranchised, those of African descent—yet I have no reason to disdain Rara the way many of the "elite" and foreigners are conditioned to in Haiti. Into this ethnography I wish to imbue a deep respect for Rara members, admiration of their artistry, their memories, and their perseverance, and acknowledgment of their creativity and talent in the face of grinding poverty and chaotic political changes.

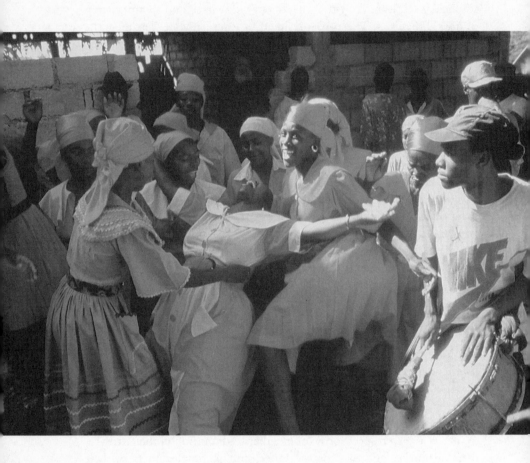

A Rara queen sings into a swoon (photo © Chantal Regnault)

Work and Play, Pleasure and Performance

It's my Rara I do to have my pleasure

This year I'm not dancing Rara at
    anyone's house
It's my Rara I do to have my pleasure
Look at a Rara I started so I can party

Se Rara'm mwen fè pou'm pran plèzi
    mwen

Ane si la, mwen p'ap danse Rara kay
    moun
Se Rara'm mwen fè pou'm pran plèzi
    mwen
Gade yon Rara'm leve pou'm
    banboche

Rara Inorab Kapab, Cité Soleil,
Port-au-Prince, 1 April 1993

SETTING THE SCENE: RARA LA BELLE FRAÎCHEUR DE L'ANGLADE

*Midway through Lent in 1992 I was invited to walk with a Rara in
the mountains above Petionville. My host, Madame Giselle (a
pseudonym), was a highly unlikely Rara participant, a member of
Haiti's French-educated "mulatto elite." She had done a very radical
thing: she had made friends with the Rara band in the valley behind
her house. A large extended family of farmers, the band members
lived without plumbing or electricity in small, one- or two-room houses
that dotted the valley, and worked hard at cultivating corn, peas,
and beets for sale.*

*Madame Giselle lived in a modern house above the valley, with
beautiful landscaped gardens and a picture window looking out over
the glade. Although her house was originally built with running water
and electricity, she had forgone both in the increasingly difficult time
after the Aristide coup. A visual artist herself, she saw her involvement
with the Rara as a meditation on the creative process and used Rara
as an opportunity to learn a side of Afro-Haitian culture of which she
and most of her class were ignorant. In this, Madame Giselle was a
unique woman, and the Rara members valued her friendship. She
contributed what she could and collected money for the Rara from
her friends. In return the Rara extended their friendship and made her
the* marenn, *or godmother, of the band.*

*"Drive up," said Madame Giselle, "and you will see the Rara on
the road. They will be wearing blue and yellow. Tell them that you are
my friends, and everything will be fine." Driving up the winding
road to Kenskoff, my companion Jacques and I were stopped by one
Rara band after another. Groups as small as fifteen members and
as large as fifty walked or danced on the road, the women in colorful
dresses with matching head scarves, and the men in blue jeans sporting
shirts made from the same cloth as the dresses. The groups were led
by a few men with whips in their hands and whistles in their mouths
who were energetically directing the groups' movement. The men
with whips were flanked by other men with drums slung around their
shoulders, who were playing fast and furiously. Other men held
percussion instruments or machetes. As we slowed the car, the groups
surrounded us dancing along slowly. Crowding against one another,
they showed us their* gouyad, *a dance in which hands are clasped against
the backs of heads, chins tilt to the side, knees are bent, and hips roll
in circles sensually. The men holding the whips stretched out their*

arms toward us. It was a scene that could be frightening, I thought, if one were unprepared, or paranoid, or had enemies in the group. Equipped with a small bundle of two-gourde notes, we cheerfully gave one away at each checkpoint, making sure to comment appreciatively about each Rara.[1] "Bèl mizik, bèl rad, bèl Rara" (Beautiful music, beautiful clothes, beautiful Rara), we shouted, anxious to let them know we were not their run-of-the-mill bourgeoisie. Satisfied that we were properly respectful, the groups would either insist that we hear a song, or they would wave us through matter-of-factly. Finally, high up the road, we saw Madame Giselle's Rara. They were dressed in yellow and blue, as promised, and held aloft a sign that proclaimed the group's name: La Belle Fraîcheur de l'Anglade (The Beautiful Fresh Air of the Glade).

We reached for our gift of a bottle of rum, and when the group stopped us, we shouted that we were friends of Madame Giselle. Smiles broke out all around, and the leader of the group came forward. He looked to be in his forties and had the strong build of a farmer, a pleasant face, and a wide, gap-toothed smile. "I am the General of the army," he said. "My name is Kanep. We've been waiting for you."

Kanep had a whip wrapped around one hand; he took my arm with the other, and we began to walk. The musicians were directly behind us: three drummers, four banbou players, and three tin klewon (trumpet) players. Behind them other men walked and sang, and behind them were about thirty women who wore dresses in different styles made of the same yellow and blue material. Everybody there seemed to be between the ages of six and sixty. As I looked back, I saw Jacques walking along, flanked by two older women who each held one of his arms ceremoniously.

Our role had been transformed: instead of driving through Rara checkpoints, we were now part of a Rara. The road we walked along was a direct route from Port-au-Prince to Kenskoff, the mountain retreat of the very wealthy, and Sunday afternoons such as this one brought a steady stream of Mercedes Benzes, BMWs, and four-wheel-drive jeeps returning to the capital. I noticed the range of reactions on the part of the drivers coming through. Some people were clearly amused, nodding their heads to the music and smiling, handing out a coin or two. Others came through with windows rolled up, air-conditioning on, heads held stiffly, staring straight ahead. If these drivers made the mistake of going too fast, honking, or looking upset, Rara members might pound their fists on the cars in frustration.

"The Rara is working," Kanep said, "but those drivers don't want to participate." "This is incredible," said Jacques at one point as we danced in place to let a string of cars past. He was a Port-au-Prince doctor. "I know most of these people—that is Dr. Elie, and that is Madame Leopold, people I went to school with, coming down from their weekend houses. But nobody has recognized me here. They don't even see me. They refuse to look at people's faces in this Rara."

After a while the Rara turned off the main road and faced a wide dirt path descending into the valley, the "glade" where the members lived. Kanep placed my arm on that of a young man named Claude and ran to the intersection of the road and the wide path, blowing his whistle. The musicians stood back, playing and singing, while Kanep danced in a small counterclockwise circle in the crossroads. He cracked his whip deftly on the roadway, scattering children who had ventured forward. Using every inch of his body in a stylish, theatrical show, Kanep blew his whistle and ran down the dirt path, holding the wooden handle of his whip up and pointing it forward like a general in battle yelling "charge." The rest of the band tumbled after him, playing and singing, running down the path at top speed as dogs barked and excited children ran alongside. We descended into the glade, an unusually dense, forested section of mountain, whose air was as beautiful and fresh as the Rara's sign had advertised.

After a small break in the music while everyone caught their breath, the drumming started up again, the banbou *joined in with a melody line, and a woman's voice sang out. Once her verse was sung, the other women joined in straightforward unison, with one woman singing an octave above the others. The music echoed dramatically across the valley on this sleepy, sunny Sunday afternoon, announcing the coming of the Rara.*[2]

I don't walk on the ground, Ay Yey
I don't walk on the ground, help me
Brother Dieuve has a fleet of airplanes
I don't walk on the ground, Ay Yey

Mwen p'ap mache a tè Anye
Mwen p'ap mache a tè Amwe
Kay Frè Dieuvè ki gen yon bann avyon
Mwen p'ap mache a tè Anye

The footing was uneven as we made our way down a dirt road past corn fields, gardens with potatoes and peas, and small houses with goats grazing in the yard. We stopped at one of the small houses, and the drums and banbou *players crowded under a thatched awning adjoining the house while the chorus of women stood to the side singing.*[3]

House, House, Oh House of Ile, Oh
House, House, Oh House of Ile, Oh
House of Ile, Oh House of Ile, the House, Oh

Kay kay O Kay Ile O
Kay kay O Kay Ile O
Kay Ile O Kay Ile La kay O

The area beneath the thatched awning was the family peristil, *or religious dance space, and the song was sung as a religious* ochan *(salute), reserved for priests and priestesses in Afro-Haitian religion. The music is simple and slow, heavy on the downbeats, where the word* kay *is sung.* Kay *means "house" in Kreyòl, and* Ile *means the same thing in Yoruba. In Kreyòl, this song salutes the "House of Ile," while at the same time it simply states the concept of "the House" in Afro-Haitian and Yoruba religion. In both traditions, "the House" is an overarching concept that refers not only to a dwelling place but also to the people who live within and to their principles and values.*

After what seemed like a long while, the priest came out of his house and the ochan *broke into a fast and furious* banda *rhythm. This rhythm features fast slaps and rolls. Banda is the distinctive rhythm and dance of the Gede spirits, the* lwa *of sex, death, and healing. As soon as the* banda *started, the kings and queen of the Rara were presented to the priest, and they began to dance.*

The role of the kings and queens is similar to the function of the majò jon *(baton major) in Rara: to perform short, choreographed dance routines for the amusement and honor of the person being saluted. This year the Rara La Belle Fraîcheur de l'Anglade had chosen three young teenagers to* jwe *(play) king and queen. Two tall, thin boys of thirteen were the kings. They wore dazzling capes covered in red and gold sequins depicting a phoenix on their backs, with matching sequined knickers. The sun caught bits of the costume so that every movement was accompanied by flashing lights. Straw hats with long fronds dripping down the front obscured their faces and gave them the cool appearance of royalty. They executed a dance known as* mazoun, *in which the primary movement is a graceful heel-to-toe step like the start of a minuet. They were supposed to be performing in perfect unison, but they did not always succeed and thus were prompted by the older* kolonèl *(colonels) who were directing the action.*

As the young kings danced, the priest's family brought the Rara an enormous gallon jug of kleren, *the pure cane liquor that keeps Rara bands fueled with calories for much of their journey. They dispensed it to the* kolonèl, *and after the* kolonèl *had drunk, the rest of the crowd took little sips of the liquor.*

When the kings finished dancing, it was time for the crowd-pleaser — the queen. This young Rara queen was only thirteen and very shy. A short, round girl, she wore a straw hat and red and white dress with horizontal pleats. She was responsible for seducing a contribution from the priest by dancing banda. *With all eyes fastened on her, this shy teenager, looking down, chin tilted to the side, clasped her hands behind her head and began the hip-rolling moves of the dance. Each time the drummers cued her with the distinctive "slap!" at the end of each phrase, she performed the "Yas!" — the pushing backward of the pelvis. The more the drum slapped, the closer she got to the priest, until finally one of the* kolonèl *pushed her right against him. At that point the priest passed her some money, which was quickly handed over to the* trezorye *(treasurer), who was close at hand, carrying a huge wooden box into which he stuffed the precious contribution. Whirling around in a danced recovery, she struck a pose, and the dance was over.*

Seeing that there was no more kleren *left and nothing else being offered, the* kolonèl *turned the group around while the musicians continued to play and the women to sing. Filing out just as they had come in, the troupe walked onward through the glade toward the bright light of the sun. We danced on for the rest of the day and well into the night, and I learned many names, heard many stories, and began to understand the intrigues and melodramas that were being played out between band members and with the spirit world. "Rara gen anpil bagay ladann," Madame Giselle said repeatedly over the course of the next three weeks: "Rara has a lot within."*

Folklorist Harold Courlander, devoting a short section to the festival in *The Drum and the Hoe,* wrote that "The general tone of Rara is non-religious. The dancing is free from the decorous restraints which characterize most religious ritual, and some early observers of the festival were shocked by what they saw."[4] Gerson Alexis wrote that "Rara is a public gathering whose purpose is the merriment of the rural counties and their surroundings."[5] Verna Gillis remarks that "The Haitian, typically a religious person like the African, says prayers for protection before many kinds of activities. The recitation of prayers before rara, therefore, does not mark the celebration itself as religious."[6]

My own research on Rara suggests that while the "tone" or "ambiance" of Rara parading may seem secular, the festival should more properly be understood as a synthesis of Carnival behavior and religious practice. Specifically, Rara consists of an outer, secular layer of Carnival "play" surrounding a protected, secret inner layer of religious "work." These two values are enacted structurally through performance codes, use of private and public space, gender relations, and social hierarchy. The outer Carnival layer of Rara members and fans is comprised of young people exhibiting their talent at singing and dancing in a boisterous, rebellious atmosphere. The inner core of Rara leaders forms an extensive hierarchy borrowed from Afro-Creole religious societies or the semireligious, semijuridical Bizango societies. They, in turn, are going about the business of performing serious ritual obligations to the *lwa.*

In order to understand how Rara bands are both "playing" and "working," it will be useful to look at these concepts in the broader context of West Indian culture. In their volume *After Africa,* Roger Abrahams and John Szwed analyze the ways in which European-American concepts of work and play differ from African-American ones. They argue that in European-American cultures, work tends to be associated with productivity outside the home and constitutes one's identity as an individual. In contrast, play means freedom from work and is the arena where one learns to coordinate with others. While work is carried out in public, playing "remains as private as one can maintain."[7]

For many cultures in the African-American context, the reverse has been true. Work is learned within the home under the direction of the mother, and is "*the* most important feature of (extended) family living." Work is generally associated with seriousness and cooperation with the family and by extension with the home and with women. In contrast, play is learned outside the home and comes to be "the activity by which

Afro-American individuality is asserted and maintained. Thus, playing comes to be associated with public places, as work begins in the home and remains, in the main, as a kind of private (or at least guarded) range of behaviors." For many African-American cultures, work is associated with seriousness and cooperation, with the family, and by extension with the home and with women. Play is associated with the crossroads or the street, with men, and with establishing one's reputation through performance. Abrahams and Szwed caution that "in the Afro-American order of behaviors, 'play' is not distinguished from 'real' or 'work' but from 'respectable behavior.' "[8]

If we look at the Rara in these terms, the carnivalesque aspects of the festival are clearly a form of "play," the singing and dancing an occasion to move away from the home, to perform competitively, and to enhance one's reputation. As Abrahams and Szwed note, "In the anglophonic Afro-American sense of the term, *play* is not commonly allowed in the house because it is generally used to refer to some of the central practices by which masculine, crossroads, reputation-centered values are enacted. Play in this sense means highly unruly behavior, engaging in noisy verbal dueling."[9] In the Rara bands I observed, the young *fanatik* who emerged from his house to follow the Rara was enacting this African-American ethos of play. The Rara member participated in order to sing and dance through the countryside and to drink and socialize with the opposite sex. Rara in this sense is considered *vakabondaj* (vagabondage), *dezòd* (unruly, or, literally, disorder), and even *danje* (danger). It is these aspects of Rara, the *fete* or partying behavior, that creates its overall ambiance, and this has led many observers to dismiss Rara as a "rural carnival."

The word *play* has had an expanded, communal meaning in the Afro-Atlantic experience as a performance that evolved out of plantation slavery. This kind of play (the noun) includes performances such as dances, wakes, Christmas, Thanksgiving, tea meetings, Carnival, Jonkonnu, and Afro-Caribbean religious services. A nineteenth-century observer in Jamaica wrote, "The dance, or play as it is sometimes called, commences about eight o'clock . . . and . . . continues to day-break with scarcely an intermission."[10] In Barbados as early as 1729, there were slave gatherings on Sundays "which they call their plays . . . in which with their various instruments of horrid music howling and dancing about the graves of the dead, they [give] victuals and strong liquor to the souls of the deceased."[11] As an all-night, public popular performance, "the play" is an occasion for men to enhance their reputations as songwriters, drummers, and dancers.

An important aspect of Rara (and also of Vodou dances) that links it to Anglophone Caribbean play practices is its all-night quality. Remember Bob Marley's line that "If it's all night, it's got to be alright!" Since their days of enslavement in the colonies, African peoples throughout the Caribbean have engaged in wakes, dances, and holidays that last all night. Abrahams and Szwed note that "the value placed on playing any celebration all night has remained evident to this day. Whether it is a wake, Christmas, carnival, tea meeting, or Thanksgiving, it is felt that if the celebration cannot be sustained all night it is a sad commentary on the performers, and the community."[12] Often these "plays" originally had religious components, which in many cases have diminished with Protestant conversion and economic change in the British West Indies.[13]

The tradition of all-night play practices remains strong in Haiti and is linked to religious activity. Currently most Afro-Haitian religious ritual takes place at night, and so do many other community events that might be considered "plays": Bizango (secret society) meetings, Masonic ceremonies, Carnival, wakes, *fèt chanpèt* (village patron saint's feasts), and Rara. The Rara leadership has a very serious agenda that consists of attending to the spiritual work of the band. It is almost always an *oungan* (priest) or *bòkò* (sorcerer) who directs this spiritual work. The *oungan* or *bòkò* deals with the important matters of fulfilling spiritual contracts, performing rituals for the *lwa* along the route of the band, waging war on other Raras, and last but not least, collecting money.

Rara performance, then, spans the values of "work" and "play" in Afro-Haitian culture. In the "play" mode, with its attendant masculine values, Rara performance codes involve reputation-enhancing public competition. In the "work" mode, Rara fulfills mystical obligations to the *lwa* and thus renews and strengthens the group. Rara is also "working" to bring the group's spiritual power into the public arena and compete magically with other groups. The women who take part in the Rara are away from the sphere of their power, the home compound. But their participation is intimately related to their association with "work," in that the Rara queens' role is to lend seriousness to the band and render it capable of delivering a sustained performance of music and dance.

THE BIRTH OF THE BAND: MYSTICAL CONTRACTS, PLEASURE, AND PILGRIMAGES

> Crossroads, Oh, This crossroads
> Crossroads, Oh, Don't you see I have
> problems
> [or: Crossroads, Oh, Don't you see I am
> under contract]
>
> *Kalfou O kalfou sa*
> *Kalfou O, pa we'm engage*

The reasons to start a Rara band in Haiti are many and include both secular and religious factors. A strong motivation is to enhance one's reputation in the neighborhood. Rara is a loud walking advertisement for its leaders. In Port-au-Prince and the provincial cities, straw hats or t-shirts proclaim the name of the Rara or the name of its business sponsors (like Celeste Borlette, the lottery.) Most people in the local neighborhoods are aware of the name of the president who sponsors a Rara financially and the *oungan* who leads the band mystically. In a country with low "professional" employment and a low literacy rate, this sort of reputation is a major form of social capital.

A Rara started by young people for fun, without an *oungan*, is called a *"ti Rara naïf"* (little naive Rara). But as these bands grow they inevitably "attract" one or more *lwa* who *reklame* (reclaim) them. In these cases, Raras are transformed from carnival bands with a popular ambiance to *bann dangajman*, bands "under contract" with the *lwa*. To be *angaje* (under contract) is probably a term derived from the early Frenchmen who arrived in the colony of Saint-Domingue as indentured servants. Called *Engagés*, they sold themselves for three years to French planters.[14]

In a student paper on Rara at the Faculty of Ethnology, Pierre Isnard Romain shows how a Rara band in Archaie that was started in a family *lakou* (compound) by the young children came to be *angaje* and to do important spiritual work for the family. "La Meprise came from the compound of Madame Pierrot, performed by the children of the area who wanted to amuse themselves and the family. . . . Soon enough the *lwa* from the Pierrot lakou came to join. They required the family to take the Rara out every year. If they did not, members of the family might die instantly." In this case, the family *lwa* "reclaimed" the Rara by announcing (through a possessed person) that they wanted to adopt the already-existing Rara. Romain goes on to say that the Rara became very successful; so popular that even François Duvalier sent donations.[15]

A number of common narratives occurred in the stories of Rara members with whom I spoke, especially in connection to the bands' "spiritual work." One such narrative focused on the process of *reklamasyon,* a Vodou concept that applies to individual people "serving the spirits." A *lwa* who appears repeatedly before a person, either in dreams or in possession, to demand that the person become initiated is said to be "reclaiming" the person. Although it is a different social and psychological process from Christian conversion, it is somewhat analogous: as in Christian conversion, people who experience *reklamasyon* construct a narrative that tends to follow a common pattern. People who are reclaimed by the *lwa* usually or always resist initiation until they receive signals and suffer bad luck or illness. At this point, they are forced to succumb to the spirits' wishes, and they become more seriously involved with serving the *lwa.*[16] In *reklamasyon* stories involving Rara, the pattern is less dramatic because Rara members do not seem to resist a *lwa*'s reclaiming the band. This is probably because it is widely understood that to start a Rara is to attract a mystical component.

An *oungan* and Chanpwèl (secret society) leader told a similar story about his Rara, which he started as a form of amusement. The very first time the band went out, they attracted the *lwa* and ended up acquiring a "work" component:

> We thought we'd have some fun. Take our drums, take some guys to have some fun and drink some booze. Meanwhile, the first time the Rara went out, a spirit came on some of the members. Even the drummers felt an energy. That's why I'm telling you, Rara is not a game. Rara is always serious. As soon as you start a Rara for fun, your feet get stuck. Next year, you have to go out again.[17]

In some cases, a Rara *bann dangajman* is not reclaimed by a *lwa* but is founded in response to a specific request by the *lwa.* Many Rara presidents told me that a *lwa* was the actual founder of the Rara: a spirit had informed the family or the community that it wanted a Rara to be formed. Usually the *lwa* who ask for a Rara to be formed are already served by that group or someone in the group. If it is a family Rara, then it is the important family *lwa* who are considered to "walk with" the Rara. If an *oungan* is a Rara leader, then the *lwa* that his society serves will likely be the ones to demand that he form a Rara. Like the Rara leaders themselves, who adopt titles from an elaborate hierarchy including presidents and vice-presidents, kings and queens, colonels and captains, the *lwa* who patronize the band are often given a military, royal, or state title.

Usually the spiritual work done in a Rara has specific terms. A *bann dangajman* is considered to be under contract with the *lwa* to perform the Rara for a certain number of years, usually seven. Says *oungan* Simeon, "Rara is a contract. It has a limit. We start with the Rara this year, and we have six more years. Because a Rara has to go out for seven years."[18] Some bands maintain a cohesive identity for decades: Rara Chen Mechan (Angry Dog) was founded in 1884 and is still going strong in Léogâne.[19]

In exchange for entering into a contract with a *lwa* to start a Rara, there is a benefit, as there is a perceived benefit for serving the spirits generally in Vodou.[20] Rara members and their families report that the *lwa* protects them, helps their businesses financially, and ensures a successful crop. There are many miracle stories of people having good luck or receiving extra profits because of their activity in the Rara.

In contrast, if the Rara fails to go out, there will be serious consequences. There are stories of disasters befalling people who did not fulfill their Rara contract, and it is said that the *lwa* can take revenge on Rara members who leave the group. One member of a Rara admitted in a matter-of-fact way, "Rara has a lot of demons in it. If you start to attend it, and then stop, that can kill you. The Rara demons can kill you. That's one of the reasons people avoid Rara."[21]

Stories circulate about Raras who go out despite obstacles because their contract to fulfill the spiritual work and bring out the Rara is more important than any adversity they face. There are stories of members dying en route, and after a hasty funeral, the band dances on. During my field research in 1992, two members of a Rara near the one I studied in Fermathe were hit by a car early in the day, as they were performing. Both died instantly. The Rara spent the morning tending to the bodies and reacting to the trauma, then continued its musical walk down the mountain later the same day.

There is a way to sever a Rara's contract with the *lwa*, but this requires a great concentration of spiritual work. The Rara band must do a final year of Rara as a pilgrimage, with specific rituals to satisfy the *lwa* before and after Rara season. One *oungan* reported that on this sort of pilgrimage, members' clothes are made of burlap sacks. A second told me of a Rara band that folded the year before in Léogâne, after performing a pilgrimage dressed in blue and mauve. Another explained: "If we wanted to stop in the middle [of the contract], we'd have to do a pilgrimage. If you don't do that, people will die, get sick, people will have all kinds of problems. You have to do a big ceremony, cut some banana trees, do a *mange* [food offering]. Then it's okay." By the same token, individuals may be reclaimed by Rara. They must participate in the Rara each year, or face spiritual sanctions. This is true even if they have moved abroad into the diaspora:

> Some Haitians live abroad. When they see Rara is coming up, even if they don't want to return home, there are *lwa* in the Rara that give them revelations in their dreams. They say that they are required to come home for the Rara. They are obligated to come. If they don't come, they get sick, they have a lot of problems. You can be driving and have a car accident.[22]

The Weekly Exercises during Lent

We escaped the political insecurity of Port-au-Prince in 1992 by high-tailing it to the lush mountain district of Fermathe. The problem was that it rained for most of Holy Week. We would sit in Madame Giselle's compound under her tall pine trees listening for the Rara to signal to us with the long tones of their banbou. As soon as they gathered outside the gate they would play an ochan, and that was our cue to join the Rara. No sooner would we emerge than it would start to pour. This made things extremely slippery, and sometimes an unbelievably thick white fog would prevent us from seeing the road ahead. "Lapli, lapli, lapli [Rain, rain, rain]," everybody would shout in panicked tones. We usually kept walking, except when it got so bad the drummers couldn't play, and then we huddled under roofs and trees until it lessened.

One night, after returning us to Madame Giselle's house, General Kanep sat down to drink a rum and tell us the inside story. The reason people were edgy was that the rain was ruining their reputation. You see, a strong Rara is supposed to be able to mystically mare lapli *(tie up the rain) and make it stop. But there was more, said Kanep. It wasn't their fault that they couldn't control the rain. It seemed that they had begun—and fulfilled—a contract with the* lwa *Simbi an Dezo (Simbi of the Two Waters). For seven years they had gone out, with Simbi mystically leading the band as its spiritual patron. Then Simbi decided to take a vacation, and he let the* lwa *Ti-Jan Dantò adopt the Rara. Right now, Kanep explained, the Rara was under the*

Rara musicians play *banbou*, plastic *vaksin*, and metal *konè*. They make their own recording with a portable cassette recorder. (photo © Chantal Regnault)

auspices of Ti-Jan Dantò, but Simbi was in the background and had grown envious. It was he who sent the rain, out of jealousy.[23]

Simbi's jealousy cost them a great prize when the rain stopped them from reaching the house one of the gwo nèg *in the region. La Belle Fraîcheur de l'Anglade had planned to visit General Abraham, the mysterious military figure who played a key role in the transition of power from Madame Ertha Pascal Trouillot to Father Jean-Bertrand Aristide. He lived in the mountains near Fermathe, and paying him respect was important for the Rara. They considered themselves an army on a march to salute a general. No doubt his monetary contribution was also anticipated. General Abraham never knew that a melodrama between Simbi and Ti-Jan Dantò cost him the pleasure of having a Rara band dance for him.*

Over the course of its years as a band, each Rara weaves a story, beginning with the way it was founded and ending with the exciting events of the last Rara season. Because Raras, especially rural ones, are composed of large extended families, they tend to be a site for the furthering of the social narrative, a time for the local "plot to thicken," both for individuals and for the group as a whole.

Every band has a history in relation to the larger events of the local community and the country, and songs and stories are created every year in commentary. Performing Rara in the rain became part of the ordeal of fulfilling the contract for Rara La Belle Fraîcheur de l'Anglade that year. The rain came to have a meaning and a value in terms of the strength of the band to overcome hardship and complete their mission together.

A Rara from La Plenn had a dramatic story to tell about how it got its name, Kat Sèkèy (Four Coffins). It seems that four people were killed during Rara season, and the *lwa* made them continue their march anyway:

> A long time ago, on a Good Friday, the Rara went out to have fun. A car passed, and killed four people from one household. They did one single funeral, with four coffins. On Holy Saturday, the *lwa* said the Rara had to go out. You have people crying in the morgue, and yet they're supposed to go out in the Rara. We had to go dance. Okay, we'd do the burial afterwards. But every year, we must go out with the Rara.[24]

The plot develops and thickens during the weekly Lenten *ekzèsis* (exercises) also called *repetisyon* (rehearsals) of the band. Different regions had different protocols about which nights a Rara could go out to rehearse. Port-au-Prince bands tended to go out on Tuesdays, Thursdays, and Saturdays, starting at about nine o'clock in the evening and ending at dawn. Bands in the countryside tended to choose Saturday night through Sunday morning for their weekly rehearsal. The Rara members come together in a group with the sense that they are bound in a common adventure, a common mission. Part of the mission is for the group to build its spiritual and physical stamina. During the final Holy Week the groups cover miles of territory, an especially rigorous feat in the mountainous areas of the countryside. On that week the story intensifies, moving into sacred, liminal time.

The Rara band has a general plan, which the leaders have drawn up together, involving whom to visit and which routes to take, which Raras to avoid, and if and when to enter into battle with another group. The plan is in place, but it can change depending on events, and so the feeling during the nightly outing, or *sòti,* is one of spontaneity. An encounter with another band, an offer of food by a household, or a traffic jam on the road can make the Rara unpredictable. This unpredictability intensifies the feeling of being on an adventure and of being in "event time," or "out of time" altogether. The events, rituals, scandals, and contributions found en route during the weekly *sòti* of the Rara are all part of the intense adventure of the group.

Current events in Haiti that affect everyone can be part of the metanarrative of a Rara band. The rise and fall of political figures is a common theme, and many satirical songs are written by Carnival street bands (or Rara bands who function as Carnival bands before Rara season). During Rara season these songs can be passed along from band to band. These songs can be kept and sung in following years, but more likely they are abandoned when the issue is no longer of concern to the community. Writing new songs is one of the ways that a Rara competes with other bands. Songs present new material that speaks to current situations in order to attract potential fans each year.

During my field research from 1990 to 1995, Raras sang about national and international current events, including the coup d'état against Aristide and the U.S. refugee camp for Haitians at the Guantanamo naval base. In 1993 a great tragedy struck Haiti, affecting many who lived in Port-au-Prince: *The Neptune,* a ship carrying more than two thousand people, sank between the southern city of Jérémie and Port-au-Prince. Almost all those who had been aboard died. Among those lost were members of a community of Jérémian migrants, who had relocated to the Port-au-Prince slum of Cité Soleil. The community's Rara sang a plaintive song about the tragedy:

> Look what bad luck happened to me
> Bad luck almost happened to me
> *The Neptune* left Jérémie, it sank beneath the sea
> Madam Louki, look what bad luck happened to me

> Look at the pot that turned over, Oh
> I don't have family to bury the dead for me, Oh
> The boat sank, Oh
> I don't have family to bury the dead for me, Oh

> *Men malè rantre sou mwen*
> *Men malè manke rive'm*
> *Neptun sot Jeremi li koule nan fon lanmè sa*
> *Gade Devenn rantre sou mwen*

> *Naptun sot Jeremi li koule nan fon lamè sa*
> *Madan Louki men malè manke rantre sou mwen*
> *Men chodyè-a tombe O*
> *M' pa gen fanmi O pou entere mò-yo pou mwen O*
> *Batiman koule woy*
> *M' pa gen fanmi O pou entere mò-yo pou mwen O*[25]

Not only had this Rara lost members in the sinking of *The Neptune*, but they had members who had tried to leave Haiti and were repatriated after spending months at Guantanamo. They wrote about this hardship in the following song, which you can hear on track 17 of the CD that accompanies this book:[26]

> We sold our pigs, we sold our goats
> To go to Miami
> Where we landed we were returned

> We sold our pigs, we sold our goats
> At Guantanamo they sent us back
> We got to Guantanamo
> We sold our pigs, we sold our goats
> The advice of friends is not sweet, Oh
> Guantanamo is no good, Oh

> *Nou vann kochon, nou vann kabrit*
> *Pou'n ale Miami*
> *Kote nou rive nou retournen*

Nou vann kochon, nou vann kabrit
Guantanamo yo voye'n tounen
Guantanamo nou rive
Nou vann kochon, nou vann kabrit
Konsèy zanmi pa dous O
Guantanamo pa bon O

Just as national events can be part of a Rara's story, so too can local current events become part of the "plot" of the Rara. Dignitaries in each community are approached and saluted in hopes that they will contribute generously to the band. Each Rara must chart a route to be sure that no notable is left out and offended. If any notable does take offense, this event becomes part of the Rara's story for that year, just as will an encounter with another Rara, a problem with a *lwa,* or an accident en route.

Songs about local events are almost always sung in metaphor, heavily obscured so as to prevent retribution by anyone powerful who might be offended. When local *gwo nèg* are sung about or local scandals are aired publicly in the Rara, this sort of critique is usually done in a communication style called *voye pwen* (sending a point). *Voye pwen* is a Haitian Kreyòl technique used in Vodou, in all levels of politics, and in Rara. It involves speaking about something in metaphor, using great innuendo. It is roughly equivalent to the African-American style known as "signifying." One such song that I heard in Fermathe in 1992 involved a young woman named Asefi who, it seems, aborted a child at seven months. ("Asefi" is a *non pwen* [nickname], which means "enough girls"—from the French, *assez de filles.* It is often given to little girls in families who wish to have boys.)

Talk about it, Oh, Talk about it, Oh
The family of Asefi will talk, Oh
Asefi who threw away a seven-month baby
Asefi who threw away a seven-month baby
Children are wealth, Oh, Talk about it, Oh

Pale O, Pale O
La fanmi Asefi a pale O
Asefi ki jete yon pitit sèt mwa
Asefi ki jete yon pitit sèt mwa
Pitit se byen O, pale O

This song clearly names the crime, names the guilty party, and provides a moral point: the Haitian proverb and tenet that children are wealth ("*Pitit se byen*").

The next year, in 1993, the same Rara was still talking about Asefi. She had done something else scandalous, and the community wove it into the story of their Rara:

I'm going to write a letter
I'm going to write a letter from Tomasin and send it to Fermathe
Asefi went down to Tomasin to steal cigarettes
Asefi went down to Tomasin to steal cigarettes
If I were a gossip, I would talk about it

M pral fè yon lèt
M pral fè yon lèt Tomasin voye'l Fermathe
Asefi desann Tomasin, al volè cigarèt
Asefi desann Tomasin, al volè cigarèt
Si'm te jouda m't'ap pale sa

Besides making musical points about the national situation, sexual mores, and politics within the local community, Rara bands also enact stories about their relationships to their patron *lwa*. In the story at the beginning of this section, the Rara recounts how Simbi gave the band up for adoption and then sent a jealous rain. This is a potent story, whose characters are family metaphors, negative emotions, and the weather. Over the years of a band's career and in the weeks of a Rara season's engagement with the *lwa*, the group comes together and plays out an intense drama with each other, with the spirits, and with members of other Raras.

RARA MUSIC, DANCE, AND PERFORMANCE

No study of Rara would be complete without attention to its public, performative nature. For the sake of analysis I will distinguish three general performative codes in Rara: the carnivalesque, "dancing down the road" style; the *ochan* and choreographed dances; and religious ritual. The range of music and dance protocols in Rara—dancing freely to move down the road, performing for contributions, and performing religious ritual—forms a continuum from the "play" values of Rara to the "work" of Rara.

While lithely dancing a two-step down the road amid one's family and neighbors, singing together and sharing what little food, coffee, and *kleren* there is, any Rara band spends most of its time moving from one destination to another in a carnivalesque, *pou plezi* (for pleasure) performance style. Because its movement through the local territory can take the members miles away from their starting point, there is no Rara audience per se. The people passing by on the roads or the households that line the roads to view the procession become momentary audiences who stop and watch or join in the Rara.

There are specific moments, however, when Rara bands have an audience, and these moments form a second, more precise performance situation. When it reaches targeted points on its route, the Rara band assembles in short, intense, choreographed routines before an audience, usually a local notable, an *ounfò* (religious house), or the community's dead at a cemetery or burial ground. They perform an *ochan,* usually followed by a short, stylized begging performance, for which the band hopes to obtain a *peye sòti* (a contribution; literally, "pay to go").

The third kind of performance in Rara is the enactment of religious rituals. Because they are so dense, these rituals will be discussed at length in chapter 3. They include baptizing the musical instruments, administering *benyen* (protective baths) to musicians, creating *wanga* (magical "works"), and holding *dans Petwo* (a religious ceremony) or *dans Bizango* (a secret society ceremony) in the temple before going out. Music and dance animate the more intense ritual actions of the *oungan;* together the ritual actions produce an effect like an improvisational opera.

These three generalized performative moments in the Rara are fluid and overlapping, and a band can enact all three styles in a short space of time. For instance, a Rara may dance a carnivalesque dance into an *peristil,* stop and play a formal *ochan,* and then segue into a Petwo rhythm while the host priest pours libations to the *lwa.* But Carnival, *ochan,* and religious performance moments are three separate performative codes that move the band from "play-time" into "work-time," all within the context of this form of Caribbean "play."

Music

Rara music itself is very much a communal effort, with around twenty people, including the singers, forming its core. It is important to note that there are probably as many configurations of Rara orchestras as there are regions in Haiti. A musical continuum, as it were, spans from simplicity to complexity. At one end are the a capella *charyio-pye* (foot bands). These bands stomp the feet in a marching rhythm that creates the tempo of the song.[27] At the other end of the spectrum are the Rara bands in Léogâne that achieve national reputations by employing brass musicians from *konpa* (popular dance) bands. These bands produce catchy melodies at a high volume that can be heard far away.

The typical Rara orchestra consists of three drums followed by three or more bamboo instruments called *banbou* or *vaksin,* then several waves of percussion players with small, hand-held instruments, and finally a chorus of singers. Also there is usually a core group of performers—either *majò jon* (baton majors), or *wa* and *renn* (kings and queens) who dance for contributions.

The drums played in Rara vary from region to region, but they are almost always goatskin drums in the Petwo family. These drums are strung with cord and tuned by adjusting small pegs in the interlaced cords along the drum body. The Rara orchestra differs from the Petwo ceremonial battery in that all of the drums must be portable for Rara and must be light enough to carry for miles of walking and playing. So the *manman, segon,* and *kata* of Petwo ceremonial drumming are replaced by a more portable ensemble of *manman, kata,* and *bas.* The first two are single-headed drums, strapped to the body by a cord across the shoulder. A *kès* (a double-headed goatskin drum played with two sticks) can be used as the *kata.* The *bas* is a hand-held round wooden frame with goatskin stretched across the top and interlacing tuning cords creating a web along the inside of the drum.

Rara rhythms fall into three categories of performance protocol: the Carnival rhythms of Maskawon, Nazon, and Raboday; the musical salute called *ochan,* played every time an important person or *lwa* is recognized; and the religious musics of Petwo, Kita, Banda, Kongo, or Bizango. While the Carnival and religious musics are African-derived, the *ochan* is probably historically derived from French military signal-corps drumming.[28]

Music, as well as dance and religious ritual, reflects the presence of the specific *lwa* "walking in the Rara," and the variations are many, both from region to region and from band to band. For example, the Raras near the Lakou Badjo, the stronghold of the Nago (historically Yoruba) nation in Vodou, reflect the *rit Nago* (Nago rite) in their drumming styles and ritual. The Raras near the Lakou Soukri likewise incorporate the styles of this "royal Kongo" center.[29] By the same token, bands that are formed by Bizango societies may use the drumming styles of the Bizango in that area.

The *banbou*, or *vaksin*, are the instruments most immediately associated with Rara music.[30] They are hollowed-out bamboo tubes with a mouthpiece fashioned at one end. Besides Rara, they are only played in Carnival *bann a pye* (literally, "band on foot") and *konbit* and *èskwad* (work brigades). Haitian ethnographers trace the *banbou* to the indigenous peoples of precolonial Haiti.[31] Robert Farris Thompson has identified them with the BaKongo instrument called "disoso" with a possible origin in Central African Mbutu (Pygmy) hocketing music.[32] Similar trumpets are used in the "broto" music of the Bambara people along the Niger River, as well as in Jamaican Kumina.[33]

Each *banbou* is cut shorter or longer so as to produce a higher or lower tone: *bas banbou* is long and gives a bass sound, and *charlemagne banbou* is short and is pitched high.[34] Other tones fall in the middle, often forming stacked minor thirds in relation to one another.[35] The musicians play the *banbou* using a method called hocketing. Each player takes the instrument and blows a single tone (or a tone plus an octave above it). By blowing rhythmically, the group of *banbou* players improvise until they find a pleasing, catchy *ostinato* (short repeated melody). It surprises many outsiders who listen to Rara music on recordings, without seeing it, that the melodies are created by players who only blow one note each. To help their timing, the *banbou* players beat a *kata* part on the bamboo with a long stick, making the instrument both melodic and percussive. Playing the *banbou* while walking takes a great deal of coordination, rhythm, and lung capacity.

This ostinato becomes the aural "flag" or sonic "logo" of the band, and the townspeople in the local area can tell which Rara is approaching by which melody rises over the drum rhythms. More than once, I learned that humorous song-slogans match the *vaksin* riffs, making them doubly memorable. The young people of Verettes, located in the Artibonite Valley, came back from Rara exercises each week singing slogans like "*Gwosè bagay sa, mwen pa kapab ankò*" ("The size of that thing—I can't endure it any longer"). This slogan has sexual connotations, referring to a woman who cannot tolerate a sex partner who is too large.[36]

The *banbou* instruments can also be engaged in hocketing melodies with instruments called *konè* (also called *klewon)*, hand-made metal trumpets with a yard-long tube and a flared horn at the end. Musicians also blow *lanbi,* or conch shells, in this manner. The line of drummers and the line of *banbou* players tend to form military-like flanks, walking closely behind one another to fit through tiny spaces along mountain paths or between cars, as the nature of their locale demands.

After these instruments come waves of percussion players and singers. The Raboday, Nazon, and Maskawon rhythms are all in 4/4 meter with "sustainer" patterns played by percussion instruments. These include the *ogan* (a hoe-blade beaten with a piece of metal, also an important instrument in a religious *dans*), *graj* (aluminum scrapers that are twelve to twenty-four inches long), and *tcha-tcha* (small gourds filled with seeds). The *tchancy* looks like a can with a handle on it, and is twisted back and forth so the seeds inside will create a sound.

After the percussionists come the singers. If the Rara is a strictly disciplined, serious group, then the singers tend to be women who may be *ounsi* (religious society members) and who are expert vocalists capable of singing a large repertoire of songs for days on end. The women rarely, if ever, play instruments. Less disciplined urban Rara bands tend to have fewer women in their ranks, and the work of the chorus is taken over by men.

Gage Averill is the only ethnomusicologist yet to analyze Rara music. He has suggested that the tuning scales of the *banbou* or *vaksin* instruments and the song melodies are different. He notes that while the *vaksin* are tuned in minor thirds, the two highest-pitched *vaksin* (and smallest in length) will be tuned a minor second apart. The melody that they play will often form arpeggiated diminished triads with a minor or diminished seventh. What is also interesting here is that in analyzing the vocal parts, Averill found them to be a pentatonic or hexatonic vocal melody. The pentatonic Rara melodies "often studiously avoid making much reference to the *vaksin* tonality."[37] This means that two tonalities are present in the same musical form. It is true that for a listener accustomed to European classical music, the interlaying of Rara vocals on the *banbou* melodies can be confusing. It also creates an aural "flag" for a Haitian listener, who can identify this music as singularly Haitian. This singularness is important in diaspora, where the distinct sounds of Rara take on a particular, and sensory, association with "home."

The musical leader of a Rara band is the *sanba* or *simidò* (songwriter), usually a man, who is a recognized as an artist in his community. The *sanba* may take a local event and create a scandal song, a political song, or a song boasting about the Rara or his own abilities. The term *sanba* can be used as a gloss for "everyman" in song lyrics. "Sanba, sa fè'm mal O" (Sanba, that hurt me, Oh) was a song from a Rara in the Gonaives area that the "roots" band Boukman Eksperyans borrowed and turned into a song about the pre-Aristide military government. Another song composed by a Rara *sanba* in the Beaufort area of the Artibonite said, "*Yo mare sanba yo, Yo mare pitit mwen, M pa ka pale*" ("They tied up the *sanba,* they tied up my child, I can't speak out").

Songs, then, can be especially created by a *sanba* to sing in Rara, and they can send a point to an intended hearer. *Voye pwen* function as social texts about local community affairs. They can be commentaries on neighborhood gossip, social judgments about specific scandals, or they can make wider pronouncements about the tribulations of the community in its struggle against landowners, national politics, or even international relations. At any given moment, a Rara is capable of singing a locally produced song about a community issue or a song borrowed from Afro-Haitian religion, which are, in effect, part of the Haitian national religious repertoire.

Dance

Almost any given kind of celebration in Haiti has an appropriate accompanying music and dance. It is possible to conceive of a distinct continuum in Haitian dance ranging from purely social, secular dance, whose purpose is to amuse, all the way to specific, sacred dances that are considered an integral and serious part of the work of serving the spirits.

An essential point about music and dance in the Caribbean is that every rhythm generates a specific dance, and every dance has its proper accompanying rhythm. I have noticed that the combined rhythm and dance create new kinesthetic information and sensory experience for the dancer. In other words, one cannot know the entirety of a rhythm without knowing and experiencing its dance at the same time, because with the dance moves, additional rhythms are generated. Specific rhythms and their accompanying dances are performative phrases that go hand in hand.

On the purely social, play end of the scale, we can find a variety of couples dances used in courtship. This is the sort of dancing one finds at a nightclub that plays *konpa dirèk,* the merengue-based pop music of Haiti. This includes *tèt kole* (cheek to cheek) or *ploge* and *kole* (slow dancing; literally, "stuck together"). Variations include *klere bouk sentiwon* (literally, "shine the belt buckle," which involves moving the hips in a figure eight). Other kinds of social dancing to *konpa* included *disko* (from American disco), *gogo* (surely from American go-go dancing), and *palaso* ("the bump" from the United States), but these styles came and went in the 1970s. In the 1990s one could find *bigup,* an appropriation of the Jamaican dance-hall style with its accompanying musical "signal," a distinctive bass-line ostinato woven into *konpa* songs. Country dances that are secular in nature include *kontredans* and *kalinda.* These dances are not associated with the concept of work, but rather with after-work pleasures of courtship and sexual expression, relaxing and "letting go."[38]

Afro-Haitian ritual dance in the *peristil* (religious dance space) is performed during ceremonies as part of the method of attracting spirit possession. Each *dans* or ceremony is held for a specific reason, and all of the ritual actions, music, and performances are part of the work of carrying out the ritual. The dances performed in Afro-Haitian religious contexts are numerous.[39] Although it is certainly not viewed as equivalent to the work of cultivating crops or cooking, ritual dance is a serious activity with a purpose and can be classified as one of the many activities involved in performing spiritual work.[40]

Dances that may be located in the middle of this play-to-work continuum include work-dances that go together with work-songs. For example, in the course of a *konbit,* a *sanba* may call out songs to men hoeing a garden. The men answer the song phrase, knock their hoes together twice with a partner, and swing the hoe into the earth. According to Rachel Beauvoir and Didier Dominique,

> It's not common to find a single peasant hoeing his garden alone. Usually a line of workers stands shoulder to shoulder as they work the earth together. Each movement they make together creates a rhythm, their breathing, the resistance of the earth, backed up by a drum and the call of the *sanba.* This total music created by all this movement, that is what is meant by "work."[41]

Rara dances mirror Rara musical styles and span the play-to-work continuum found within Haitian dance. The Rara dance *pou plezi* does not include couples dancing, but it features carnivalesque dance styles, danced to the "Rara" rhythms of Maskawon, Nazon, and Raboday. In his work on Haitian dance band music, Averill writes helpfully about Carnival bodily experience. He analyzes the movements of people in the *foul* (big crowd). Normally people are packed tightly against one another along the back streets, following the source of Carnival music, whether flatbed truck or *bann a pye*. "The goal," writes Averill, "is for the crowd to reach a peak experience of involvement, a state that Haitians often describe with words that connote 'overflowing' such as *debòde* (overflowing, exuberant)."[42] He notes that

> Carnival singers will exhort the crowd to "mete menn an lè" (put your hands in the air) to help the exuberance along or to get the entire crowd in the act. The raised hands gesture is generally accompanied by a leaning back and swaying of the upper part of the body, a motor response encouraged by the singer's call to "balanse" (sway). . . . The expressed goal is to "*lage kò-w*" (let go of yourself).[43]

The ultimate end point of *lage kò-w* (let go of yourself) in Carnival is not giving oneself over to the *lwa* in possession, but rather a sort of giving oneself over to the rest of the crowd in a move called *apiye pa frape* (literally, "leaning not hitting"). As the crowd is dancing down the streets, people lean backward into each other, moving onto one foot, and are even swept away on people in the crowd itself, feet dangling down in a *toubiyon* (whirlpool). Another way to *lage kò-w* is in *lese frape* (literally, "let hit") by simply allowing one's body to lean so far into someone else's that it collides.

Lese frape can lead to a serious physical competition called *gagann,* in which two young men hurl themselves at one another, landing destabilizing blows in the upper chest. Often *lese frape* gets out of hand and a collision is received as an act of hostility. *Gagann* can lead to *wozèt* (strangling; literally, "bow-tie") and end in outright fights. Ideally, however, the crowd remains in its "let go" jubilant state and exhausts itself happily into the early hours of the morning.

The basic form of Carnival dancing—two-stepping with hands raised, hips strutting forward, and chest back—is the primary dance style in Rara. But it is also possible to see *apiye pa frape* and *lese frape* in Rara. I see all of these carnivalesque idioms as having as their goal the exuberance Averill describes. These styles are heavily masculine, feature reputation-enhancing displays of Haitian machismo, and can degenerate into physical fights. Carnivalesque dancing is often accompanied by singing *betiz*. We can see how Rara's masculine, exhibitionistic, all-night dancing in its Carnival mode is a classic form of West Indian play.

Surrounded by the carnivalesque play of Rara, the core of religious work is also evidenced in performative codes. This work value is embodied in the choreographed Rara dances designed to solicit money, as well as the moments when Rara bands perform Vodou dances in local *peristil*. Let us examine the *ochan*, Rara's militaristic musical salutes. *Ochan* are usually the first phase of a Rara's performance upon its entering a compound. The sound announces the arrival of the Rara and carries with it an implied directive, signaling that the band is communicating to the patron or *gwo nèg*, summoning him or her to appear before the band. *Ochan* can also be used to signal respect toward other bands and indicate the intention to avoid a fight. *Ochan* feature long unified notes sounded by all the *banbou*, accompanied by drum rolls sounded in unison, often making a phrase that says "one-two, one-two-three."

Elements of *ochan*, including its musical style, are of French origin. In his study of Vodou musical history, David Yih notes that *"Aux Champs"* ("to the fields") was a command in the French military signal drumming repertoire meaning "Forward march!" In contrast to the polyrhythmic style of most Afro-Haitian drumming, *ochan* "shows stylistic features of European drumming, as exemplified by the rudiments, including flams, ruffs and rolls." Yih goes on to point out that "a manual of regulations issued in 1754 states that 'soldiers will cease marching every time the beating of the drum stops,' thus, as long as the soldiers were to keep marching the music had to be played continuously."[44] This principle is true in Rara as well, because an informal code ensures that if the music stops, the entire band halts. In fact, one band will seek to *kraze* (crash, ruin) the next by somehow stopping their music.

The military ethos in Rara music and in *ochan* in particular extends to the songs that accompany *ochan*. "Ochan songs make frequent reference to military leaders," writes Yih. He recorded the following militaristic *ochan* song:

The General was not there, he is going into the government
If I could find a flag corps I would celebrate his return

Jeneral-la pa te la l ap antre nan gouvènman
Si m te jwenn yon kò drapo m ta fete laretounen[45]

When I visited the popular neighborhood of Cité Soleil to record the Rara band that had composed songs about their experience at the U.S. Guantanamo refugee camp, the band used an *ochan* as a *pwen*, sending a message to everyone present that a policeman had arrived in the vicinity.

> Good evening, good evening, Corporal
> How are you
> Good evening, good evening, Corporal
>
> *Bonswa Bonswa mon kaporal*
> *Kouman ou ye la*
> *Bonswa Bonswa mon kaporal*

Later, at the end of the evening, the band sounded another *ochan* to signal that it was time for us to make our contribution.

> Look at the salute I'm doing for you
> You have to pay me
>
> *Gade yon Ochan mwen frape pou ou*
> *Se pou peye'm*

They were using this *ochan* in its classic way to exact payment from people of stature. In this sense, *ochan* can be seen as a traditionally sanctioned negotiation of power and status between classes. *Ochan* is a ritualized moment of political patronage whereby Rara groups align themselves with local notables through a performance of loyalty and homage but at the same time make a monetary demand, asserting the ideal of responsibility on the part of the more powerful.

Immediately following the musical *ochan*, and in the same category of performance-for-pay, is the dance of the *majò jon*, which derives from both African and European historical sources. The baton jugglers are dressed in flashy, sequined costumes, for which Rara bands are famous. Bands usually have two to six jugglers, or they may eschew the baton dancers altogether and have only kings and queens. Today the *majò jon* costumes consist of white tennis shoes, white socks or stockings reaching the knee, a matching set of sequined knee-length pants, a fringed sequined tunic, and a cape around the shoulders. It is possible that the design of this costume is modeled on the Roman Catholic priest's "fiddleback" chasuble, worn by French missionaries to the colony.[46] The *majò*

Majò jon pose in sequined costumes (photo © Elizabeth McAlister)

jon may also wear many colorful scarves tucked in at the waist and hanging down to achieve the effect of a palm-frond skirt. As the dancer moves and spins the baton, the scarves whirl and the sequins flash in an eye-catching spectacle. Often the *majò* will wear hats with sequins or round mirrors attached; they may also wear mirrors on a belt around the waist. They inevitably sport sunglasses and whistles in their mouths.

The batons the *majò* carry are two to three feet long and are made of wood covered with embossed aluminum. The two ends are flared into a round ball, giving it the same shape as the twirling baton commonly used in the United States.[47] The batons are infused with mystical energy when they are baptized on Holy Thursday in a ritual in the *peristil;* they spend that night "sleeping" under the *poto mitan* (ritual centerpost). On Good Friday they are fully "charged" and can help the dancers execute deft and stunning moves.

When a Rara band enters a family compound or stops in front of a house to perform, the group clears a space for the *majò jon* to dance. Much of the dancing is executed with the knees bent, placing the *majò*'s body low and fully balanced in his center of gravity. With the music playing, the *majò* begins to dance and twirl the baton simultaneously, sometimes throwing it up in the air, sometimes passing it across his own back. After a few minutes, the *majò* approaches the notable from whom money is being asked. He then executes the *twa limyè* (three lights), or *zèklè* (lightning), by passing the baton over the neck and shoulders of the potential contributor. By making a circle around the person with the mystically charged baton, this gesture of respect symbolically draws the person into relationship with the Rara.[48]

A second type of *majò jon* costume, which I saw in the Artibonite, consisted of colorful streaming ribbons hung over knickers and hanging from hats, reminiscent of Yoruba Egungun maskers. Both these sorts of festival costume have their origins in plantation society and are similar to other Caribbean festival masquerades. David H. Brown reports an account of an Epiphany street festival in nineteenth-century Cuba. We can read through its ethnocentric and racist stance in order to cull the important description: "[T]he chief object in the group was an athletic negro, with a fantastic straw helmet, an immensely thick *girdle of strips of palm-leaves around his waist,* and other uncouth articles of dress. Whenever they stopped . . . this frightful figure would commence a devil's dance, which was the signal for all his court to join in a general fandango" (emphasis added).[49]

The use of palm-leaves in Cuba and of sequins, ribbons, fringe, and mirrors in Haiti reflects a general aesthetic of assemblage found commonly across Caribbean festivals. West Indians borrowed costume elements from African masquerade, including bones, raffia, beads, shells, metal, and textiles, and created creolized festival costumes out of materials at hand.[50] Clearly the popular artists of the Caribbean also included European elements in their creolized works. Jonkonnu, mumming, and other Carnival costumes feature knee-length knickers, stockings, white shoes, and capes, most likely originating in European courtly styles.[51]

The sources of Rara probably include indigenous American ritual as well. Verna Gillis reports that the *majò jon* is "modeled after the *kasik,* a legendary Haitian Indian king. The baton he twirls is both African and Indian in origin. The Indian used the baton for fighting as well as dancing; there are batons used in dance in Benin (formerly Dahomey), Sudan and the Congo."[52] Popular knowledge in Haiti holds that Rara was something "African slaves learned from the Indians." (It was also said to be a "Jewish" festival; this will be discussed later.)

In contrast, the *mazoun* dance of the Wa Rara (Rara King) mainly reflects European styles and may be derived from the French minuet. In *mazoun,* the knees are bent, the head is tilted, the chin is down, and the eyes are focused on the feet. The dancer balances on one foot while touching the other foot softly on the ground: first the heel, then the toe, then the toe again, then the heel. The proficient dancer manages also to shimmy the shoulders slightly at the same time. Then the feet are switched, and the opposite foot displays the heel to toe movement under the dancer's own cool gaze, often hidden from view by ribbons or palm-fronds streaming from his hat. Folklore choreographer Lyonel St. Surin explained the movement to me thus: "The dancer is saying 'Look at my white shoes! Look at my white shoes!'" The white shoes, white stockings, knickers, and cape that reference the European court all display the royal idiom at work in Rara, now all but subsumed under the syntaxes and symbols of republican government and the ethos of militarization.

The moments of carnivalesque performance that are broken with precise *ochan* salutes and choreographed dance performances can be understood as a cultural creolization known as "code-switching" in which actors contrast Afro-Creole cultural forms with European ones. Linguistic analyses of Creole languages have shown that a speaker's moving back and forth from English to Patois (known now as Nation Language), or from French to Kreyòl, signals the "awareness of the differences between the performance rules and strategies of culture in contact, and of the behavioral consequences of adopting these forms."[53] The works of Karl Reisman, Roger Abrahams and John Szwed, and David H. Brown have applied the concept of code-switching to a wider variety of cultural forms. In its wider application, "style-switching" is the practice of alternating between African-Creole and European-Creole social or performance codes, where the cultural politics between these two groups position the African as "low" and "disorderly" and the European as "high" and "formal."[54] But as David H. Brown notes, "the 'formal,' 'European-derived' styles were less European in their essence than European signs which were creatively borrowed to reconstitute formal varieties of public speech and act which existed in Africa."[55] The choreographed performance moments of ritual reciprocity in Rara may reflect a historical process whereby European courtly styles were learned and inserted into otherwise Afro-Creole performances as a signal of formality and prestige within the general universe of Afro-Creole logic. Szwed and Abrahams describe these moments as "loan translations"— the insertion of a single performance "sign" into another performance system.

> With *plays,* as with the majority of performance events introduced into Afro-American life from Europe, the focus and uses of the ceremony were changed along with some aspects of the pattern of performance, and these changes were in accord with the ethical and esthetic demands of a conceptual system shared by Africans and Afro-Americans. . . .
>
> Many of these features . . . were introduced into ceremonial proceedings as a substitution for similar prestige varieties used for oratory in West Africa. . . . [I]t is the inevitable by-product of cultural fascination and renewal that occurs when different groups encounter each other.[56]

Rara features distinct performance characteristics—hocketed *banbou* melodies, sequined and striped cloth costumes, and baton twirling—not found together in any other festival. However, by comparing Rara with other Caribbean festival processions, we can understand Rara as a form of West Indian "play" in which Afro-Creole masculine codes of carnivalesque *pou plezi* dancing are contrasted with intense stylized ritual begging salutes borrowed from European courtly tradition. Viewed along a play-to-work continuum, Rara is a time of all-night play during which short periods of work occur.

Queens hitch up their skirts and dance (photo © Chantal Regnault)

Vulgarity and the Politics of the Small Man

Aristide, the country is for you
Screw whores however you want

Aristide, Peyi-a se pou ou
Konyen bouzen jan ou vle

Rara season, 1991

On the side, on the side of the clitoris
God sent me there to have fun
That's where I get my pleasure

Arebò arebò arebò langèt
Bondye voye'm se la pou'm amuse'm
Se la pou'm pran plezi'm

Rara Baby Cool, Port-au-Prince, 1993

INTRODUCTION: *BETIZ* AND ABSURD VULGARITY

Part of Rara's creativity as a form of West Indian "play" involves the bravado of sexual innuendo. Rara bands will usually launch Vodou prayer songs during their morning outings, but somewhere around mid-afternoon the cane liquor flows freely, and songs take on an irreverent vulgarity. The humor of innuendo not only is found in Rara lyrics but is firmly established in Haitian culture as a form of Kreyòl speech called *betiz*. Despite its wide usage by all classes in Haiti, Kreyòl sexual innuendo and *betiz* have never been taken seriously as a category to be studied. I want to move toward such an analysis by treating the *betiz* in Rara as a popular form of speech that reveals certain truths about gender and sexuality in Haiti, truths that are not merely analytical categories in themselves but must be related to political, economic, and cultural forces.[1] I believe that Rara's *betiz* songs are as much about order, subordination, exploitation, and dictatorship as they are about sex and sexuality.

To speak of gender and sexuality in Haiti is a charged subject, because Vodou has too often been hypersexualized by foreign writers. Since the colonial period, the sexual lives of Africans have been the object of fascination for outsiders. It is true for Haitians that "the exoticization of colonized peoples was achieved by the eroticization of their lives."[2] So I want to be careful in treating this subject and look beyond the sexual life to view the performance of vulgarity and obscenity in its national, political context. I want to connect vulgarity with power, and thus I take up the idea advanced by Achille Mbembe that "the grotesque and the obscene are two essential characteristics that identify postcolonial regimes of domination."[3] My analysis of Rara necessarily links the micro—the intimacy of gender roles, sexuality, and machismo—with the macro—economic conditions, political insecurity, and the class divide.

Singing along with the Raras during the coup period convinced me that sexualizing *betiz* songs are a form of popular laughter that comprises the only public form of speech possible for the Rara *ti nèg* (small man), the singing follower. On the most basic level, *betiz* songs perform the cultural work of affirming not only the existence but also the creative life of a people in the face of insecurity and everyday violence.

The Rara *ti nèg* who sings obscenities in the streets is borrowing a form of knowledge and performance from religious ritual. In Vodou, jokes using *betiz* are the special province of Papa Gede, the bawdy spirit of sex and death who tirelessly works, jokes, and heals. The Gede are quick to satirize the ruling order in general, and with it, anybody in authority or in a position of respect. Elsewhere I have written that by linking sex irrevocably with satire, the Gede spirits are the ultimate social critics in Vodou, uniquely able to make political commentary in both domestic and national arenas.[4] Through the jokes and *betiz,* both Papa Gede and the Rara bands become free to parody, to question, and to laugh. While this politics is not an engaged political movement, it is a politics of liberation nonetheless. This is because *betiz* opens a philosophical space for opposition and rejection of the suffering of the world through laughter.

Sexualized popular laughter constitutes a national politics in which Rara *ti nèg* use sexual imagery to "read" the social order as well as current events and issues in the local and national arena. While other forms of Rara songs are explicit political critiques and can occasion violent response from the state, the politics of *betiz* songs are obscured and generally go unremarked. Sexual Rara songs can be political "readings" at the deepest level of Haitian Kreyòl. Circulated from year to year and updated to fit the present circumstances, *betiz* songs are dialogic and contain multiple levels of meaning.

Betiz can thus be understood to be the only tolerated form of popular public speech that subaltern actors in Haiti may voice in what James Scott calls the "public transcript," the space of open interaction shared by the dominant and those they dominate.[5] *Betiz* is a form of "the privileged outspokenness of carnival [that] might even come to constitute a kind of national politics in societies in which direct commentary might be treasonous."[6] When you are not permitted to say anything else, at least you can swear, drink, and sing vulgar songs.

From this perspective, *betiz* can be seen as the last bastion of uncensored speech in Haiti. This characteristic of the postcolonial condition results from a long-standing, unwritten pact between the classes, which asserts that the populace will perform ritual vulgarity en masse during seasons sanctioned by tradition. The military and the literate bourgeoisie will leave the people unmolested, thereby distinguishing themselves from the childlike and vulgar *mas pèp-la* (common people) and confirming their own status as civilized, refined Haitians. The dominant classes adopt a Turner-esque analysis, viewing the obscene lyrics in Carnival and Rara as *defoulman,* the overflowing excitement of the crowd who is "blowing off steam" as a "safety valve" against real revolution.

Sexual speech, obscenity, and vulgarity have therefore been tolerated by the state and have even been encouraged. Both François Duvalier and his son Jean-Claude promoted *konpa dirèk,* the popular dance music. Although *konpa* can wax nationalistic and has been used as a critique (especially from vantage points outside of Haiti in the diaspora), it is known primarily for its benign lyrics about "Island life—women, beaches and rum."[7] Like its other Caribbean dance music counterparts—

calypso, salsa, merengue, soca, zouk, and Jamaican dance-hall—*konpa* is typically loaded with sexual double entendres.

Most of the sexual songs in Rara feature tongue-in-cheek, humorous lyrics. The most blatantly obscene Rara songs are those that describe genitals or sex acts. These songs are meant to be funny in their absurdity and rebellious in their vulgarity. Some songs are hardly songs at all; they're more like sung slogans. The following slogan had a distinctive and catchy melody line played on the *banbou,* and because of the wide association of the music with the lyric, the ostinato and the slogan stood in for one another:

Take out the dick, stick the dick under the clitoris

Rale zozo foure zozo anba langèt-la[8]

Singing *betiz,* Rara band members raise their voices, smile, and take pleasure in the sheer silliness and immodesty of the songs. The queens sing as loudly as the men or louder, in the spirit of competition. They may hike up their skirts and grasp them in their hands out to the side at waist-level, displaying their white slips. When they are intent on collecting money at the height of Easter Week, the slips may come up too, to reveal *kilòt* (underpants) and the prized *pwèl* (pubic hair) that may show at the top of the thigh and will surely be enthusiastically remarked upon by male passersby. Women's full participation in *betiz* makes the following song even more absurd, as it humorously describes passion and sexual frustration in a (presumably) male voice:

When I see you I want to come
The heat of your pussy makes me not able to come

Depi mwen wè ou la m'anvi voye
Chalè koko ou fè'm pa ka voye[9]

As I have indicated, the humor of these sexualizing Rara songs lies partly in their inherent absurdity. The following song was the refrain in Carnival and Rara songs in almost every region I visited in the early 1990s, making it a nationally known *betiz.* You can hear it at the end of the song on track 6 of the CD that accompanies this book. Men, women, and children sang it, often as a refrain of other songs:

Go roll titties
Go roll your mama's titties

Al roule tete
Al roule tete maman ou

Besides their absurdity, a crucial dimension of these songs' humor is their irreverent attitude toward Catholicism. This makes sense, as the parody of the Church has historically been a common Carnival theme. In early modern Europe, sacred rites were satirized in Carnival theater: sermons in praise of thieves, travesties of the catechism, and parodies of the Psalms and the Ten Commandments.[10] Insofar as they rebel against bourgeois Catholic constructions of the body, sexuality, and decorum, obscene Rara songs, like Carnival songs and Gede's songs, represent a confrontation with the pious morality and conservative gender ideology of the ruling Haitian bourgeoisie.

All of the sexual songs in Rara implicitly satirize Catholicism, but the connection can be made explicitly when a crowd sings a Catholic prayer song and follows it with a song about sex. The following song is particularly blasphemous, suggesting that the Virgin Mother has AIDS:

> Our Lady of Perpetual Help
> Watch over your children
> Our Lady of Perpetual Help
> Pray for us
> If I fuck her I'll get AIDS
> Your mama's clitoris [or, Fuck your mother]

> *Notre Dame de Perpétuel Secours*
> *Vueillez sur vos enfants toujours*
> *Notre Dame de Perpétuel Secours*
> *Priez pour nous toujours.*
> *Si'm konyen'l m'ap pran sida*
> *Kou langèt manman ou*[11]

This is a "straight" French hymn until it delivers its ridiculous punch line in Kreyòl. It uses language in a classic example of the code-switch, where the alternating use of "high" and "low" language is employed strategically for humorous effect. It is a twist on the Immaculate Conception and the international perception of Haitians as AIDS carriers: in this scenario, an Immaculate Infection makes the Virgin Mary the source of the disease.

Just as "straight" Catholics depend on Vodou as an oppositional evil, so too does the sexualized silliness of Rara depend on Catholic (and more recently, Protestant) decorum for its humor. In this sense, these songs share the politics of "slackness," the sexually explicit lyrics in contemporary Jamaican dance-hall music. Sexual explicitness in the context of conservative morality can be read as a politics undermining order. According to Carolyn Cooper, "slackness is potentially a politics of subversion. Slackness is not mere sexual looseness—though it certainly is that. Slackness is a metaphorical revolt against law and order; an undermining of consensual standards of decency. It is the antithesis of Culture."[12]

Rara *sanba,* like hip-hop MCs and Jamaican DJs, are cultural producers at the "lowest" ends of culture, who exploit the only unrepressed speech in the public transcript: obscenity. Vulgarities, expected of the poor by the rich, are the lyrical route by which disenfranchised Haitians carve out expressive space in the public arena. Because of the cultural politics wherein obscenities are disdained and dismissed, obscenity becomes a form of speech that allows the powerless to navigate into spaces of opposition, community, and a certain kind of powerful publicity.

And yet the *sanba* is broadcasting more than sheer vulgarity. There are repetitive themes in sexualized Rara songs. Usually these are expressed from a male perspective, although there are instances in which women's voices produce textual meaning as well. The male-voiced texts betray an implicit misogyny, with adultery and prostitution the most common subjects. Often these two subjects are linked, so that the adulterous mate is simultaneously and necessarily a *bouzen* (prostitute, or loose woman). (She may also be called a *madivin* [lesbian], which, along with *bouzen,* is the most ruinous challenge to Haitian women's reputations.) Other songs caution against gossip and verbal betrayal, describe genitalia and sex acts, discuss homosexuality, or express fear of contracting AIDS. As a dialogic form, however, the songs are usually about many things at once. As subsequent discussion will illustrate, lyrics about whores also refer to corrupt politicians, and songs that involve domestic themes often contain critiques that have national and transnational meaning.

In the following song, composed by a Rara in the Artibonite Valley, a man laments that he has given his money to his wife and she has cheated on him. You can hear the song on track 12 of the CD that accompanies this book:

There are no women you can trust by God
No women you can trust, Oh
I work hard to give you food
Why do you cheat on me?

Give me my things so I can go
That woman has fire under her butt
The stuff is sweet; she can't go

Pa gen fan'm konfyans devan Bondye
Pa gen fan'm konfyans O
Valè redi m redi pou ba ou mange
Pou ki sa wap banm zoklo
Ban'm pakèt mwen pou'm ale
Fan'm nan gen yon dife kap limen na bonda'l
Bagay la dous li pa ka ale

It is unclear who has "a fire under her butt" and who can't go. Surely part of the meaning of this song lies in its local historical specificity: the *sanba* probably wrote this as a *pwen,* a coded message meant to reveal a hidden truth, an opinion, or scandal. The woman who has "a fire under her butt" goes unnamed, and the use of both "she" and "I" obscures who it is that can't go. The song begins by addressing a domestic partner in the first person, and then the perspective shifts to refer to the partner in the third person, suggesting that a wider audience is being invoked to consider the issue. These sort of ambiguities may allow the song to have political as well as domestic meaning.

Haitian popular songs commonly reference domestic and national political situations simultaneously. Another song about adultery says:

Whoa, you can't leave your house
To go screw in a guy's room

Way, ou pa ka kite lakay ou
Pou al taye nan chanm gason[13]

This song may have been composed to discourage a young woman's sexual conduct. But it may simultaneously have carried meanings with national connotations. It was sung by a Rara band whose members included people who had escaped from Haiti as *bòt pipol* (boat people) and been repatriated from Guantanamo. At the time, President Aristide had been ousted and was living in Washington, D.C. It is possible that the song contains a political barb implying that Aristide was prostituting himself to the United States. By dialogically referencing a local story in front of, as it were, the national, historical one, the Rara can claim that the song carries only the local meaning. This way the band is protected from political pressure by those who might read the song in terms of the larger context.

Themes about adultery and loose women reflect an overarching anxiety over the relationships between men, women, and money. The following song may be read as a male-voiced resignation that women require money and must be paid for their sexual services. The song gives both women and money a positive value:

> Silvera doesn't hate whores, Oh [Repeat]
> If you hate the whores, they will know
> They'll hide their pussies
> Money is good
> Whores are good too
> Ago ago

> *Silvera pa rayi bouzen O [Repeat]*
> *Si ou rayi bouzen yo, se wè ou a wè yo*
> *Y'a sere koko yo*
> *L'ajan bon*
> *Bouzen-an bon tou*
> *Ago ago*[14]

But while Silvera, a Rara *kolonèl,* likes "whores" in the preceding song, he wants to bar them from the valley and lock them up in the following song, which is recorded by Silvera's Rara on track 15 of the CD:

> Key, give me a key, give me a key
> So I can lock up the whores, Oh [Repeat]
> Dieuvè won't let whores in Fermathe
> Silvera won't let whores in the valley
> Sanba, ask for a key to lock up the whores

> *Kle, prete'm yon kle, prete'm yon kle*
> *Pou'm klete bouzen Owo [Repeat]*
> *Dieuvè pa kite bouzen kay Fermathe*
> *Silvera pa kite bouzen kay Anglade*
> *Sanba mande yon kle pou klete bouzen Anye*

In Haitian Kreyòl, "whores" can signify undesirable exploiters—politicians, lawyers, thieves, or con-men (often associated with literacy by the nonliterate)—making this song a possible injunction against some generally immoral behavior or person. Simultaneously it can be read as a critique of politicians, coup leaders, and corrupt nationalists who would keep the government from majority rule.

GENDER AND THE *TI NÈG* IN THE RARA

There are a number of ways in which to analyze themes of prostitution and adultery in Rara. To start, it makes sense to examine the lyrics at face value and begin with a gender role analysis before moving on to consider their meanings within Haitian nationalism. In much of the Afro-Caribbean world, as in West Africa, women are the primary vendors in the local marketplace and also control the finances of the domestic space of the *lakou* (family compound). The man who does not own land (half the peasantry) or have a job (80 percent of urban males) becomes dependent on female family members. This division of paid labor and the absence thereof tends to institutionalize working-class female domestic rule within the broader condition of middle- and upper-class male dominance in Caribbean societies.[15] Lyrics dealing with women, money, and sexuality may reflect a discursive revolt on the part of this disenfranchised, relatively powerless male against the classed and gendered structure of Haitian society. This analysis echoes others' thinking about the misogyny of hip-hop and dance-hall music, and while it needs to be complicated and elaborated, such analysis is a logical starting point in considering Rara.[16]

While the Rara *gwo nèg* (big man) rises to a position of wealth, attracts followers, and augments his reputation, we may look at the Rara follower as a sort of "small man" counterpart—unemployed, wageless, dependent, and socially devalued—who occupies the lowest end of the social order. The *ti nèg* voices his opposition to the financial advantages of women in West Indian society in what Carolyn Cooper calls a "chain of disempowerment."[17] Seen this way, certain paradoxes about the themes of adultery and prostitution can be understood as assertions by the economically dependent male. The lyrics of the *ti nèg* can be seen as a response to the complex and often contradictory conditions that govern his own circumstances.

Other themes of male-voiced Rara songs are also contradictory and inconsistent. The generative schemes of Haitian-style popular machismo comprise rebellion against Catholic moral codes and resentment over the relative economic empowerment of women and the African-based polygamous ethos of domestic partnership (which is beyond the scope of this discussion but which extends into Haitian society).[18] These male-voiced Rara lyrics subvert the Catholic sanctions on "illegitimate" relationships, but at the same time they impose their sanctions about adultery onto women of their own class.

An adulterous woman is by definition a *bouzen* and is denigrated by the *ti nèg* in the Rara. Prostitution certainly exists in Haiti: it is a reality of extreme poverty that some women are led to commodify their sexuality. During the military coup and the international embargo on Haiti, women faced severe economic hardship, and unprotected sex sold for a dollar and seventy-five cents and virginity for five dollars.[19] Karen McCarthy Brown has written about the ways in which Haitian women from the disenfranchised classes piece together sources of income. Encountering a market woman on a country path, Brown asked what she was selling. "Beans, tomatoes, and my land," she replied. Brown was surprised: "You're going to sell your land?" The woman reached down and grabbed her own crotch.[20]

The attitude of Haitian machismo toward women and money expressed in *betiz* may be understood, then, as a series of lyrical revolts against gender roles and economic structures on the part of *ti nèg* in the Rara. One of the scant resources that *ti nèg* may have access to are domestic female partners who have greater structural access to financial opportunity. Therefore, as Cooper puts it, "undomesticated female sexuality—erotic marronage—must be repudiated."[21] However, sex is one of the few (oft-commodified) activities, along with music, that Haitians from all classes can produce and enjoy for free. Within the ethos of Haitian machismo, lesbianism or free female sexuality outside of male control carries a tinge of prostitution. In Haitian Rara and Carnival, any unranked woman walking in the procession who is not a queen doing the spiritual work of singing and dancing is considered a *bouzen* by association. Other scholars have commented upon the frequent association of women's musical activities with implied or real prostitution.[22]

Consider the attitude toward prostitution in the following *betiz* song-slogan:

> For the way I fuck whores, whores hate me
> *Jan m konyen bouzen, bouzen rayi m*[23]

Betiz are so short and cryptic that they are open to many interpretations simultaneously. For example, the "whores hate me" lyric carries a double meaning. In one way it is violent and misogynist. Read another way, it may be an ironic statement of love-making prowess. The singer may be stating that he makes love so well that women want to marry him, then come to hate him because he doesn't want to marry. In this interpretation his prowess reminds the women of their own oppressed situation: his sexual prowess transforms him from a paying customer to a powerful erotic partner, but they remain paid laborers. Both of these interpretations ascribe to the singer a kind of power. They comment on a political economy that forces women away from pleasure when relationships between people become relationships between money and bodies.

The sexual prowess of the *ti nèg* is an important aspect of Haitian machismo and is a common theme in Haitian *betiz,* giving the prostitution theme a second valence. Because of his disadvantaged position in the economic structure, the *ti nèg* sometimes trades on his love-making skills to secure women's loyalty. One Rara slogan says:

> If you don't have a pretty dick
> You won't have a pretty woman

> *Si ou pa gen bèl bwa*
> *Ou pa'p gen bèl fanm*[24]

The slang use of *bwa* (wood) for "penis" is also found in Jamaican language. Cooper cites the proverb "Oman an hood never quarrel" ("Woman and wood never quarrel"), which affirms a common Haitian male view that women's primary pursuit in life is chasing sex and, specifically, penetration.[25]

A common Rara song in 1992 was a satirical revision of a serious Vodou song, which you can hear on track 6 of the CD that accompanies this book. The original song said:

> Bowl in my hand, I'm begging [Repeat]
> It's not because I'm poor that I'm begging
> I'm seeking a relationship with the *lwa*

> *Kwi nan men, ma'p mande [Repeat]*
> *Se pa pòv mwen pòv m'ap mande*
> *Se relasyon gwo lwa m'ap chache*

This was inverted to:

Bowl in my hand, I'm begging [Repeat]
It's not because I'm poor that I'm begging
I'm seeking a relationship with a penis

Kwi nan men, ma'p mande [Repeat]
Se pa pòv mwen pòv m'ap mande
Se relasyon zozo m'ap chache

It was spun into even more vulgar heights by one band late in the evening:

Pubic hair in your butt cries out [Repeat]
It's not a little penis that will make you cry out
It's the big penis that will make you cry out

Pwèl nan bonda ou ap rele [Repeat]
Se pa ti zozo ki fè ou ap rele
Se gwo zozo ki fè ou ap rele[26]

Some of these songs from a decidedly male perspective contain undertones of sexual pleasure together with sexual violence. In the following song, even if "they" like small *bwa,* the singer will "give them" big *bwa.* (Although *dada* can literally be the buttocks, it can also be slang for the whole person, as in the English phrase "I took my butt home.") In call and response, the song says:

They like little dick
I'll give them big dick
I say
Dick!
Dick in your butt
Dick!
Dick in your butt

Yo renmen ti bwa
M'a ba yo gwo bwa
Mwen di
Bwa!
Bwa nan dada ou[27]

WOMEN'S VOICES: JUSTICE AND THE SEXUAL MAROON WOMAN

It is important to remember that Rara songs are performed by both men and women, and although the songs usually express a male voice, there are a few songs where a female positionality may be located. Like their male-voiced counterparts, these songs often link women, sexual activity, and money, but these lyrics display the plight of women in the commodification of sexuality and assert that they have sexual rights. The female-voiced songs can be seen as women's perspectives on sex and the contradictions of the Haitian economy. Female-voiced lyrics point to a dialogical process where women and men are engaged in exchanges concerning the political and sexual economy they find themselves in. Not necessarily in complete opposition to the male-voiced Rara songs, the female-voiced songs take up the themes within *betiz* and work within and against them.

Consider this businesswoman's assertion that she is not being paid enough for the strain placed on her body:

Dieuvè, get up off my belly, Oh [Repeat]
You don't hear my pussy crying
Bum, that's not enough money

Dieuvè leve sou vent mwen O [Repeat]
Ou pa tende koko'm ap rele
Salòp se pa lajanm sa[28]

The following female-voiced song is the story of a young girl who was taken into domestic partnership by a poor man and faces the violence of unwanted sex. This song is on track 14 of the CD that accompanies this book.

Charitab, Oh, send me away [Repeat]
You who took me as a virgin from my mother's house
You don't even give me a wooden spoon
The sun isn't set yet, you're putting cheese in my butt

Charitab O, voye'm ale [Repeat]
Ou-menm ki pran'm ti-moun kay manman'm
Ou pa ban'm yon kiyè bwa wayo
Solèy poko kouche, ou'ap mete fwomaj nan bounda'm[29]

Cheese here probably alludes to semen. *Fwomaj* (cheese) is also a vernacular usage for the symptoms of sexually transmitted disease.[30] Or the lyrics may be using *bounda'm* (butt) in its more general sense. In any event, this is a woman's voice critical of her husband's poverty (his inability to give her even a wooden spoon) and his sexual aggression. The song is the protest of a woman caught in a domestic trap of poverty and sexual violence.

These women's songs are important because they point to instances in the Rara where women may be producers of meaning and not simply bearers of meaning. From this perspective, women's singing obscene songs in Rara may be seen from the *bouzen*'s position, as a positive deployment of sexuality and an argument for the rights of sexual women. Consider this song in which a woman asserts herself as a prostitute and astute businesswoman:

> Good day madam, Good day sir
> How much are you bringing, it's ten cents
> Where are you going with your ten cents?
> The dick is too big; it will tear my pussy [or, clitoris]

> *Bonjou Madanm, Bonjou Msye*
> *Konbyen ou pote, se de gouden*
> *Kote ou pral avèk de gouden ou la*
> *Zozo a trò gwo, l'a chire langèt mwen*[31]

These voices provide the female counterpoint to the Rara *ti nèg* and dialogically answer his revolt with political expression of their own. They respond to the gendered dimensions of power in Haiti, and they create a position within the reality of these terms.

I noted earlier that any unranked woman *fanatik* in the Rara who is not a queen is open to the suspicion that she is committing "erotic marronage" and flaunting her sexuality as a *bouzen madivin* (lesbian whore). Her wholehearted singing of *betiz* and her dancing the hip-swiveling *gouyad* pose interesting questions. Why do Haitian women sing in the voice of the "whore"? Why do they also sing "The way I fuck whores, whores hate me" as loudly as the men? What is the meaning of women's blatant, sexualized performances?

This is a complex subject, not unlike the paradoxes of women's involvement in blues, Carnival, hip-hop, and dance-hall. And again, we can look to women's participation in these other "masculinist" forms for common ground. Perhaps, as Judith Bettelheim suggests, "Rather than assuming the role of victim, some African and African American women have asserted their sexuality in performance as an oppositional practice. They manipulate a colonial or racist or patriarchal authority by means of that which is often used to subjugate them, their sexuality."[32] Like the Gede spirits' own politics of liberation through sexualized laughter, women in the Rara use their sexualized personas to present ways of knowing and ways of acting in the world that are different from dominant, masculinist, and Catholic narratives.

A quality Rara queens seem to share with their hip-hop counterparts is their irreverence toward the dominant culture's moral stance, which would seek to repress their sexuality as women. In her pioneering book on Rap music, Tricia Rose talks about female rappers' performances, in which "black women's bodies are centered, possessed by women, and are explicitly sexual."[33] Rara queens, as well as rappers and other women artists in Black Atlantic performance traditions, fashion and perform a publicity that projects images of female sexual freedom and economic control. One common feature of many forms is the centrality and celebration of the African female behind. Future scholarship might well look into the possibility that the "bottom-heavy" hip-rotating dances like *gouyad*, whinin', and "doin' da butt" "had one meaning in African culture and came to be integrated into bodily performances of opposition in the American setting."[34]

In performances by the *mizik rasin* band Boukman Eksperyans, the women vocalists perform many of the dances of Afro-Haitian religion, including the *banda* with its sexually suggestive, pelvis-rotating *gouyad*. During one show at the height of the postcoup violence, the group sang its 1993 Carnival song about fearlessness in the face of military repression. After singing a verse that said, "They can bring Uzis, they can bring batons, I'm not afraid of them," the lead singer launched immediately into a sexualizing *banda,* her hands outstretched, chin up, in a pose of centered defiance. That song often gave me the shivers, because the military *did* bring Uzis against the people, and I, personally, *was* afraid of them. I was quite struck by her direct connection of defiance and *gouyad* at that moment, on that stage. The connection between resistance to military rule and her physical liberation was clearly illustrated in a bodily, performed way. Audience members dancing along with her likewise developed a kind of muscle memory that connected freedom of movement, sexuality, and political redemption.

The Clitoris and the Beautiful Vagina

Besides the female-voiced songs about sexual rights, there are a number of other elements in *betiz* that offset the themes of sexism and sexual violence. Two striking aspects of Rara *betiz* songs are not found in any other musical genre that I am aware of. First is the distinction in Kreyòl terminology between *koko, krèk,* and *langèt. Koko* roughly means vagina, whereas *krèk* and *langèt* can be used to describe the clitoris. Interestingly, the clitoris is commonly referenced in *betiz*. Second, women's genitalia are often described as beautiful. A Rara band near Gonaives is named La Bèl Krèk de Janine (Janine's Beautiful Clitoris). Consider this song:

Come and see, come and see Klodet's pussy
What a clitoris!
This woman is a beautiful woman

Vin wè, vin wè koko Klodèt
Ala youn langèt
Fanm sa a bèl fanm[35]

This genre of *betiz* songs can be intentionally humorous. The following song circulates in the New York City Raras:

Oh Suzette
Who is walking up the Marniet mountain
Her clitoris is longer than a wooden plank
She has to pay to have sex [literally, "get it cut"]

O Suzèt
K'ap monte mòn marinèt
Krèk li long pase youn goyin
Se peye' l peye koupe'l

Part of the complex of Haitian constructions of sexuality, then, is an awareness of the central role of the clitoris in female sexuality. *Betiz* songs point to an aesthetic within Haitian sexuality that values female genitals, pays attention to the size and shape of the clitoris and the vaginal area, and values an abundance of pubic hair.

HOMOSEXUALITY

So far my discussion has implicitly centered on an assumed heterosexual orientation. But Rara bands are liberal in their discussion of homosexuality, both male and female. Like the subject of *betiz,* very little has been written about Haitian homosexuality, despite the important relationships between homosexuality and Afro-Haitian religion and between homosexuality and AIDS, one of the leading causes of death in urban Haiti.[36] Some Carnival bands in Port-au-Prince are made up of a majority of *masisi* (gay men) who cross-dress in long gowns and makeup. These bands come out of Vodou societies that have gay congregations. I did not find any Rara bands that had a majority of gay members, perhaps because of Rara's proximity to Petwo, the aggressive and conventionally masculine side of the religion, and to Bizango, the secret societies. However, there is a tradition of cross-dressing in Rara, and of singing about *masisi* and *madivin.*[37]

Unlike the homophobia of Jamaican dance-hall, made famous by Buju Banton (whose lyrics "Bye Bye Boom" advocate attacking gay men), the *betiz* about *masisi* and *madivin* in Haiti are not violent but are in keeping with the general irreverence of other songs. Rara Modèl in a pro-Aristide neighborhood in Carrefour sang this song as they finished their Holy Week activities on Easter Monday 1993:

Nasty—
Faggots are the sweetest
Nasty—
Faggots are the sweetest

Chawonj—
Masisi pi dous
Chawonj—
Masisi pi dous

Difficult to translate, *chawonj* means something smelly and nasty, or as one person explained, "like a dead dog in the street." *Chawonj* describes someone who will have sex with anyone, any place. Interestingly, I heard Silva Joseph's gay Carnival band sing the same song early in the year as they descended the Bel Air hill into downtown in full drag. Carnival is one of the few times Haitian homosexuals may be openly gay with a reasonable measure of security. Under Duvalier it was a crime to be gay in Haiti, despite an underground international gay tourist trade. After the fall of Duvalier, Haitian society remains markedly homophobic. In keeping with the popular license on vulgarity for Carnival and Rara, however, homosexual themes are tolerated as appropriate subjects for *betiz*. Another song declares:

I just know I'm not a faggot [Repeat]
A dyke gave me the explanation!

Sèlman mwen konnen mwen pa masisi [Repeat]
Madivin te fèm eksplikasyon!

And the following song, shouted at full volume by the extended family in the mountains of Fermathe, was performed late in the day, right after a Catholic song:

Faggots and dykes, they're twins [Repeat twice]
They fuck, they fuck and they come

Masisi a madivin se marasa [Repeat twice]
Yo konyen, yo konyen, yo voye

Within the Haitian majority classes there is a range of gender practices and sexualities. However, it is unclear (to us outsiders) how these Creole sexualities are practiced by Haitians and what their meanings are. More research is needed on the full practices and meanings of Haitian gender and sexuality and their relationships to other social structures.

My own research on same-sex relationships in Haiti indicates that, as with heterosexual relationships, gay relationships are conditioned by finances and access to resources. Gay women, for example, may have husbands who assist them financially, and discreet female lovers. By the same token, men forge alliances that crosscut lust and desire with economic resources. As in other parts of Latin America, homosexuality in the popular classes in Haiti takes a shape similar to the "butch-femme" categories in the United States. Both men and women are called *masisi fanm* and *masisi gason* (girl faggots and boy faggots) and are distinguished by the gender roles they assume. Afro-Haitian religion is sympathetic to gay men and women, and many talented gay people establish reputations as openly gay singers, dancers, or artists. For the enfran-

chised classes, homosexuality is fraught with anxieties over public reputation and potential police attack. Only a very small, wealthy, elite
circle of young people live relatively open gay lives, and there is nothing
resembling a gay movement.

Haitian homophobic machismo links the French with ideas of false
masculinity and by extension, homosexuality. All things French are privileged in Haiti, and association with French language and culture is
a form of cultural capital that the middle classes draw upon to reach
for upward mobility. However, the French are also associated with
physical weakness and the inability to perform physical labor, and
this association makes the French language a sign of femininity. Haitians shift between French and Kreyòl speech in sophisticated ways
during the course of daily interactions with social inferiors and superi-
ors. Failing to make these code-switches (for occasions of intimacy,
aggression, and humor) can constitute a political act in Haiti. This
was tragically reinforced in 1994 when an upper-class gay man was
arrested outside a nightclub and attacked for six hours by armed civilians in league with the military—ostensibly for speaking "too much
French."[38]

AIDS

One of the newer additions to the repertoire of *betiz* in Carnival and
Rara is an awareness of AIDS, as in the following song:

> If I fuck her [or him] I'll get AIDS
> Your mother's clitoris [or, Fuck your mother]
>
> *Si'm konyen'n m'ap pran sida*
> *Kou langèt manman ou*[39]

New *betiz* about AIDS are explicit about its transmission through sex
and its prevention through condoms. In the following song, lesbians
were interchangeable with whores in a joke about lesbian sexuality and
safe sex:

> A lesbian (or whore) in the band asked me to screw
> I don't have a condom, lend me a false penis

Youn madivin (bouzen) nan bann-nan ki mande'm konyen
Pa gen kapòt, prete'm yon fo zozo[40]

ELITE CONSUMPTION AND POPULAR VULGARITY

I have argued that Rara is the season in the Haitian calendar during which the popular classes are given sanction to produce displays of vulgarity in public. In so doing they rebel against Catholic morality and allow the bourgeois classes to reactively perform distaste, refinement, and sophistication. The theatrical quality of interactions between Haitian class groups is heightened during Carnival and Rara, when thousands of (Black, poor, thin) bodies from the populace take to the streets with (lighter-complexioned, rich, healthier) bodies as their disdainful and ambivalent audience.

M. M. Bakhtin has argued that popular displays of vulgarity are parodies that undermine dominant culture by exposing its absurdity.[41] I want to suggest that the vulgarity of the popular classes must be considered in light of the decadence of the rich that is continually displayed in the Haitian "public transcript." I extend the performance metaphor to view the bodies of the rich who also produce performances of display. These performances of conspicuous consumption are vulgar and obscene in a deeper, more profound sense than those of the downtown Rara bands. Furthermore, in a cultural dialectic between "high" and "low" cultural forms, the poor read and interpret the vulgarity of the rich, and it is these readings that become incorporated into their own performances of obscenity on the public stage.

As we have seen in the preceding song texts, orifices and genitals are the primary signifiers through which the poor produce *betiz* in the public transcript. Achille Mbembe describes a similar relation of popular laughter and body imagery, suggesting that vulgarity is used as a method of deconstruction by subalterns in sub-Saharan Africa:

Ultimately, the obsession with orifices and genital organs came to dominate Togolese popular laughter. But the same is also to be found in writings and speech in other Sub-Saharan countries. . . . [O]bscenity and vulgarity—when regarded as more than a moral category—constitute one of the modalities of power in the postcolony. But it is also one of the arenas of its deconstruction or its ratification by subalterns. . . . It is here, within the confines of this intimacy, that the forces of tyranny in Sub-Saharan Africa have to be studied.[42]

Only through a shift in perspective can we understand the vulgarity of the populace as a reading of the generative vulgarity and obscene decadence of the dominant classes. Thus "The people who laugh kidnap power and force it, as if by accident, to contemplate its own vulgarity."[43] From this orientation, the popular classes can be seen to be enacting, in a ritual way, the vulgar decadence of the rich. Performed vulgarity, then, must be understood in light of displays of decadence, repression, and the power relations of dictatorship.

Michel-Rolph Trouillot has suggested that there is a kind of intimacy that characterizes contact between classes in Haiti, usually at points of exchange, often in domestic service.[44] Sexual, emotional, and physical services are traded or exacted, and the body becomes a central site of power relations. Based on a combination of factors including physique, comportment, complexion, dress, and speech, any actor in Haitian society can instantly read the class position of another. In any bourgeois household at the present writing one can find thinner, darker bodies nurturing, nursing, feeding, pleasuring, and guarding heavier-set, lighter ones.

Many writers have pointed out the ritual importance of feasting in the maintaining of supremacy by dominant classes. Literate, enfranchised Haitians, convinced of their inherent humanity and their refinement and superiority compared to the general populace, take pleasure in European forms of consumption, including eating, drinking, dressing, and adorning and scenting the body, with the inevitable assistance of the servant. Scott notes that "Those forms of domination based on a premise or claim to inherent superiority by ruling elites would seem to depend heavily on lavish display, sumptuary laws, regalia, and public acts of deference or tribute by subordinates."[45] In Haiti there has been no shortage of conspicuous consumption. The lavish display of the wedding and general consumption patterns of Jean-Claude "Baby Doc" Duvalier to Michelle Bennett represented the height of the decadence of the dictatorship and became an international scandal. After their multimillion-dollar wedding ceremony, the couple continued to consume with money taken directly out of the state treasury and invited the public to watch their consumption on television as a sort of spectator sport. "Ostentatious presidential parties, televised on presidential demand, showed officials and bourgeois alike, flaunting expensive designer gowns, jewels, champagne, and caviar."[46] It was common knowledge that the family was consuming the funds in the national treasury; this was routine behavior for the president-for-life whose father had rewritten the Lord's Prayer to insert himself in God's place.[47]

Though they represented the extreme end of consumption in this era of Haitian history, the workings of power in society made the first family the model of everything desirable, imitated by those who wished to create an appearance of social parity. Haitian parties of the era (and to this day) feature a lavish "buffet" of diverse dishes and a series of alcohol choices, privileging imported whiskey over domestic rum.[48] Through the actions of assistance at these events, the servant affirms the humanity of the master, which is displayed through the process of consumption. In the pure political economy of the modern age, humanity is linked with purchasing power, and feasting is linked with display. Mbembe speaks of the *commandement* as the phrase denoting colonial authority, "the images and structures of power and coercion and the instruments and agents of their enactment." He suggests that bodily orifices are a central signifier within performances of wealth and power in postcolonial societies. "[I]f . . . ceremonies and festivities constitute the pre-eminent means by which the *commandement* speaks and the way in which it dramatizes its magnificence and prodigality, then the body to which we are referring is, foremost, the body that eats and drinks, and which (in both cases) is thus open."[49]

In Haiti the genitals are the favorite subject of absurd vulgarity, but *betiz* also includes scatological humor. *Kaka* (shit) can be an exclamation point for any given song. An example was the 1993 Carnival song by *konpa* superstar Michel Martely (whose nickname, "Sweet Mickey," the populace cynically gave to the notorious torturer and chief of police, Michel François). The song featured various verses and then stretches of instrumental breaks where Mickey would exhort the crowd to repeat after him, "Oh Oh, Ah Ah." Carnival followers immediately turned this into "*Koko, kaka*" (Vagina, shit), which became a standard *betiz* throughout the rest of Carnival and Rara seasons.

The popular laughter over bodily orifices included the favored choice for president, Jean-Bertrand Aristide. Inaugurated on 7 February 1991, Aristide presided over the Carnival that began three days later. Aristide had spent his adult life as a Catholic priest in the Salesian order, teaching and ministering to the poor of Port-au-Prince. Nevertheless, his emblem for the election ballot was the *kòk kalite* (good fighting cock). The logical double entendre followed, and a series of songs were launched by the Rara *ti nèg:*

> Aristide, the country is yours,
> Bare your butt however you want
>
> *Aristide, Peyi-a se pou ou,*
> *Kale bonda-ou jan ou vle.*

Variations on this theme included

> Bare your dick however you want
> *Kale zozo-ou jan ou vle*

and

> Screw whores however you want
> *Konyen bouzen jan ou vle*

Carnival 1991 also gave the *ti nèg* the chance to "read" and critique those who had caused harm to their beloved President Aristide. A failed coup d'état had been launched by *tonton makout* Roger Lafontant before the inauguration of the new president. The transitional president, Madame Ertha Pascale Trouillot, was blamed by the *ti nèg* for her alleged collusion in the coup. They broadcast the following song, which had been composed and recorded by the *mizik rasin* band Koudjay:

> Mama Caca Trouillot
> Shit Mama
> Look how you let the guinea fowl
> Get into the national coop
>
> *Manman kaka trouyo*
> *Mama Kaka*
> *Gade pentad ou kite*
> *Antre nan kalòj la*

Folklorist Donald Cosentino reported the following image from that year's Carnival, in full obscene form: "On a wooden platform . . . across from the Presidential Palace, a signboard had been painted with all the same characters from the national soap. Lafontant was tied up nude to a pole. His zozo (penis) was bound with cords. Trouillot, her coco (vagina) hugely magnified, was bent over and bare for the divebombing kok kalite. During Carnival, symbols aren't subtle."[50]

In 1991 the repression of the military coup changed the public transcript. The military government showed no signs of relinquishing power despite a crippling economic embargo. The financial distress of the poor was matched by the repression of the Cedras regime, which brutally revoked the free speech rights of the press and the people. Military and armed civilians arrested and tortured journalists, closed radio stations, and allowed only one television channel.[51] The vulgarity of *betiz* dominated Carnival, Rara, and most forms of joking in the public transcript. It seemed that as the repression became worse, the *betiz* grew louder.

If this analysis is correct, then increased repression will generate an intensification of the obscene lyrics in popular music. There is some evidence that the historical moment at which the vulgarity in Carnival went from sophisticated sexual double entendres to blatant obscenity occurred at the consolidation of the Duvalier takeover of the Haitian state. During the Carnival of 1959, the famous *konpa* bandleader Weber Sicot hired a woman to stand at the front of the Carnival truck and sing *betiz* and dance *gouyad*. Called Ti-Simone, the woman had the same name as the dictator's wife, Simone Duvalier, and therefore was sanctioned, by synonymous relations with the dictatorship, to near-complete freedom. Some recall that moment as a turning point in both the repression of the state and the vulgarity of Carnival.

This chapter has sought to link a micro analysis of gender, sexuality, machismo, and vulgarity with a macro analysis of class inequalities, political insecurity, and postcolonial military dictatorship. I have suggested that sexualized humor in Kreyòl speech is popular laughter that constitutes a kind of national politics in which the relatively powerless can perform political readings at the deepest level of speech.

This chapter views the *ti nèg,* who follows and complements his local *gwo nèg* counterpart, as a master of *betiz,* the last form of uncensored expression in the public transcript. *Betiz* is a reaffirmation of the "low" and vulgar tastes of the populace and therefore functions as a performance of subservience. At the same time, *betiz* is a political reading of the particularities of Afro-Caribbean gender relations, the social order, current events, and issues in the local and national arena.

Mystical Work

Spirits on Parade

Mama asked me where I'm going
I said to my father's house
Papa asked me where I'm going
I said to the crossroads
Master Crossroads asked me where
    I'm going
I'm going to the cemetery

*Manman mande mwen kote mwen
    prale
Mwen di kay Papa
Papa mande mwen kote mwen prale
Mwen di nan kalfou
Met Kalfou mande mwen kote'm prale
Mwen pral nan cimityè*

Afro-Haitian prayer song

Young Rara kings and a queen dance for the ancestors at a tomb (photo © Chantal Regnault)

Although the carnivalesque "play" values of Rara are important, Rara also can be a serious religious act required of committed members. Rara festivals are concerned with carrying out spirit work that is considered a matter of life and death within the community. There is a great deal of evidence that Rara is religious and that it comprises the Lenten season's spiritual activities. During these six weeks, *ounfò* (religious houses) suspend ritual activity until after Easter, diverting their energies into Rara bands. As you will see from my descriptions of religious rituals later in this chapter, Rara can be understood as one of the rites in the Afro-Haitian religious complex. It is produced locally in multiple places by multiple groups, drawing participants in numbers ranging from thirty members to thousands, and lasting all the six weeks of Lent.

Performing Rara is considered a service to the *lwa,* and aspects of the performance adhere to protocols in Afro-Haitian religion, drawing on its ritual prayers, songs, and dances. Rara bands interact with the spiritual energy that resides in specific natural sites by pouring libations, lighting fires, and cracking whips to appropriate that energy. Priests baptize material objects used in Rara performance—batons, drums, and costumes—during Easter Holy Week.

During these moments when Rara bands perform religious rituals at the home temple, at crossroads, trees, bridges, and stones, and in cemeteries, Rara members shift from carnivalesque, vulgar, play activities into a mode focused on work. More precisely, Rara bands are "working the spirits" and engaging *lwa, zonbi,* and *pwen* (purchased spirits; literally, "points").

"Work" is a cultural concept with many levels of resonance in Haiti, a society that was formed in plantation slavery, where people were routinely worked to death. As the chapter epigraph shows, Rara bands systematically make their way from a home compound to a nearby intersection and then on to the cemetery in order to perform spiritual work required of them. The song—which goes from Mama to Papa to crossroads to cemetery—also hints that work and space in Rara are gendered. I believe that there are deep links between memory—the memory of slavery—the crossroads, and the cemetery. When they work the unseen spirit world, the priests and sorcerers in the Raras revisit and engage these memories. Understanding Rara—and the Afro-Haitian religion it is part of—means seeing Rara performance and the spiritual work of Vodou in terms of the many profound and lasting effects of slavery.

Much of the initial spirit work of Rara consists of gathering energy from the outside, invoking spiritual powers and attaching them mystically to the band. This principle of infusing a group with supernatural energy is common to many African-based religions, where practitioners bring spiritual power from outside the boundaries of society to use for their benefit.[1] One way they activate this mystical force is through the invisible enslaving of the community's recently dead. In these moments the trauma of the experience of slavery is revisited, ritually reenacted, and controlled by the priests and sorcerers of the Rara.

The energy brought in can be Rada *lwa*, Petwo or Bizango *lwa*, *pwen cho* ("hot" magic forces), or *zonbi*. In order to understand the differences between these various spirit entities, previous scholars have focused on the division between the Rada and Petwo branches of the Afro-Haitian religion. The "cool" and regal Rada rituals and spirits were thought to have derived historically from Dahomey, whereas the "hot" and "violent" Petwo branch was presumed to be "Creole," "born out of slavery in the New World."[2] Much of the Petwo symbology was assumed to be indigenous American, but the gunpowder, whips, and whistles in Petwo were thought to have been incorporated from elements of slavery. Now things seem both simpler and more complicated. The Rada rituals do largely derive from Dahomean and Yoruba religions. But closer attention to the Petwo and Bizango branches shows that they are rooted in the Kongo societies of Central Africa.[3] Some words in Petwo song prayers are from the KiKongo language. Gunpowder, whistles, flags, and the colors red, white, and black are all central features in the Kongo religious complex. "Petwo and Kongo, it's the same path," the spirits will tell you.[4]

Things are also more complicated than they once looked because all the branches of the religious system were creolized with European Catholicism and with one another. (Not to mention that many of the Kongo were already converted Christians when they were enslaved.) All of the branches of Afro-Haitian religion, then, can be said to be rooted in African societies and also to be fully Creole systems, transformed and evolving in the West.

Perhaps a more salient division in Afro-Haitian religion than "African" versus "Creole" or even "cool" Rada versus "hot" Petwo is a moral distinction that Vodouists make themselves between "Ginen" and "magic." "L'Afrik Ginen" (literally, Guinea Africa) is the originary Africa across the waters, from whence the slaves were taken and to which the Vodouist will return after death. Ginen is a mythical place, but it is also an ethos. Someone who is "Ginen" follows family ways, is morally upright, and does not meddle in a neighbor's affairs. To work in the

Ginen tradition is to work "with the right hand" and to accept the will of God and the spirits.

In contrast, "magic" (meaning sorcery) is spiritual work that may not accept the will of God and may instead manipulate *pwen* created by sorcerers who "work with both hands." These spirits are mystical mercenaries who will activate change on behalf of whoever pays them. Their ceremonies are "hot" and often use fire and gunpowder to *chofe* (heat up) ritual materials. Petwo ceremonies and prayers sometimes—although not always—involve working *maji* (magic). Petwo and Bizango rites (of the Chanpwèl secret societies) are often militaristic, concerned with aggression or self-defense. Bizango rites seem to be centrally focused in working *maji* and consolidating power in both local and national territories. But these categories are also complex. The terms *Ginen* and *maji* depend on one another to make sense, and they too are intertwined in various ways.[5]

Rara is rooted in the Petwo-Kongo-Bizango rites, then, which are positioned in folk categories as the "military," "hot" branch of the religious complex. Rara leaders repeatedly told me that "*Rara sòti sou Petwo*" ("Rara goes out under [the auspices of] Petwo"). Petwo *lwa* are commonly invoked in songs, Petwo rhythms are played, and there is an emphasis on the entire Petwo symbology, including the colors red and black, and the use of the whip, gunpowder, and whistles. *Lwa* who are commonly associated with Rara bands include Mèt Kalfou, Ti-Jan Petwo, and Simbi Makaya, which mark these rituals as Petwo-Bizango. The spiritual "heat" and violence of Rara mirror these two specific divisions of Afro-Haitian religion.

The Bizango, or Chanpwèl societies, are a major source producing Rara personnel and ritual. Several people repeated to me that "any Rara can become a Chanpwèl," and that the core leadership of a Rara can carry out the agenda of the Bizango society at any moment—usually at midnight. A hidden signal will go through the crowd, and anyone who is not a member of the society will be sent a message to turn back and go home. At this point the Bizango members are said to *wete po, mete po* (change skins) and transform into nocturnal beings with magical power. Bizango members parading as a Rara have the opportunity to advertise their status as Bizango members to the community—a possible form of preemptive social self-defense.

As we will see, yet another rite—Banda—is important to Rara, forming a ritual logic of a Petwo-Bizango-Banda trilogy. Banda is the rite of the Gede spirits of the cemetery, with a specific drum rhythm and dance (*banda*) featuring the hip-undulating *gouyad*. Coming at the end of the evening in a domestic urban religious ritual, Banda signals the journey to death but also celebration of the outrageous: the inverting of polite society. Rara bands can play stretches of *banda* rhythm while saluting a house in order to receive its *peye sòti* contribution. The Rara queens often dance a *banda* for the person from whom money is being asked. Thus the progression of a Rara band from home to streets to the cross-roads to the cemetery is also spatially gendered. We can see this in the work of the queens who sing in the chorus and dance.

WORK AND GENDER IN RARA

> The queen, Oh, works
> The queen, Oh, works
> Walk to see where the healer-priest works
>
> *La renn O travay*
> *La renn O travay*
> *Mache pou wè kote oungan travay*
>
> Rara Belle Fraîcheur de l'Anglade, Fermathe,
> Easter morning 1992

As in the English-speaking Caribbean, the word for *work* in Haiti connotes seriousness and family-based activity, and by extension it is identified with the *lakou*. To the extent that the *lakou* is opposed to public space (or "the crossroads"), work is identified with women and with the domestic sphere where women control much of the resources and labor.[6] In *The Man-of-Words in the West Indies: Performance and the Emergence of Creole Culture*, Roger Abrahams explores the gendered implications of work values. He notes that in West Indian family structures, it is the women who are charged with keeping discipline in the yard (the outdoor cooking area) and states that "Work is learned within the home as the most important feature of (extended) family living." Abrahams argues that a primary way West Indian family life is organized is in terms of gendered spheres, where women control the household and men dominate the street corner. "This distinction is pursued in terms of the differences of orientation, activity, and value systems between the female system of respectability and the male valuation of reputation maintenance."[7]

The division of labor in Haiti is, indeed, gendered; there are definite sets of women's work and men's work. But work in Haiti is even more complex than this gendered set of associations. Labor is structured through social class and skin color, with certain classes of the country performing work that other classes never perform. Work also expands in Afro-Haitian culture to include religious actions undertaken in order to effect change. Thus *oungan* and *manbo* (priests or priestesses) work when they receive clients, pray on their behalf, or perform rituals centered on healing or justice. As in Anglo cultures, this work can include "acts aimed at fulfilling religious ideals or acts done in compliance with religious laws."[8] Within the Afro-Haitian religious complex, work includes singing, dancing, drumming, ritual cooking, attending services, and performing rituals.

A priest or priestess is said to *fè yon travay* (do a work) for clients when they initiate people, perform divinations, make protective baths, or construct any number of mystically infused objects. A sorcerer is said to be one who "works with both hands," the righteous right hand and the sinister left hand. By extension, a ritually created object that results from an *oungan*'s work is itself a "work," a *wanga*, or a *travay maji* (magic work). (*Wanga* are material objects infused with spirits and medicines; they use a series of visual puns to admonish the spirits to work. These *wanga* are then said to be "working" for their owners.)[9] Work in the Afro-Haitian context carries with it values of seriousness and of effecting change through actions, and it can range from the physical labor of farming to the singing and dancing of a religious service.

We can see an association between women, religion, and work in the section epigraph: "The queen works, the queen works, walk to see where the *oungan* works." The gendered qualities of play values and work values are present in Rara, and the religious work of the band is linked to femaleness in two important ways. First, when work is being done inside the *peristil* or the *lakou* before the Rara takes to the streets, this work is situated in a domain that is symbolically female (although, in the majority of cases I saw, even the religious preparations of Rara are overwhelmingly undertaken by men). This first sense, then, links women to Rara work in terms of symbolic space. Second, women in the Rara are usually directly involved in the spiritual work of the band when the Rara goes out. As queens and chorus members, they are an organized group of singers and dancers who are there not to establish their individual reputations through competition, but rather to sing prayer songs, collect money, and "bring honor to the Rara."[10] Women who are not dressed up and in the Rara's chorus but who dance in the crowd as *fanatik* are engaged in "play" and are inevitably labeled *bouzin*.[11]

Recent studies of women's folklore and culture suggest that in many societies, women and men appear to occupy separate expressive spheres, creating two differentiated yet complementary halves of culture. Dichotomous oppositions between men and women are rooted in basic religious and class structures, linking male and female musical domains to traditional dualisms such as sacred or profane, holy or sordid, monied or slave, and instrumentalist or singer.[12] The presence of the working queens at the core of the Rara is likewise one element in a conceptual complex of oppositions. The outer periphery of play values is a carnivalesque, male realm of artistic competition. It is public and open, allowing for the display of reputation-enhancing feats of music and dance. The carnivalesque periphery protects a hidden core of mystical work, seriousness, and the presence of high-ranking women—the queens.

The most profound work of Rara takes place inside the cemetery. Here both men and women participate in spiritual obligations, although the most intense work—capturing and enslaving the recently dead—is the province of the male captains, priests, and sorcerers. Here the Rara leaders generate the *maji* that will empower the band. In so doing, they simultaneously remember and reenact the condition of slavery.

WORKING THE CEMETERY

The cemetery is the core site of religious work in Rara. The cemetery in Haiti is a mystical metropolis populated by spirits of the dead as well as higher-ranking spirits who "own," guard, and direct the dead. It is conceived as a small city ruled by leaders, with codes, rules, and regulations all its own. Saint Victor is an entity who lives at and owns the cemetery gates. Inside, Bawon and Brijit own the cemetery itself and direct the affairs of the dead. They are assisted by second-ranking *lwa* like Kapitèn La Kwa, Kapitèn Zonbi, Pike La Kwa, Grann Seli, and Mèt Minwi. Following them in rank comes the "nation" of Gede *lwa,* the spirits of people whose personalities and powers were so strong that they became *lwa* over time. Under the Gede rank are the *zonbi,* the recently dead. Rara bands that make the trip to the cemetery conduct mystical negotiations and make contracts with these entities in order to infuse the band with magical force.

Before the cemetery, however, necessarily comes the crossroads. This theme of a progressive link between the crossroads and the cemetery is a fundamental way that landscape and cosmology are theorized together in Vodou. Numerous people told me that *"Si kalfou pa bay, simityè-a pa ka pran,"* meaning literally, "If the crossroads won't give [passage], the cemetery can't take."[13] In the ritual logic of Afro-Haitian religion, certain deities must be "saluted," or invoked, before others; this is called the *regleman* (rule). While Legba is the first *lwa* to be invoked for the Rada rites, Mèt Kalfou (Master Crossroads) is the first *lwa* in the Bizango rite of the Chanpwèl secret societies.[14] It is considered impossible to get to the healing and magical properties of the *lwa* Bawon Simityè (Baron Cemetery) without first propitiating the *lwa* of the crossroads. Rara bands enact this inner religious *regleman* in a public, literal way when they adopt and work certain physical crossroads by performing rituals there before moving on to the cemetery gates, and then to work inside the cemetery itself.

President Moriset of Rara Ti-Malis in Léogâne was not particularly religious; instead, he viewed Rara philosophically. He interpreted the Rara as a public ritual about walking down life's road: "The road is what gets you to the crossroads. After you pass the crossroads you can get to the cemetery. And that's where you end up. You can't go any further."[15] Other Rara presidents, especially if they were members of Chanpwèl societies, envisioned the symbolic progression—from the home *peristil* or *lakou* into the public space of the crossroads and on to the cemetery—as a mystical route that leads to the center of the Rara's work. As a Port-au-Prince *oungan* explained to me, "Each crossroads has a master; is owned by a *lwa*. You can't go through the crossroads without saluting it. Because if the crossroads doesn't let you pass, you won't make it to the cemetery. When a funeral leaves the church [for the cemetery], it goes through the crossroads."[16]

The route from crossroads to cemetery also includes two ritual sites visited during formal initiation into the Vodou priesthood. Initiation is called *pran ason* (taking the sacred rattle), and part of becoming *oungan asogwe* or *manbo asogwe* (priest or priestess holding the rattle) involves making secret nocturnal visits to the spirits Mèt Kalfou and Bawon Simityè.

Rara bands who are Chanpwèl societies pay a spiritual "toll" to the *lwa* of the crossroads, Mèt Kalfou, in order to access the mystical power in the cemetery beyond. The crossroads is a *lwa* and also a symbol for the intersection between worlds, and thus for change. As the penultimate point before the final destination of the cemetery, the crossroads is a place of judgment in many Afro-Atlantic religious schemes. Boukman Eksperyans, a *mizik rasin* band, sang a Carnival song in 1994 called "Kalfou Danjere" (Dangerous Crossroads). The song invoked the imagery of Mèt Kalfou as judge in a coded message to the military coup leaders:

> If you kill, you've got big problems
> At the crossroads, crossroads of the Kongo people
> If you steal, you've got big problems
> At the crossroads, crossroads of the Kongo people

> *Si ou touye, ou chaje ak pwoblem*
> *Nan kalfou, kalfou nèg Kongo*
> *Si ou vòlè ou chaje ak pwoblem*
> *Nan kalfou, kalfou nèg Kongo*[17]

A Petwo-Bizango Protection Ceremony

Rara La Fleur Ginen, in Port-au-Prince, consecrated their band in two different ways during two ceremonies preceding Rara *sòti* in March of 1993. In the first ritual, a mystically charged stone was brought out from the *badji* (inner sanctum of a Vodou temple) and used as the essential ingredient in making a *benyen* bath. The heads, arms, and torsos of all the members of the Rara band were bathed in the liquid, making them fit for the long ordeal ahead and any warfare that might ensue. In the second ceremony, the band processed to a local cemetery and the officiating *oungan* captured three *zonbi*. Armed with this spiritual force, the Rara were now energized and ready to walk for the rest of Easter weekend:

We arrived at the peristil, *which was the Rara headquarters, after dark, around 8:00 in the evening. The musicians were assembling to watch one of the* oungan *draw a* vèvè *(sacred cornmeal drawing) on the ground in the yard outside the* peristil *doors. He deftly traced a pattern for the* lwa *Simbi Makaya, which measured about four feet. A helper held a candle so he could see, while people called back and forth to one another, organizing themselves for the ceremony and making jokes.*[18]

Rara *kolonèl* use a bonfire to mystically heat up the band (photo © Chantal Regnault)

After the vèvè *was drawn, they all but obscured it by placing wood on top of it in preparation for a fire. The* oungan *turned and drew a second* vèvè, *this time for* Mèt Kalfou. *We could hear the* banbou *tones blow here and there like an orchestra tuning up. The air was heavy, with rain clouds hanging above us in the sky, the atmosphere of excitement before a storm. The* oungan *lit the fire and poured liberal amounts of cane liquor on it so that it would flare up. In this way the* oungan *both invoked (by drawing the* vèvè) *and "heated up" (by lighting the fire) the mystical powers of Simbi Makaya and Mèt Kalfou, two of the Petwo-Bizango* lwa *with whom the band had an* angajman, *a contract.*

Next the oungan *unwrapped a package at his feet to reveal a small mountain of rock salt. He threw huge handfuls of rock salt in the four cardinal directions and showered the remaining handfuls into the fire, which crackled and popped. Then he poured water and rum libations on the ground.*

Soon he signaled for the musicians, who assembled next to the fire and began to play. They had one Petwo *tanbou a liy (a mass-hproduced* timbale, *a small metal-framed drum with a crisp sound, played with sticks, used as a* kès), *a small goatskin* kès, *three* banbou *(one of which was made of industrial plastic PVC tubing), three* koné, *one trumpet, two huge shakers with diamond shapes on either end, and two huge* graj. *While they played, the* oungan *continued to pour alcohol on the fire to produce huge blasts of flame. He thus both allowed the fire to "heat up" the Rara band, and the music of the Rara band to "animate," or "heat up" the energy of the* lwa.

After a while we were treated to a baton twirling performance by the majò jon *wearing white shorts and a white t-shirt, not yet having donned his sequined costume. (The* oungan *wore a t-shirt bearing the logo for Tuborg Gold beer, evidence of his link to the wider hemispheric economy, in which Haiti is the recipient of vast amounts of used U.S. clothing.) The music was punctuated by shrill blasts from the small tin whistles that the* oungan *and* majò jon *had in their mouths.*

The oungan *led the band, still playing music, inside the* peristil. *On the floor inside, a group of objects had been carefully laid out along a constellation of power points. The central object was a* vèvè *for Bawon Simityè, with small piles of gunpowder on square pieces of white paper at five points along the drawing. At the head of the* vèvè *was an oblong stone, probably a* zemi, *an indigenous Taino sacred object.*[19] *The* zemi *stone sat in a white enamel plate, bathed in rum. At the foot of the* vèvè *sat a red sequined bottle. When he entered the* peristil, *the* oungan *laid two of the* majò jon's *batons on either side of the* vèvè, *crossing them at the top. The whole assemblage of objects on the floor became a focal point for the following ritual.*

The oungan, *with a whip in his hand and a whistle in his mouth, ignited the rum in the white enamel plate, producing a blue flame around the important stone. He then knelt and poured some kind of liquid on each small pile of powder. One burst immediately into flame. (The others must have been duds!) He took some of the contents of the red bottle into his mouth and sprayed a fine stream of mist in all four directions. After that, he pushed the plate, still on fire with the stone in it, into the center of the room, and the band encircled it, playing all the while. In this way he brought the energy of the stone into the room, associated it with Bawon Simityè by placing it onto his* vèvè, *heated it up by setting it in a plate of lighted rum, and activated the mystical powers that the stone held together with a reference to Bawon. Then he used all of that "charged" energy to "charge" the band, whose music further activated the stone. After cracking his whip inside the* peristil *in the four cardinal directions, the* oungan *led the band in a series of feints like a military charge to battle. Still playing, they ran forward, stopped abruptly, and then ran forward again. These movements would confuse enemy Raras—or enemy spirits—and were a rehearsal to discipline the band.*

Next the oungan *set the* zemi *stone into a white enamel basin and used it as the fundamental ingredient in a* benyen. *He bathed the stone in a red liquid he poured from a plastic gallon jug. He added Florida Water, a commercially produced cologne commonly used in Vodou. Soon the stone was sitting in a basin of liquid, and the leaders of the Rara came forward for the* benyen. *They took off their shirts, gathered around the basin, and squatted down. Then they rose, holding hands, and saluted the four corners with their hands held. Leaning over the basin and reaching toward each other like wrestlers, each bathed the other: first the head, then the arms, and then the torso. The officiating* oungan *broke into a very low dance with his arms held out and dangling, a dance associated with the rite of Bizango.*

*After the leaders were finished, one by one the ranked band
members and musicians came forward, took off their shirts, and
were bathed by a leader. The music had been playing continually
since we entered the* peristil, *but as the musicians put down
their instruments to receive their baths, the music gradually
died out.*

After the bath, the music resumed, and the oungan *led the band
in military "charges" around the* poto mitan. *Finally, infused
with spiritual energy and protection, the Rara set out into the
Port-au-Prince streets.*

The Rara I described in the introduction performed a similar commence-
ment ritual bath on March 1993, midway into Lent. The Rara leaders'
and the musicians' legs, arms, torsos, and heads were bathed with an
herbal bath around a huge *boukan* (bonfire) outside the Rara headquarters near the Mache Salomon (Salomon Market) in downtown Port-
au-Prince. The Rara president threw five packages of gunpowder into
the fire, and the band walked around the fire counterclockwise, playing
their instruments.[20] They then processed to the nearest crossroads, lit
another bonfire, and walked counterclockwise around it before regroup-
ing at the headquarters and going out into the streets to play. The Rara
proceeded to place packages containing *wanga* in the streets to "crash"
other Rara bands.

These baths display some of the classic ritual vocabulary of the
Kongo-Petwo and Bizango rites. In the case of the Rara described here,
its location in the *peristil* marks it as belonging to the world of Afro-
Haitian religion. The *vèvè* for Mèt Kalfou and Simbi are important signs
as well. Mèt Kalfou occupies the place in Bizango that Papa Legba holds
in the Rada rites: he is a spirit of the crossroads, and the first *lwa* of the
Petwo rite that must be saluted at the start of a secret society ritual. The
Petwo Simbi, in contrast, is known as a great magician. Both spirits were
invoked to "heat up" the proceedings. The use of gunpowder, whips,
and whistles are specific to the "hot" side of the religious complex, and
the core leadership in both Rara bands consisted of members of Bizango
societies.

Other aspects of Petwo, Kongo, and Bizango rites were present in the
second of the "charging up" ceremonies conducted by Rara La Fleur
Ginen on Maundy Thursday in 1993.

Capturing *Zonbi* to "Charge" the Rara

Papa Cemetery, I'm asking permission
To dance Rara, Oh

Papa Simityè m'ap mande pèmisyon
Pou'm danse Rara Wayo[21]

Lwa, pwen, and *zonbi* are believed to provide energy and strength for carrying out spiritual obligations, as well as for defensive magic against other aggressive Rara bands. When a band is affiliated with a Chanpwèl society, the spirits they invoke and the magic practices they engage in will be rooted in Chanpwèl practice. This can involve taking the band to a local cemetery and capturing *zonbi*. Spirits of the recently dead, if they were Vodouists when they were alive, are obliged to work for their fellow living Vodouists.

By ten o'clock in the evening, the poto mitan *inside the* peristil *was "dressed," in a state of readiness for ritual. There was a* kwi *(calabash bowl) filled with bread underneath the centerpost, three upside-down brooms leaned against the post's sides, and the straw hats of the* oungan *hung from nails. A few bottles were set at the base of the* poto mitan, *along with whips, the Rara band's wooden sign, and calabashes filled with popcorn with white candles propped up inside. As the instruments warmed up, people gathered inside the* peristil, *waiting for the Rara to go out. The leaders were all wearing blue shirts of varying shades. They put on their straw hats and red neck scarves, achieving the classic costume of the* lwa Kouzen Azaka.[22]

After ordering the musicians to play, two kolonèl *led them and the rest of the Rara around the* peristil. *They executed the "charge" around the* poto mitan *the way they had done during the* benyen *ceremony. Soon one of the* kolonèl *led the musicians and band followers out of the* peristil *and down the steep and slippery streets of the hilly slum, attracting many of the youth of the neighborhood who heard the music and joined the band.*

Cars approached as the band walked through the dark streets. The Rara members parted and danced past them like schools of fish,

*ignoring the potential for soliciting contributions. One older man in
the Rara carried the brooms in his hands, dancing with them down
the streets, straw facing up. The* kolonèl *carried whips, bottles, and
calabashes with bread in them. At designated crossroads, a* kolonèl
*delivered whip cracks. When the band reached the cemetery—a small,
very old local cemetery called Simityè Ti-Cheri (Little Darling
Cemetery), they stopped and the musicians played an* ochan *to
Saint Victor, the spirit who lives at the cemetery gate. Said Simeon,
the officiating* oungan*: "If you don't salute the cemetery gates
and you go in without permission, you cannot come out with*
zonbi.*"*[23]

The kolonèl *quickly organized the Rara members to hold hands
and form a human chain at the entrance of the cemetery so that no
one could break through and enter. Keeping Phenel outside with
the band, they ushered Chantal and me inside—as foreign guests—to
stand off to the side on a nearby tomb. The* kolonèl *went to Bawon's
cross in the middle of the graveyard. (Inside each Haitian cemetery is
a large cement or wood cross for Bawon, or the grave of the first
man buried there is established as Bawon; the first woman buried
within is Grann Simityè or Brijit. These spirits become the invisible
"owners" of the cemetery.) They set the three brooms upside down
against the cross. They ignited the contents of the calabash and set it
on top of the cross. Another fire was lit at the base in the front, and a
third at the back, with a candle in the middle. Bawon was thus saluted
with fire, announcing the Petwo nature of the ritual. Every so often
the leaders poured* kleren *or* rum *on the fires at the base and cracked
their whips in the four cardinal directions.*

*The purpose of this part of the ritual was to ask Bawon for
permission to remove the spirits of the recently dead from the cemetery.
Bawon will determine how many* zonbi *may be taken. The* oungan
*later told me, "When I went to the cemetery, I was planning to take
seven* zonbi. *I left the Rara outside, and I went inside to consult
Bawon. Bawon La Kwa said I could only have three. There were
others, but they could only give me three." The priest continued: "The
cemetery is not a place without rules. I could come here looking for
beer. And you have a whole case of beer. You tell me, 'Simeon, I
can only give you one.' They're yours, and if you only want to give
me one, I can only have one."*[24]

After Bawon declared how many zonbi *they could take, the* oungan *disappeared behind the tombs and captured the three* zonbi *in a technique of the Chanpwèl rite.*

I kneel down and I take a bit of earth and put it in my palm. If it's hot you have to let it go fast. You can't hold on to it. It will burn you. When you see that bit of earth is hot like that, the *zonbi* is there. But you have to know what you're doing. If you're not Bizango you can't understand it.[25]

Soon the leaders came back from behind the tombs with the captured spirits contained inside a bottle.[26] *The* oungan *cracked a whip all around Bawon's cross and called the band forward to play and process around the cross. Simeon put red ribbons on the three brooms: a signal, he said, that the band was walking with* zonbi. *Together he and another* oungan *tied knots in one of the whips. They drew the whip around the cross of Bawon, then took a short break and drank some rum.*

After the band regrouped, they processed around the cross again. Taking the brooms tied with their red ribbons off the cross, the oungan *made sweeping motions on the ground as they left the cemetery. The band filed out along with them and snaked its way through the Port-au-Prince streets toward the* peristil.

Every so often, the oungan *carrying the brooms would stop in the middle of a crossroads and sweep the streets, occasionally gathering up small piles of rubbish, which they put into red scarves and tucked into their shoulder sacks. The brooms act as spiritual cleansers, chasing away negative spirits and magic traps set by other Raras. The garbage acts as a link between the crossroads and the Rara. Taking the garbage binds the crossroads to the Rara and ensures protection. Simeon explained: "The broom chases away bad spirits, and just the same way, it adopts bad spirits. The garbage—that's a witness. That is to say, when we gather up the garbage in the crossroads, the crossroads can do work for us forever."*[27]

The band continued to play and dance through the streets, then returned to the peristil *to baptize the Rara costumes, batons, drums,* banbou, *and* zonbi.

Little has been written about ritual sweeping or ritual use of the broom in Afro-Atlantic religions. Afro-Cuban *mayomberos*, priests of Kongo-

Cuban religion, mount campaigns of spiritual espionage and warfare in which they link the mystical objects in the house with points in the neighborhood through a process of leaving and taking materials, which they put into a *prenda*, a vessel containing the spirit of a recently dead person. It is worth quoting at length from an interview conducted by David H. Brown:

The Prenda is like the whole world, there is something of everything, wherever you are you have to put something in it: If I go to New York to establish a point, I have to take something back from there and put it in the Prenda. You see, we are like warriors. When an army conquers a country, they leave an occupying army. . . . I will have to leave scouts or guards, build a perimeter, a fortress.

Q: You leave something there as well as bring something back, as you said?

Yes.

Q: What would you bring back?

I'd bring back a stone, dirt, something from the place . . . and put it in the Prenda . . . to incorporate in my world.

Q: And what would you leave?

If someone has any enemy and they come to me, the enemy becomes my enemy. I go to her house, I have to set up a perimeter around her block, on the corners; I have to make a compact with the spirits of those corners, so I have to leave something so they will work for me, look out for me. I will know what is going on there. It is a . . . constant exchange, putting something from the Prenda down and taking something else back and putting it in the Prenda. . . . I have to protect myself against my enemy, so I build a perimeter around my house, around the 12 blocks around my house so I know when my enemy enters my territory, I'll have time to prepare.

Q: Your Prenda lets you know?

Yes, sometimes I'll invade his territory and make a perimeter around him so I know what he's doing.

Q: What if your enemy has a stronger Prenda, what happens?

He will win, it all depends on the faith and the relationship you have with the Prenda, the main spirit. Now, I have the spirit of a whole man in my Prenda, Francisco Siete Rayos. I have the Kiyumba, the head, I have the arms, the hands, the legs, and the feet, all inside.

Q: Is there a right or wrong, a morality in the work?

No, whatever you pay it to do, it will do, it's not like the Santeros.[28]

The ritual process of "commanding" a territory by capturing part of its earth or dust and then magically activating it with spirit remains consistent across these two Kongo-based cultures. In the case of Rara, the bands sweep up parts of the crossroads in order to preserve, activate, and control them. Rara *kolonèl* and generals mount campaigns of spiritual proprietorship throughout their neighborhoods, endeavoring to control their territory and establish formidable reputations. Like the *mayombero,* part of the way in which they achieve this mystical force is through the invisible enslaving of the community's recently dead.

The *Zonbi* in the Afro-Haitian Religious Complex

> The Police stole a coffin with the corpse of the deceased inside, after violently breaking up a burial with their clubs in the Dwouya Cemetery. Police arrived when one of the mourners, the leader of a Mardi Gras band, started to sing songs critical of the de facto government. The police threw stones at the mourners before they took the coffin, and arrested at least ten people.
>
> *Libète,* April 27–May 4, 1993

In a general sense, the figure of the *zonbi* is a metaphor in Haitian culture for the condition of servitude that has been so central to Haitian experience. In religious practice, *zonbi* is also a spiritual category with a practical dimension. *Zonbi* are spirits of the recently dead who are captured and thence owned by a "master" and obliged to work.[29] *Zonbi* are used to perform various sorts of work, ranging from general protection to the improving of specific talents like drumming and dancing, or carpentry and tailoring. In using *zonbi* to work in the Rara, the leaders of Rara bands are displaying their power as actors in a political world that extends from local reputation-building to the complex politics between the living and the dead. Using *zonbi* broadcasts a message to neighborhood communities that the Rara leaders' supernatural power extends to making deals with Bawon, harnessing the energies and talents of the community's recently dead, and launching spiritual and military campaigns with those energies.

The notion of using the recently dead to work operates on at least three levels in Haitian culture. First, and most commonly, ritual experts extract the *zonbi* magically and use them for mystical work, as did the Rara La Fleur Ginen. Second, there is some evidence for a less frequent (and criminal) practice of poisoning people to induce a lowered metabolic rate so that they appear dead, and then reviving them after they are buried in order to force them into physical labor. The material reality of this practice is contested and has been documented at length in a controversial Harvard study.[30] Third, *zonbi* operate in Haitian culture in the realm of symbol and metaphor. The meaning of the *zonbi* centers around one person imposing his or her will onto another and forcing them to perform work. Thus the *zonbi* have become an allegory for the condition of slavery and servitude that has characterized the history and present-day life of the majority of Haitians. This trope is referenced commonly in conversations and jokes on the streets as well as in literature by Haitian intellectuals.

In order to understand the concept of the *zonbi* and how it is that the spirits of the recently dead can be captured and made to work, it is necessary to look briefly at concepts of the soul in Vodou. In Afro-Haitian thought, the *nanm* (soul) is made up of different overlapping parts. There are variations in belief, but generally it is said that a person's soul consists of a *gwo bon anj* (good big angel) and a *ti bon anj* (good little angel). The *gwo bon anj* roughly corresponds to what we might consider personality. Maya Deren writes that "the daily life of a man depends on his constant communication with his own *gwo bon anj*—his own memory, intelligence, imagination and invention."[31] The *ti bon anj* has to do with the moral soul, the soul that is changeless and that ultimately returns to the cosmos. When a Vodouist dies, the *ti bon anj* goes under the water to Ginen to be with the *lwa,* and the *gwo bon anj* lingers near the grave. This latter part of the soul is thought to retain the personality of the living man or woman.[32] Because the soul of the recently dead is considered to be present near the grave, it can be borrowed or bought from Bawon and made to work as a *zonbi*.

There are many methods for capturing a *gwo bon anj* and many reasons people may desire to capture one. It is said that concerned parents in the countryside who send their children to schools in town may extract the child's soul and encase it in a bottle, which is then kept in the home for protection. This is called *mete nanm nan boutèy* (putting the soul in a bottle).[33] In Rara, a *bòkò* may enter the cemetery, ask Bawon for a *zonbi,* and use it to mystically charge or "put on" the drummers and *majò jon* so that they can perform strenuously for long hours during Easter weekend. One drummer informed me that each Holy Week, he was given a *zonbi* by the band's *kolonèl* to put on his arms. This way his playing would be guaranteed to be fast and furious and he would never tire. Indeed, he said, he could hardly remember the intense ordeal of the climax of Rara, because to some extent his own consciousness was overshadowed by the *zonbi.* He wore a red armband for the occasion, to signal to other Rara bands the profound extent of his supernatural power.[34]

Another way to capture the spirit of the recently dead to use as a *zonbi* is to obtain the bones of the dead person, especially the skull. In this scenario, the *bòkò* goes to the cemetery and breaks open the tomb of a person he has targeted because he wants to make use of the qualities or talents the person had when alive. This is a spiritually dangerous process, because to break open a tomb exposes the intruder to a *kou'd le* (literally, "hit of bad air"), the sickness and bad fortune borne on the air inside the tomb. The breaking of the tomb must not occur too soon after the dead has been interred. Sources in Port-au-Prince reported that they customarily waited for one year to ensure that the person had fully decomposed.[35] It is also possible for *oungan* or *manbo* to have skulls brought to them on demand by cemetery workers with whom they have ongoing reciprocal relations. The priests supply the workers with cigarettes and *kleren,* and they receive bones in return.[36]

The practice of encasing the spirits of the dead inside containers and instructing them to work bears strong historical connections to the culture of the Kongo kingdom, which provided the bulk of slaves to Hispaniola in its last years of slavery.[37] In the Kongo context, containers with instructive visual codes, puns, and specific work to do were called *minkisi.* Labeled "charms" and "fetishes" by Europeans, a *nkisi* (*minkisi* is the plural) was essentially a container of spirit, constructed and controlled by humans.[38] Usually drawn from the spirits of the dead, the *nkisi* was there to activate a particular desire of its maker, the *nganga-nkisi*. More often than not, *minkisi* were used in healings and could also be used for good luck, good hunting, and the like.[39]

The bottle containing a *zonbi* is a living grave. A "spirit-embedding medicine" is activated, usually through the ritual insertion of white clay called *mpemba* (*mpemba* also refers to the land of the dead underneath the water). An alternative to clay is earth, as Robert Farris Thompson explains, "often from a grave site, for cemetery earth is considered at one with the spirit of the dead."[40] In the case of the *zonbi* in the bottle constructed by La Fleur Ginen, the spirit of the dead person was captured through the earth around the grave.[41]

Capturing *zonbi* in order to perform mystical work can be an act of sorcery, but it is also a practice that can be morally benign. *Oungan* and *manbo* use skulls for healing, to remove negative spirits that have been "thrown" on people. Some priests take the skulls of fellow Vodouists because the *zonbi* retains helpful aspects of the confrere's personality. After death, people have the same talents they had when they were alive. Rara committee member Simeon explained the practical uses of trading in *zonbi:*

> I sell *zonbi*. If somebody wants a *zonbi* to drive a car, I have to give them a chauffeur's *zonbi*. If somebody needs a *zonbi* to do business, I have to give them a market-woman's *zonbi*. Somebody who was a market-woman who had a bar and restaurant. You can't take the *zonbi* of somebody who was a tailor and give it to somebody who wants to be a chauffeur. That won't help him. What's he going to do with that?
>
> For example, you could take a *zonbi* and send it after somebody to do a bad deed, and the *zonbi* gets there and does something good. The person was a good person. If I want to use a *zonbi* to go do bad works, I have to go the cemetery looking for a *zonbi* who was mean.[42]

Almost every practitioner I spoke with maintained that the community of Vodouists carried obligations and loyalties to one another even after death. A Vodouist was morally bound to help other members of the religion even from the grave. I asked one *bòkò*, who said he routinely used *zonbi* in his work, if he wouldn't be upset if he were taken and used after he died. He answered: "I wouldn't be mad. On the contrary, there are people who are lazy and people who are not. If you take the *zonbi* of someone who liked to work, they feel happy because they didn't like to sit around doing nothing."[43] Another *bòkò* responded in a similar way but insisted that he was "too powerful" to be "taken." "They couldn't," he said. "But if they did, no problem. I'd work."[44]

Although these attitudes depict the use of *zonbi* as morally neutral, the practice of capturing and manipulating *zonbi* is most often associated with Chanpwèl societies and their reputation for sorcery. It is said that the person who goes to collect the bones of the dead is precisely the same person who killed the dead—either magically or through poison. I asked a sorcerer about a bottle that I saw him construct, which contained the shavings of two human skulls, and he replied: "The two skulls inside are working the bottle. They are *zonbi*. They died once, at the hands of man. They are working for me. When they die by God they'll finally die."[45]

Theologically, there is a fatalism at work within Vodou that says that the hour of death of each person has been preordained by God. There is nothing that can be done to kill that person before God takes them from the earth. However, the sorcerer can cause the person's physical death and use the lasting spirit to manipulate and dominate. In this way the person has died once physically, "by the hands of man," but not twice, "by the hands of God." These people are now magically obligated to perform spiritual work for the sorcerer, be it healing or harming. At the moment of their preordained death, they will "die two times" and proceed to their cosmic destiny. One Vodou song implies that there is too much sorcery in Haiti, that there are too many people dead from magic:

> The Cemetery is full of people, Oh
> Baron Samdi asks all the people
> If it's God who put them there
>
> *Simityè plen moun O*
> *Bawon mande tout moun sa yo*
> *Si se Bon Dieu ki mete yo*[46]

The implication is that if God did not put them there, then they have died magically and are potential *zonbi*. Remember the distinction in Haiti between religious magic—capturing a *zonbi* and using it for healing—and sorcery—killing a person and forcing his or her soul to work. Magic within a religious context yields, ultimately, to the will of God and the *lwa*. Sorcery is magic that "steals from God."[47]

Capturing *zonbi* and *nanm* to control them is seen by many people as a serious infraction against another person, as evidence of the malevolent nature of the Bizango and Chanpwèl societies. Boukman Eksperyans sings against the indigenous practice in a song called "Nanm Nan Boutèy" (Soul in a bottle). They stretch the image into a metaphor for the Haitian postcolonial dilemma: the bourgeois psyche that is dominated by foreign, or *blanc*, cultural standards:

Hey that's hard, Oh
Our soul in a bottle

When will we get there
When will we become conscious
My friends, this is hard.
We're going into the revolution.

Ki lè nape rive
Ki lè nap pran konsyans

Mezanmi sa rèd O
Anye sa rèd O
Nanm nou nan boutèy
Ouyee, nan revolisyon na prale[48]

A powerful and frightening concept, the *zonbi* is a potent metaphor for the slave and the lasting effects of slavery in Haiti. The "living dead" *zonbi* figure in particular (so common in American horror films) recalls the tragic and heartbreaking experience of the Haitian ancestors (as well as Africans throughout the Americas) who were transported to the colonies as slaves. Like the African sold into slavery, the *zonbi* is captured from its home, torn from family, and taken away, essentially dead to them. The *zonbi* spends time within a casket, just as the kidnapped Africans were forced to lie in the holds of slave ships. The *zonbi* is then resurrected, beaten, and forced to work as a slave on a plantation for a master. The poignant plight of the *zonbi* as it is expressed in myth and ritual is a graphic memory of the experience of capture, transport, and enslavement of the Africans in Saint-Domingue who lived and died far from home. As long as the myth of the *zonbi* exists in Haitian culture, this terrifying history is remembered.[49]

There are important political dimensions to the *zonbi* metaphor as well. Insofar as the *zonbi* represents the slave, or the worker, there is always the possibility that the *zonbi* will wake up, shake off the oppressor, and start a revolution. The trigger will be the metaphoric taste of salt, or spark of political consciousness. Haitian intellectuals have worked with the *zonbi* figure in exploring the Haitian condition. The writer Rene Depestre translates the mythology into a political symbology:

> It is not by chance that there exists in Haiti the myth of the zombi, that is, of the living dead, the man whose mind and soul have been stolen and who has been left only the ability to work. According to the myth, it was forbidden to put salt in the zombi's food since this could revitalize his spiritual energies. The history of colonization is the process of man's general zombification. It is also the quest for a revitalizing salt capable of restoring to man the use of his imagination and his culture.[50]

References to *zonbi* are common enough in Haiti, often in connection with the issues of exploited laborers. Karen Richman reports that day laborers who come into one province from another are sometimes called *zonbi*.[51] The idea of the *zonbi* is employed cynically in government, where during the corruption of the coup years, thousands of paychecks were issued for people whose faces never appeared at work; these were referred to as *tchèk zonbi* (*zonbi* checks).

While *zonbi* practices are cultural metaphors for exploited labor power and the mystification of labor relations, for Rara presidents *zonbi* are actual spiritual entities who are captured and made to walk with the band as spiritual slaves. General Gerard explained: "When I bring the Rara out, the *zonbi* walk in front with the colonel, on foot, like you and me. Normal people don't have eyes to see them. The colonel is behind the *zonbi*. The *zonbi* are in the middle of the Petwo spirits. The *zonbi* are like children for the Petwo spirits. Like slaves."[52] These Rara presidents, descendants of African slaves who fought for their own independence, are now slave masters of the dead. They envision these spirits of the dead as children, or slaves, who are working to "heat up" the Rara. Their spiritual energy is activated through the use of the whip: "When the colonel cracks his whip he's whipping the *zonbi*. It's a way to attract people so the Rara can be hot. The whip lashes are a 'condition.' When he does it, the *zonbi* know what they should do."[53]

Here the centuries of enslavement in the colony of Saint-Domingue are remembered and reenacted through ritual work. This time, it is the descendants of the former slaves who control slavery by themselves enslaving spirits as mystical helpers. It is one of the many lasting effects of slavery in the Americas. But these *zonbi* are not brutalized by their masters the way the ancestors were in the colony. Just as Rara bands hold *benyen* ceremonies before they leave the *peristil*, so too do they perform ritual closing ceremonies. In the case of a band that has captured *zonbi*, this means properly "receiving" the spirits with a small offering of food and drink. After the *zonbi* has eaten, the spirits are returned to the cemetery.

Reception for a Protestant *Zonbi*

Among the three zonbi *that we saw Rara La Fleur Ginen capture in the Little Darling Cemetery, it seems that one had been a Protestant when he was alive. Simeon, the* oungan, *knew this because as they returned to the home* peristil, *the bottle began to shake in the hands of the* kolonèl *holding it and refused to go inside. The* oungan *realized it was a Protestant* zonbi, *which means, according to the logic of Vodou, that it was not obliged to serve, help, or "heat up" the Rara.*

In Port-au-Prince there is a brotherhood and sisterhood among Vodouists that stipulates that if an oungan *or* manbo *is in need, they may ask the spirits of the recently dead for mystical help in their work. The same isn't true for Protestants. Those who converted and renounced the* lwa *won't work for Vodouists after death. This is a recent twist in the ongoing construction of Vodou logic since the rapid expansion of evangelical Protestantism into the Caribbean basin. Now a fierce ideological war wages between the Vodouist and the evangelical Protestant. Becoming Protestant protects the Vodouist from being touched by the demands and duties of any obligations to the* lwa.

The Rara walked with the Protestant zonbi *anyway, and at the end of Rara season they set about preparing the feast for the* zonbi *in order to send them away. The food was set down before the bottle so the* zonbi *could consume it mystically. Apparently the Vodouist* zonbi *ate their food peacefully, allowing Simeon to fulfill his obligations to them. The Protestant, however, would not: "The Evangelical wouldn't eat. He was mean and grouchy." Simeon was left with a stubborn* zonbi *on a hunger strike.*

Simeon told me his solution, which I thought was rather ingenious: "I've read my Bible," he said. "I served him a glass of red wine and some unsalted bread." The zonbi *consumed this symbolic communion offering, and everyone was satisfied.*

The Rara *kolonèl* tricking the dead, enslaved Protestant into taking communion strikes me as a good example of Vodou in its dealings with other systems. Vodou tries to incorporate other forces that are seen as powerful, and if it can't, it slyly and usually with great humor finds a way to co-opt them anyway. The reaction of Vodou to Catholicism has certainly been a history of absorbing and creolizing specific elements and ignoring others. For some Vodouists, the resurrection of Christ makes Jesus the first *zonbi* of all. The next chapter will take up the theme of incorporation and look further at the *zonbi* and the figure of "the Jew" in the Rara.

This chapter has argued that at its core, Rara practice is concerned with carrying out religious work. Rara societies form themselves under the patronage of the spirits and continue to carry out complex negotiations and contracts with the supernatural world. Contrary to the popular conception of Rara as a "peasant Carnival," Rara is a rite within the overarching Afro-Haitian religious complex that includes domestic family-based Ginen practice on one hand, and Bizango on the other. It is the latter—the rites of Petwo, Kongo, Bizango, and Banda—that provides the deepest symbols and structures of Rara. The ethos of these rites is focused on the militaristic and aggressive gaining of power, but also on healing, justice, and self-defense.

Perhaps most important, the group is transformed collectively through the performance of these ritual expressions. The open, public nature of the festival and the dissolution of conventional social, spatial, and temporal boundaries create an intense, dramatic, liminal climate. The purposeful nature of the religious aspects of the parade—saluting natural dwelling places of the *lwa*, visiting the dead at the cemetery— creates a kind of *communitas*, a transitory state where people are acutely conscious of joining together to effect change for the group as a whole. During Rara season, relationships between people and between humans and the spirit world are felt to be especially charged and rich. And as the next chapter will show, as Easter's Holy Week draws near, elements and characters of Christian history make their way into Afro-Haitian festivities in unusual and fascinating ways.

A country Rara in full swing (photo © Elizabeth McAlister)

Rara and "the Jew"

Premodern Anti-Judaism in Postmodern Haiti

EUROPE AND THE JEWS: A MYTHOLOGICAL BLUEPRINT FOR DEMONIZATION

So far I have talked about Rara bands' engagement with the religious work demanded by the Afro-Creole spirits. But there is another level of mythology at work during Easter's Holy Week in Haiti. Local dramas reenact the Christian ritual cycle of death and resurrection, and people play the roles of Jesus, Judas, and "the Jews." During these dramatic rituals, it is evident that Haitian culture is heir to the anti-Judaism of medieval European popular thought. But it is not a clear-cut case of anti-Judaism (or anti-Semitism). Present-day Vodou practitioners manipulate inherited, demonized images of "the Jew" in both alarming and creative ways. In the course of Easter Week, "Jews" are demonized and burned in effigy by some—but they are also honored and claimed by others as forefathers and founders of the Rara bands. Various Rara leaders embrace the identity of "the Jew" and claim a mystical Jewish ancestry. In accepting the label of "Jew," these Rara leaders might be understood as taking on a mantle of denigration as a kind of psychic resistance. They symbolically oppose the powers that historically have sought to exploit them—the Haitian Catholic elite.

As I researched the histories of anti-Judaism and of slavery, I saw that most of the negative images originally used to characterize Jews had been transferred onto Africans—in particular, African and Afro-Creole religious practice. This chapter presents a historical argument that many of the negative images of Vodou and Rara are drawn from medieval European images of Jews. These flexible popular tropes hinge on the figure of the devil and link the devil first with "the Jews" and then, in colonial Saint-Domingue, with Africans and Afro-Creole Vodouists.[1]

As figures to be manipulated, demonized, or embraced, the Jews were marked as the original "Other" of Europe, the very first object of projection, marginalization, and demonization of Christendom. Europe's demonization of the Jews became a mythological blueprint for the encounter with Native peoples and Africans in the Americas. Easter Week in Haiti tells many histories, but here I focus on the demonization by European Christianity of two groups: Jews and black Africans. This chapter is about how some Haitians have inherited, used, and manipulated European Christian anti-Judaism.

Bwile Jwif: "Burning the Jew" in Effigy

It was Holy Thursday night in 1993, and Chantal, Phenel, and I were out recording and filming a Rara band in the narrow back streets of Port-au-Prince. We were dancing down the dark hilly streets at a good clip, on our way to a small cemetery to try to get some zonbi *to "heat up" the band for the season's climax on Easter. We stopped while the band paid a musical salute to the invisible guardian of the cemetery gates in Vodou. I looked up and noticed a straw dummy sitting on the roof of the house across the street. It was a* Jwif *(Jew).*

He was sitting in a chair in the open air, on top of the one-story tin-roofed house. Made of straw and dressed in blue jeans, a shirt, suit jacket, and sneakers, this "Jew" wore a tie and had a pen sticking out of his shirt pocket. His legs were crossed, and over them sat what looked to be a laptop computer fashioned out of cardboard. A cord seemed to run from the computer down into a briefcase that sat by his chair.

I asked around for the dummy's owner. An older man missing a few teeth came forward, offering a callused, muscular handshake that revealed a life of hard physical labor. He was from the countryside in the south of the island, a migrant to Port-au-Prince. I found myself in the ridiculous position of having to compliment him on his work. "Nice Jew ya got there," I said. "Ou gen yon bèl Jwif la, wi." "Oh yes, we leave it up for the Rara band to pass by. Tomorrow afternoon we'll burn it," he said. "Aha . . . well . . . great . . . ," said my research partners and I, flaring our eyes at each other. I guess nobody told the guy that Jean-Claude Duvalier banned the practice in the 1970s,

A stuffed "Jew" sits waiting to be burned (photo © Elizabeth McAlister)

*around the time of a rush of tourism and foreign industrial investment.
I bet other people still "burn the Jew," here and there.*

The Easter ritual of burning "the Jew" or burning "Judas" in effigy was
practiced until recently by all classes in Haiti. There were many local
variations, but usually by Maundy Thursday an effigy had been erected
in some central location, and at 3:00 in the afternoon on Good Friday
it was burned by the local community.[2] This was done in a ritual retal-
iation against Judas, who betrayed Jesus, or against "the Jews" who
"killed Jesus."

The burning in effigy of the *Jwif* around Easter was found in all
classes and in most regions, from local peasant communities to wealthy
plantation households. Thérèse Roumer, a writer from the provincial
city of Jérémie, remembered the *Juifs errants,* the "wandering Jews" of
her childhood. Her father owned expansive tracts of land in the region
and maintained a large family home. A *Jwif* was erected at the beginning
of Lent. He had stuffed pants and shirt, with a pillow for a head, and
he sat in a chair on the veranda by the front door. The idea, said Madam
Roumer, was to kick the *Jwif* whenever you went in or out of the door,
"say any bad words you had," and scold him for killing Jesus. On the
Saturday morning before Easter, all of the children from town would
find wooden sticks, come to the house to beat him, and burn him in a
bonfire.[3] Children were exhorted by the grown-ups to "pray for the
conversion of the Jews."[4] The family would then go to church to collect
Holy Water, with which to wash the verandah.[5]

Most remembered that the Jew in effigy was part of a child's game,
in which "the Jew" represented Judas and was hidden by the adults in
the neighborhood. William Seabrook, whose book *The Magic Island*
has sustained many critical blows since its publication in 1929, wrote
this tongue-in-cheek account, worth reproducing in its entirety:

> On the last bright Easter morning which I spent in Port-au-Prince—this
> was only a year ago—the Champs de Mars, a fashionable park adjacent to
> the presidential palace and new government buildings, resembled an untidied
> battlefield on which scenes of wholesale carnage had been recently enacted.
> It was impossible to drive through it without swerving to avoid mangled
> torsos; it was impossible to stroll through it without stepping aside to avoid
> arms, legs, heads, and other detached fragments of human anatomies.
> It was impossible also to refrain from smiling, for these mangled remains
> were not gory; they exuded nothing more dreadful than sawdust, straw and

cotton batting. They were, in fact, life-sized effigies of Judas and Pontius Pilate's soldiers—done to death annually by naive mobs bent on avenging at this somewhat late day an event which occurred in Palestine during the reign of Tiberius.

. . . I had made the acquaintance, so to speak, of one Judas before he betrayed our Lord and fled to the woods. All the little community had contributed toward his construction. He sat propped in a chair outside the doorway. They had stuffed an old coat, a shirt, and a long pair of trousers with straw, fastened old shoes and cotton gloves, also stuffed, to the legs and arms, and had made ingeniously a head of cloth, stuffed with rags, with the face painted on it and a pipe stuck in its mouth. They introduced me to this creature very politely. They were rather proud of him. He was Monsieur Judas, and I was expected to shake hands with him. You see—or perhaps you will not see unless you can recall the transcendental logic which controlled the make-believe games you used to play in childhood—that Judas had *not yet* betrayed Jesus. He was, therefore, an honored guest in their house, as Peter or Paul might have been.

And so their righteous wrath will be all the more justified when they learn on Saturday morning that Judas has turned traitor. Then it is that all the neighbors, armed and shouting, the men with machetes and *cocomacaque* bludgeons, the women with knives, even more bloodthirsty in their vociferations, invade the habitation where Judas has been a guest, demanding, "*Qui bo' li?*" (Where is the traitor hiding?)

Under the bed they peer, if there is a bed; behind doors, in closets—I happened to witness this ceremony in a city suburbs, where they do have beds and closets—while members of the household aid in the search and make excited suggestions. But nowhere can Judas be found. It seems that he has fled. (What has really occurred is that the head of the house has carried him off during the night and hidden him, usually in some jungle ravine or thicket close on the city's edge. Judas usually takes to the forest as any man would, fleeing for his life. But this is not always predictable. A Judas has been known to hide in a boat, in a public garage yard, even under the bandstand in that Champs de Mars whither so many of them, wherever found, are dragged for execution.)

So tracking Judas becomes a really exciting game. A group collects, shouting, beating drums, marching in the streets, racing up side-alleys; meeting other groups, each intent on finding the Judas planted by its own neighborhood, but nothing loath to find some other Judas and rend him to pieces *en passant*. Crowds may be heard also crashing and beating through the jungle hillsides. It is rather like an Easter-egg hunt on a huge and somewhat mad scale.[6]

The tradition of burning Judas in effigy at Easter Week has been practiced in various cultures, notably in Mexico and other parts of Latin America.[7] The practice may stem from the liturgical dramas, or "evangelizing rituals," practiced by early Jesuit missionaries to the Americas. The Jesuits are known to have staged elaborate dramas in the communities where they worked, playing out scenes from Jesus' life.[8] Passion Plays spread the idea of Jews as "Christ-killers." According to this ritual logic, Judas, who betrayed Jesus, is conflated with "the Jews" who "mistreated Jesus," making all Jews into "Judases."[9] The supposed role that the Jews played in the Crucifixion, as described in the New Testament, embellished in legend, and portrayed on the stage, was familiar to both cleric and layperson. It was a good starting point for moral teaching.

The idea that the Jews killed Jesus is rooted, of course, in the New Testament, which can be read as a polemic that displays the anti-Judaism of the early Church towards the Jews. Sander Gilman has argued that the negative image of difference of the Jew found in the Gospels (and especially, we might note, the figure of Judas) became the central referent for all definitions of difference in the West.[10] During the medieval period, European Christianity produced the image of "the demonic Jew," an inhuman creature working directly for Satan. Joshua Trachtenberg writes in his classic work *The Devil and the Jews* that "the two inexorable enemies of Jesus, then, in Christian legend, were the devil and the Jew, and it was inevitable that the legend should establish a causal relation between them."[11] By the medieval period, the devil was cast as the master of the Jews, directing them in a diabolical plot to destroy Christendom.

After all, Christopher Columbus and the early colonists of Hispaniola were products of the religious worldview of the late Middle Ages, when the Inquisition was in full force. In a telling coincidence of history, Columbus sets sail for what he would call the *outro mondo* (other world) in August of 1492, only three days after the final departure of the Jews from Spain. This was the era during which Spain expelled its entire Jewish population, and the Inquisition reserved special tribunals for any *anusim,* or *conversos,* converted Jews who were suspected of "Judaizing."[12]

In the medieval Passion Plays that set the tone for the popular Christianity of Columbus's Europe and the colonial Jesuit missions, the Jews are handed the entire weight of blame for Jesus' death, and Pontius Pilate and the Roman participants in the narrative fade into the background.[13] Medieval European Mystery Plays were popular liturgical dramas, reenacting various scenes from scripture. They grew into village festivals performed in marketplaces and guildhalls, taking on the "secular, boisterous, disorderly and exuberant life of the folk."[14] In *Le Mystere de la*

Passion, a fourteenth-century French play depicting the Crucifixion, the Jews are the villains of the piece, egged on by devils. In the climax, the devils instigate Judas to betray his master and howl with glee when they are successful.[15] The idea of Jews as demonic Christ-killers is enhanced throughout the medieval period, forming a central theme of anti-Judaism that will authorize the expulsion of Jews during the Inquisition.

The clergy of Spanish Hispaniola, like the French that followed them, were small in number and faced the overwhelming project of establishing and maintaining Christianity. It is likely that the Jesuit, Dominican, and Franciscan missionaries made use of the theatrical tactics deployed by their colleagues in New Spain to convert the Native Americans. In that colony, large-scale popular dramas were modeled after the Mystery Plays of Spain and France, depicting the winners and losers in the Christian story and making clear parallels to the colonists and the conquered. Judas, "the Jews," Jesus, and the apostles made for casts of characters that would illustrate the larger drama of power relations at the start of the colonial enterprise.[16] The Christian story and theatrical public rituals generated narratives meant to authorize and display the technologies—chains and whips—of servitude. European Christendom dramatically set itself up as a sole civilizing force, against the barbaric and demonic forces of Jews, Native Americans, and Africans.[17]

The historical antecedents of the Haitian *bwile Jwif* (Jew burning) rituals may well be in these sorts of Passion Plays that referenced the events of the Spanish Inquisition. In the late fifteenth and sixteenth centuries—as the Spanish were establishing the slave trade to the colonies—*conversos* believed to have secretly practiced Judaism were sentenced to be burned alive in Spain. *Conversos* in hiding were sentenced in absentia and burned in effigy.[18] These auto-da-fé practices were likely the model upon which the Latin American rituals are based. Although the Inquisition was never organized in Hispaniola, the Easter effigy-burnings are most probably rooted in Inquisition symbolism and its attendant public ritual terror.[19]

Other bits of cultural flotsam and jetsam may have trickled down from Inquisition history. The *lwa* Papa Gede, in his own code language, calls the pig "Jwif." Surely Papa Gede is remembering one of the most common caricatures of the Jew in the Middle Ages, the notorious figure of the *Judensau,* in which a sow feeds her Jewish offspring with the devil looking on.[20] Perhaps the expression is an inverted survival of the fifteenth-century term for the Spanish *conversos,* who were called *marranos* (swine) after the Christians conquered the Moors.[21]

Anti-Jewish sentiment was an implicit part of the ruling process of the French colony of Saint-Domingue. The Church itself was among the largest of the slave-owning landholders in the colony, and it won an advantage with the establishment of the Code Noir.[22] This edict by King Louis XIV mandated the planter class to baptize and Christianize the slaves, just as it simultaneously outlawed the exercise of any religion other than Catholicism. The Jesuits, working as an order before the 1704 official establishment of their mission, manifested a marked dislike of Jews and their religion. In 1669 they appealed to the Crown representative to take actions against "tavern keepers, undesirable women and Jews."[23] In 1683 the Church induced King Louis XIV to expel all Jews from the colony and to impose a religious test on new immigrants.[24]

It would have been only logical for the colonial clergy to take the image of the Jews as an evil, anti-Christian force and hold them up in comparison to early forms of Vodou—the real threat to Christianity in the colony. Although the Christianization of the Africans in colonial Saint-Domingue was a half-hearted and badly organized enterprise, enslaved people were mandated by the Code Noir to be baptized, and they sporadically attended mass, married, and were directed in catechism.[25] In their efforts to control the enslaved, the clergy probably preached Paul's letters to the Ephesians and other biblical passages exhorting slaves to obey their masters.[26] Most of their practical worries revolved around the "superstition" of the Africans, their magical abilities and their knowledge of poison, for greater than the fear of diabolism was the more imminent threat of uprising and rebellion. Numerous regulations were passed in the colonial period and after, making various religious and magical practices illegal. Underlying anti-Vodou sentiment was the notion that the Africans, like the Jews before them, were acting in consort with the devil.

The litany of charges that were leveled against Jews in medieval Europe was transferred wholesale onto the Vodouist. The list of devilish crimes attributed to European Jews was an elaborate series of evil activities aimed at destroying Christendom. Jews were accused of a range of magical crimes, from superstition, sorcery, and desecration of the host, all the way to ritual murder, the drinking of Christian blood, the eating of human flesh, and poisonings.[27] It is striking that this list is replicated in the colony, attributing these crimes to Africans and Creoles of Saint-Domingue.

Like the converted Jews constantly under suspicion of "Judaizing," African converts to Christianity were suspected of sorcery. Joan Dayan writes of the late eighteenth century, "It seemed as if the more Christian you claimed to be, the more certainly you could be accused of conniving with the devil."[28] A decree passed in 1761 complained that slaves' religious meetings at night in churches and catechizing in houses and plantations were actually veiled opportunities for prostitution and marronage. Slaves who had taken on roles of "cantors, vergers, churchwardens, and preachers" were charged with "contamination" of sacred relics with "idolatrous" intentions.[29] Africans requested to be baptized over and over, believing in the mystical properties of the rite.[30]

The legal codes from colonial times to the present criminalize numerous practices of sorcery, linking the devil with the Africans and Creoles. A decree passed in 1758, for example, prohibited the use of "*garde-corps* or *makandals*."[31] Still in use today as *pwen* (literally, "points"), these "body-guards" were objects infused with spiritual force, directed to protect their wearers. "Makandal" was also the name of the famous maroon leader in the Haitian revolution. An adept botanist as well as a revolutionary, Makandal was convicted of instigating a campaign of poisoning planters' wells in 1757, during which more than six thousand whites were poisoned.[32] Besides being labeled sorcerers, poisoners, superstitious heathens, and false Christians, Africans and Creoles were accused of stealing and desecrating the host, drinking blood, and practicing cannibalism, accusations that rounded out and replicated the litany of anti-Christian charges against Jews.

SATAN'S SLAVES: VODOUISTS IN THE CATHOLIC IMAGINARY

Throughout Haitian history, the Catholic clergy and the enfranchised classes have cast Vodou as a cult of Satan, a complex of African superstitions to be purged from the beliefs of the Haitian majority. In cycles of violent repression, Vodou practitioners have been jailed, tortured, and killed, and their sacred objects have been burned. Using the image of slavery so salient to a population once enslaved and perpetually negotiating its sovereignty, the Church's antisuperstition campaigns figure Vodouists as slaves of Satan, who is himself working to contaminate and destroy Christianity. Consider this rhetoric from a Haitian catechism of the antisuperstition campaigns of the 1940s:

—Who is the principal slave of Satan?
The principal slave of Satan is the *oungan*. [Vodou priest]

—What names do the *oungan* give to Satan?

The names the *oungan* give to Satan are the *lwa,* the angels, the saints, the dead, the twins.

—Why do the *oungan* take the names of the angels, the saints, and the dead for Satan?

The *oungan* give the names angels, the saints, and the dead to Satan to deceive us more easily.

—Do we have the right to mix with the slaves of Satan?

No, because they are evil-doers and liars like Satan.[33]

In Haitian cultural politics, Catholicism has positioned itself against Vodou as an official, European, legitimate, orthodox tradition associated with ruling power and authority. Vodou occupies an oppositional space that is Creole, homegrown, unorthodox, diverse, and by extension illegitimate, impure, and evil—even Satanic. Politically, then, the two traditions have been constructed as polar opposites. The Lenten period becomes an interesting and tense time when Catholic and Vodou practices clash. The performance of Rara during Lent, within the Roman Catholic yearly calendar, reveals its historical evolution as a festival celebrated in a world dominated by Catholicism. The Rara festival unfolded in an Afro-Creole cultural space juxtaposed against a Catholic order, and its performance each year underscores the political oppositions between the two symbolic systems.

The political uses each tradition makes of the other are only the most public face of culture; these uses obscure the complex interactions between the traditions, the ways they combine themselves theologically, and the ways individual people combine them in practice. Focusing on their political opposition obscures the dialectic figuring and reconfiguring inherent in historical processes of creolization. Writing on Afro-Cuban religion, David H. Brown points out that "An over-emphasis on 'religion,' the binary positioning of 'African' and 'European/Catholic' systems, and the stark racial opposition of 'white' and 'black' limits our comprehension of the multiplicity of experiences, influences, and roles Afro-Americans *chose* in complex Caribbean creole societies. 'African' and 'European' interacted less as static capsules than as historical processes."[34]

American cultures evolved through processes of creolization, wherein cultural tropes and symbols shift and reconfigure themselves within unequal power relations. Both the Afro-Haitian religion and the Catholicism that evolved in Haiti were constructed in dialectical relation to each

other. To a significant degree, both Vodou and Catholicism have incorporated the other into its philosophies and practices. Each tradition is
constitutive and revealing of the other.

Cultural complexes that evolve in unequal relations of power take on
a process similar to the wars between "high" and "low" culture articulated by Peter Stallybrass and Allon White:

> A recurrent pattern emerges: the "top" attempts to reject and eliminate the
> "bottom" for reasons of prestige and status, only to discover, not only that
> it is in some way frequently dependent upon the low-Other . . . but also that
> the top includes that low symbolically, as a primary eroticized constituent of
> its own fantasy life. The result is a mobile, conflictual fusion of power, fear,
> and desire in the construction of subjectivity; a psychological dependence
> upon precisely those others which are being rigorously opposed and excluded
> at the social level.[35]

Institutional Catholicism depends on its opposition to Vodou, because
Catholicism's position against what is impure and illegitimate strengthens Catholic virtue in Haiti. In the Christian story, the trope of the Jew
is used by the enfranchised classes as a fantasy "low-Other" that au-
thorizes Catholic bourgeois superiority. The equation of non-Christians
with Jews gave bourgeois Haitians one more cultural difference between
themselves and the nonliterate Vodouists. Besides being dark-skinned,
nonliterate, Kreyòl-speaking peasants, they also were pagans and anti-
Christians. Symbolically, they were Jews. Haitian Catholics came to depend on the trope of the Vodouist-Jew as a force to oppose and exclude,
a way to define the Catholic self through a negative referent.

The myths and rituals that surface at Easter yield particularly illus-
trative readings for the way in which groups in both "high" and "low"
cultures reach for symbols and embrace, perform, and transform them
in the ongoing process of negotiating power. The performances of Easter
myths range from the strictest Catholic mass, to the popular Easter rituals sanctioned by Catholicism, all the way to the oppositional readings
of Rara bands.

Theologically, Easter is the most important holiday in the Catholic
calendar, celebrated in Haiti both in official church mass and in popular
rituals. One of the Easter traditions practiced by all classes is the reenactment of the stations of the cross after church on Good Friday. For
this Passion Play, a series of ritual stations are set in place, and bare-
footed pilgrims, some dressed in burlap, visit each station, fasting, without water, reciting prayers before each spot. A local man plays the role

of Jesus, and other actors portray various figures in the story. The Passion Play was honed as a genre in medieval Europe, and this somber drama drawn from the four gospels still enacts itself in numerous locations on Good Friday all over the Christian world.

At the same time that Catholics engage in these Easter rituals, Rara bands are busy parading through public thoroughfares. In fact, some Raras deliberately plan to walk past churches on Sunday to annoy the Christians. In 1993, a priest in Pont Sonde ended mass with the admonishment "Don't go in the Rara," worried he might lose some parishioners to this "devil's dance." In the imaginary of the Haitian bourgeoisie, Vodouists have been cast as evil slaves in Satan's army. As anti-Christians, they become symbolic Jews.

"IF YOU GO IN THE RARA, YOU ARE A JEW"

On Good Friday 1993, Rara Ya Sezi (Rara They Will Be Surprised) walked for miles all day along the banks of a tributary of the Artibonite River. They were on their way to the compound of Papa Dieupè, a bòkò *and wealthy landowner in the region who also served as the "emperor" of a Chanpwèl society. Chantal, Phenel, and I had chosen Papa Dieupè's as the best place to be for Rara; we figured we could stay comfortably in one place and watch the bands come to salute a "big man" in the countryside.*

Papa Dieupè has a great deal of land under cultivation, and with his talents as an oungan *and* bòkò *he has developed solid links with the Haitian military, who come to him as clients to make* wanga. *He has five wives and never travels without thirty to forty* ounsi, *who augment his presence when he goes away to baptize boats and gas pumps.*

Many people make the journey to Dieupè's lakou, *asking him to adjudicate cases of theft, abuse, or labor conflicts. He leans back on his chair under the mango tree and drinks Johnny Walker White Label Whiskey out of a glass soda bottle. Each visitor is offered a beverage appropriate to his or her social status. The farmer is welcomed with* kleren. *Rum is for the youth traveling from Port-au-Prince. Ice, if there is any. Whiskey for the military. Soda for the Protestant pastor, who stops by because Dieupè, while "pagan," is, after all, a cousin.*

During Easter season, Rara bands of hundreds of people come from miles around to honor Dieupè and "animate" his lakou. *They are shown to a table well-stocked with whiskey and rum and are given a place to sleep. In the morning they are given coffee, and they dance away, making room for the next Rara. We were well-received, given a little house with a bed to sleep in, introduced to an* ounsi *named Veronique, and told to ask her if we needed anything. During the day we could swim in the Artibonite River, and in the evening a solid dinner was served. We got to know the compound, waiting for the Raras to come.*

Ya Sezi's entrance was spectacular. It was a sleepy country day, and we could hear the banbou *blowing from miles away. Children ran through the compound to announce breathlessly that the army was coming to salute the emperor. Then the Rara came up the path and saluted the spirits in the compound and Papa Dieupè's ounsi. Finally, after they'd played until about midnight, Papa Dieupè himself greeted them.*

After playing music in the compound for much of the night, the group slept. They awoke early Saturday morning to play and warm up before they left. While the musicians played, each of the dancers (who were all women) took turns holding the whip belonging to the leader and ran in circles through the compound. The other dancers set off in hot pursuit, their dresses streaming out behind. Papa Dieupè told me they were taking turns being Jesus, running from the "Jewish soldiers." Pilate's Roman soldiers were nowhere in evidence; they had been collapsed into a new bloodthirsty figure of "Jewish soldiers." Comically enacting Jesus' suffering on his walk to Calvary, the Rara members were amusing themselves by taking turns portraying both Jesus and his "killers, the Jews."[36]

During the Easter Rara festivals, the story of Jesus' life and death replays itself in the churches and streets of the country, and Jesus, Judas, and "the Jews" join the spirits of Vodou as dramatic characters to be performed and interpreted.[37] Good Friday in particular becomes a day of stark contrasts between the devoted Catholics who pray, fast, and walk the stations of the cross and the Rara bands who parade noisily through the streets singing and working to *chofe* relationships with Vodou spirits and the recently dead. Catholic Haitians make a clear connection between the exuberant celebrations of Rara on the anniversary of Jesus' death and "the Jews who killed him." A popular expression says, "*Ou al nan Rara, se Jwif ou ye*" ("If you go in the Rara, you are a Jew").

Because Haitian Catholicism equates Vodou, the devil, and "the Jews who killed Christ," it is clear how celebrating Rara in the streets on the day Christ died "makes you a Jew" in the Catholic view. Even some university-educated Haitians have a vague concept that "Rara is a Jewish festival." At a fancy cocktail party in the wealthy enclave above Petionville, I was introduced to a young Haitian architect from the mulatto class. "Studying Rara?" he asked incredulously. "Well, you'll find that it's a Jewish thing." Pressed to explain how a Jewish festival could have found its way through history to be adopted by the Haitian peasantry, the man shrugged his shoulders and reached for his rum punch.

In contrast, every Rara member I interviewed remembered that Rara "came from Africa" with the slaves. This seems a clear historical fact: Rara continues and extends a number of African cultural principles, including the centrality of community enterprise, relationships with the ancestors and the deities, a kind of politics of "big man-ism," the use of natural sites for spiritual work, and the performative African-based drumming, call and response singing, and dance in public festival.

After establishing the African roots of the festival, however, Rara leaders would invariably go on to articulate the idea that Rara was linked to the Jews. Many of them cited the precise origin of Rara as the celebration of the Crucifixion itself. "It was the Jews who crucified Christ who made the first Rara." One *oungan* explained it this way: "Long ago, after they finished nailing Jesus to the cross, the soldiers who did that saw that it would be even more satisfying to put out a Rara to show that they were the winners. They put out a Rara, they made music. They were rejoicing, singing, and dancing."[38]

This idea that "the Jews who crucified Christ" rejoiced and made the first Rara was stated to me repeatedly by Rara members. The historical genealogy of the notion is obscured here, as is the cultural history of most dispossessed groups. Yet one returns to the Passion Plays of the Colonial Church, modeled after the ones in medieval France, England, and Germany. The Jews are the central villains of these stories and are directed by demons and devils hovering in the background. Together the devils and the Jews convince Judas to betray his master, and they celebrate when they succeed. Joshua Trachtenberg describes it thus: "Around the cross on which Jesus hangs the Jews whirl in a dance of abandon and joy, mocking their victim and exulting in their achievement." This explicit scenario of a crucified Christ surrounded by joyful, dancing Jews celebrating their victory seems to have made its way from the popular European imaginary to become a memory of former African slaves.[39] Another Rara president states that "Rara is what they did when they crucified Jesus, on Good Friday. At that point, all the Jews were happy. They put the Rara out, they masked, they danced, they dressed in sequins, they drank their liquor and had fun."[40]

The link between Rara and "the Jews who killed Christ" was strong enough in the Haitian imagination that Rara members became Jews in their own rememberings. An *oungan* told me that "It was the Jews who came with this tradition. Now it's become our tradition."[41] The *oungan* provided an explanation that implicitly described how the Africans could have inherited this celebration of the ancient Hebrews. "Rara is something that comes from the Jewish nation. So, mystically speaking, Haitians are descended from Africa. The Africans always kept their mystical rites."[42] In this logic, Africans are equated with the ancient Israelites, and it is this linkage that explains how Haitians have inherited Rara from the Jews. Through Rara, these Haitians embraced the subversive identity of "the Jew" and see Jews somehow as forerunners of their African ancestors.

When Rara members embrace the negative cultural category of "the Jew," the mythology they generate may be understood as a repressed people's subversion of the ruling order. This class resistance to Catholic hegemony is a form of theatrical positioning on the part of the peasants that says, "Yes, we are the Jews, the enemy of the French Catholic landowners." Like other groups that take on the negative terms ascribed to them by the powerful, Haitians take on a mantle of denigration in the face of a hostile dominant class. Just as "high culture" includes "low culture" symbolically in its self-construction, so here the "popular culture" includes the "elite." Laënnec Hurbon understands this dynamic historically as a creative appropriation of cultural goods: "[The slaves'] diverting of Christianity to their own ends . . . had nothing to do with the systematic denial of Christianity, nor was it a sign of inadequacy of evangelization, but a process of making off with those elements of Christianity which could be useful in the struggle and in the construction of their new culture."[43]

Vodouists' interpretations of biblical stories can be understood as creative subversions of official discourse. Like the Rastafari of Jamaica, Vodouists are adept orators and creative interpreters of myth and scripture. Every imaginative Vodou practitioner may offer a new visionary

interpretation of the Bible and of history. These versions allow Vodouists and Rara members to authorize their own history while positioning
themselves, for themselves, in terms of the dominant class and its religious ideology.

Jesus Christ is the subject of much theorizing on the part of Vodouists.
In one myth, God created the twelve apostles just after he created the
earth and the animals. The apostles were rebellious and challenged God.
In punishment, God sent them to Ginen, the mythical Africa of Vodou's
past and future. The apostles and their descendants became the *lwa,*
while a renegade apostle who refused to go to Ginen became a sorcerer
and took the name Lucifer.[44] Throughout the oral mythologies of Vodou
is a clear theme of morality and a distinction between working with the
Ginen spirits and working with the forces of sorcery. Usually the sorcerer
is also a slave master of captured spirits and souls, and thus themes of
morality are bound together with philosophical issues of slavery and
freedom.

One story I was told posits Jesus as the first *zonbi,* a soul that has
been captured and sold in order to work for its owner. Although I have
written of this elsewhere, it bears reiterating here. This myth creatively positions Jesus and God as the innocent victims of two unscrupu-
lous Haitian soldiers who secretly witnessed the Resurrection. It was
related to me by a sorcerer who confided that he knew the techniques
of capturing the spirit of the recently dead and ordering the *zonbi*
to work:

> The reason that we are able to raise people after they die goes back to when
> they crucified Jesus Christ. Christ was sent by Gran Jehovah, by Gran Mèt
> [God]. He also sent Mary Magdelene, along with two bodyguards for Jesus
> from the Haitian Armed Forces. When Jehovah gave the password to raise
> up Jesus from the dead, the soldiers stole the password and sold it. It's been
> handed down from father to son, which is how I could get it.[45]

Vodou takes what it can use theologically and constantly re-creates
itself with fresh material. The Vodouist fits biblical figures into an already-existing Afro-Creole scheme. Jesus is problematic for the Vodouist: the heavy catholicizing of the French and, later, the Haitian elite
makes him the god of the dominant classes. This story subtly acknowledges the teller's opposition to Christianity: a worker (a Haitian foot-
soldier) stole something from Jesus (the god of the elite). The stolen

knowledge becomes a tool for the subordinates, because it is Vodouists who now control the resurrection secrets of God. This tale illustrates how the Vodouist uses oppositional mythology as one of the ongoing weapons in everyday Haitian class warfare.[46]

Rara leaders I interviewed accepted the Catholic labels of pagan, Satanist, and Jew and theorized their position in a specific Vodou theology. In doing so, they agreed that Rara is anti-Christian. As one leader explained, "Rara is basically against the power of God. Because Rara is what they did when they crucified Jesus, on Good Friday." This view understands Rara to be "against the power of God," in Catholic terms.[47]

On some level, however, God has abandoned Haitians. The president of Rara Mande Gran Moun (Ask the Elders) in Léogâne explained: "God made the king Lucifer. God commands the sky, and the king Lucifer commands the earth. Everybody who is poor on this earth is in hell."[48] In this interpretation, God rules the heavens but has given Lucifer control over the earth, and humans are the political subjects of the king Lucifer. The president adds that "everybody who is poor on earth is in hell." In the face of a class structure divided by access to the means of production but marked, in many ways, by religious affiliation, the response of Vodouists is to embrace and creatively rework the identity given them by Catholics. Commenting directly on the suffering generated by extreme economic exploitation, the figure of Lucifer stands as moral commentary on the state of Haitian government and its history of class inequality.

Rara leaders construct theology through the appropriation of "high" cultural elements into allegories of empowerment. The stories of the Jewish Rara and the *zonbi* Christ construct an engagement with the texts of the Catholic dominant classes in which the power of the Vodouists or Rara members is hidden inside the images of demonization. Haitian sorcerers construct themselves as active enemies of the Catholic order, as Jews, or as allies of thieves who stole from God. The narratives support Hurbon's statement that "In the eyes of the Voodooist, his mysticism is his power. Thus it may be correct to say that the Voodoo cult, since its inception with a creole coloration, is used by Voodoo believers as a power base from which to deal with the power elite."[49]

These myths can be seen as antihegemonic counternarratives that reconfigure histories and genealogies to cast power with the popular classes. In repressive contexts, cultural expression often generates double-voiced, allegorical strategies so that the dominant culture is turned back on itself, transformed by the subordinate. The myths generated and performed by Rara reveal how "high" Catholic culture and "low" Vodou culture are constructed in relation to one another, each mystically exoticizing the other in the ongoing performance of class in Haitian society. Each end of the class spectrum reaches for the figure of "the Jew" to authorize its own power in the imaginary of Haitian class warfare. "The Jew" in Haiti remains largely a figure constructed from the leftovers of medieval Christianity and sustained through Catholic popular culture. Inherited by Afro-Haitians, "the Jew" is creatively presented as a figure allied in opposition to the Church, the landowners, and the Franco-Haitian elite.

THE JEWISH PRESENCE IN HAITI

A popular expression of surprise in Haiti roughly corresponds to the phrase "I'll be damned!" It says, simply, "*Jesu, roi des Juifs!*" ("Jesus, king of the Jews!"). "The Jews" are a stock figure in Haitian popular culture, inherited in the process of Catholic European missionizing that was part and parcel of the Latin American plantation enterprise. A figure used at once as scapegoat and mystical forebear, "the Jew" can also be a comedian who speaks the unspeakable. He shows up in Carnival as Papa Jwif, a wandering Jew who delivers satirical political commentary or enacts problematic issues in the community. In Port-au-Prince during the coup that ousted President Aristide, Papa Jwif was both a signal of the AIDS pandemic and a symbol of the corrupt military rulers, diseased beyond redemption. Here "the Jew" was a Carnival character dying of AIDS. He was surrounded by an entourage of doctors perpetually treating him with useless remedies, coded as U.S. political forces propping up a violent and corrupt regime.

"The Jew" and Judas are most often negative markers, and to be a *jouda* (Judas) is to betray one's friends through gossip. I have heard particularly violent army officers or *tonton makoutes* described in low tones as *yon Jwif* (a Jew) in their cruelty or barbarism. To be greedy or stingy is to be *kras pase Jwif* (cheaper than a Jew). While most of the negative images of the Jew center on the premodern anti-Judaism that depicts Jews as betrayers and Christ-killers, the anti-Semitic imagery of

Jews as hoarders and usurers has crept secondarily into the Haitian cultural vocabulary.

In Vodou, "the Jew" represents a particularly potent magic centered on the figure of Moses. Haitians have canonized Moses as a Vodou spirit of their own, and handmade ceramic figures of Sen Moyiz (Saint Moses) clutching the tablets containing the Ten Commandments sit on the occasional altar. Long pictured in popular Christianity as the most famous magician of all time, who transformed serpents into staffs and parted the Red Sea, Moses' magic intrigues Haitian mystics. His magic and the magic of "the Jews" in general is an attractive source of power for disenfranchised Vodouists.

All of the myths, symbols, and rituals centered on the Jew raise the question: What was the historical Jewish presence in Haiti? While Jews never established a lasting community, it is nevertheless possible to discern a thin strand of Haitian Jewish history. It starts with the genesis of the modern Americas: at least one recently converted *converso* was aboard Columbus's ship in 1492, and five others are suspected by historians.[50] Although the forces of the Inquisition excluded Jews, Moors, and other non-Christians from the colonies, "Jews slipped through and managed to live unmolested in loosely organized communities."[51] Most colonial Jews were Sephardim, Iberian Jews of Spanish or Portuguese origin. They came often under false identities, many of them to Hispaniola, which was settled first.[52] Some came directly from France, but others made a circuitous route from initial settlements in Dutch territories, or from Spanish and Portuguese colonies after the Inquisition was established in those areas.[53] In a study on Jews in Saint-Domingue, Zvi Loker has located Jewish settlements in four zones of Haiti, including eighty Jewish families from Curaçao who settled as traders in Cap François and brought with them a prayer leader.[54]

The relationships between most Christians and the Jews in Saint-Domingue were friendly, and Jews became a subgroup of the planter and business class. As a result, the Church was not particularly successful at creating an anti-Jewish movement among the populace. The demonized images of the biblical Jews do not seem to have been converted into explicit anti-Jewish violence.

In the late nineteenth century, Azhkenazi Jewish families arrived in the country. The pattern for these arrivals and for the descendants of colonial Jews was to assimilate and convert to Catholicism, though many today acknowledge their Jewish ancestry. There were also Jews among the Middle Eastern diaspora of the early twentieth century, who settled in Haiti to become known as *Siryen* (Syrian) regardless of their nationalities as Syrian, Lebanese, or Palestinian. Later, during the Holocaust, French and German Jews made their way to Haiti on steamship. While most moved on to North America or Israel, a handful stayed in Haiti to live out the rest of their lives. In perhaps the most delightful symbolic reversal of all, the Haitian legislature in the 1930s declared all Jews to be of African ancestry, since they came from Egypt at the time of the Exodus with Moses. This justified permitting European Jews to settle in Haiti as enfranchised citizens, because the Haitian constitution had made land ownership possible only to those of African descent.

Despite the small but constant Jewish presence in Haiti, there is no evidence that a synagogue ever existed. Only one Jewish cemetery was established, centuries ago in the colonial period, and it has long since been abandoned.

As Haitians spread further abroad in their own diaspora, the founding of the state of Israel and subsequent gathering of Jews have given Jews a positive image in Haiti. The first Aristide government contracted for a study of Israel and its politics of returning citizenry, viewing Israel as a possible model for recouping the human potential lost in the brain drain of outmigration.

Despite the recent positive valence given to Jews in Haitian thought, the original anti-Judaic tropes of Christianity remain. As this chapter shows, Easter season has always set the stage for the resurfacing of the image of "the Jew," both in popular theater and in the official Church. Throughout Christendom, references to Jews were most numerous in sermons delivered during the Easter season, and the clergy used the Crucifixion story as the moment to illustrate the demonic nature of "the Jew." The rituals of Holy Week provided the clergy with a clear narrative to fix in the minds of the faithful the enormous crime that the Jews had committed against Jesus.[55]

Through the images of Jews that surface during Rara season, we can trace the process of domination that married Christianization and anti-Semitism to a process of racialized capitalist expansion in the Americas. The imaginary reserved for European "demonic" Jews is portable and easily transferred onto the Indian and African peoples of the Atlantic world. But myths, by their nature, create imminent and shifting imaginaries, less easily controlled by orthodoxy. Exploited peoples embraced the image of "the Jew" and creatively performed oppositional dramas in which they critiqued the morality of Christianity and their own place in the class structure.

Rara officers pose with batons. In the back, market women carry food to sell to the fans.

(photo © Elizabeth McAlister)

Rara as Popular Army

Hierarchy, Militarism, and Warfare

I am arriving with my regiment,
    Ossagne Oh [Repeat]
Don't you hear [about the] the
    National Palace
Let it flow
I am arriving with my regiment,
    Ossagne Oh

M'ap antre ak tout kò divizyon mwen,
    Osanj O [Repeat]
Ou pa tande Palè Nasiyonal
Lese koule
M'ap antre ak tout kò divizyon mwen,
    Osanj O

Rara La Belle Fraîcheur de l'Anglade,
Fermathe, Easter Sunday 1992

The oldest Rara leader I met was well into his hundreds, a retired farmer named Papa Dieubon who lived high in the mountains off the road to Jacmel.[1] Friends presented me to him one hot afternoon so he could bay odyans *(literally, "give me an audience"). We sat leaning back in small chairs under his porch roof, sipping* kleren *laced with sweet spices. Papa Dieubon's skin had the wizened look of a life lived*

under the hot sun, his face topped with snowy white hair. For a
long time he did not understand what I had come to ask. "I want to
talk about the Rara you led," I kept shouting. I began to have the
absurd feeling that I was talking to the wrong old man. "Ah," he said
at last, drawing himself up in his chair. "You mean the Army."

An overarching ethos of militarism pervades the Rara festival,
because bands construct themselves as small regiments and go out into
the streets in the spirit of battle. Rara bands often conceive of
themselves as small statelike entities involved in diplomacy or warfare.
Embedded in the social organization of Rara bands and underlying
the festival conceptually is the notion of an imaginary state. Furthermore,
vestiges of a royal idiom are interwoven with the military and state
symbols in Rara. The social organization of Rara, then, is an articulation
of power and rank based in military, state, and royal metaphors.

This chapter examines the social organization of Rara bands in historical
context, viewing them as a type of militarized traditional peasant organization that has frequently marched across the pages of Haitian history. These groups were (and are) traditional forms of popular organizing that political activists, especially liberation theology advocates,
tapped in the recent efforts to gain political enfranchisement.[2] As self-
organized peasant groups, they can be viewed as the prepolitical forerunners of the contemporary grassroots popular organizations that
make up the democratic peasant movement.

Rara hierarchy and organization reveal how the cultural practices of
the Haitian popular classes display and draw attention to the local social
order. In Rara, individual agents act out an implicitly political theory,
asserting their right to participate in a communal endeavor, always
ranked in strict hierarchical relationships with compatriots and *gwo nèg*
and often united in battle against other local groups. Embedded in the
bands' social relationships and performed in the roles individuals assume during their parades is the system of patronage that has fueled
Haitian politics at all levels through the present day.

In the Rara bands, royal imagery has over time been replaced by
military idiom. This change may be contextualized historically. Early
colonial accounts of Vodou described the existence of a king and queen
as the two leaders.[3] After independence in 1804, the north was headed
from 1807 to 1820 by King Henri Christophe of the Kingdom of Haiti,
and it was probably during or after this time that republican titles re-

placed royal ranks in ritual. Dolores Yonker remarks that "Royal titles formerly used such as king, queen, princess and prince, dukes, etc., are gradually being displaced by more republican ones: president, various cabinet ministers, and the military."[4] We can compare this process to the history of other Afro-Caribbean societies like the Cuban *cabildos,* where the social structure was modeled on republican government but earlier had been borrowed from monarchy.[5]

Raras are organized into elaborate hierarchies, and their members hold specific titles known by everyone in the community. At the head of the band is the president. After the president come kings, queens, colonels, majors, rear guards, prime ministers, and secretaries of state. What follows is a list of possible titles for band members. These bestow upon their bearers the prestige and honor of publicly recognized rank. Linguistically, the titles are derived from French. They invoke multiple imageries borrowed from monarchy, from republican government, and from the French army:

prezidan	president
vis prezidan	vice-president
premye minis	prime minister
dezyèm minis	second minister
pòt drapo	flag bearer
avan gad	front guard
minis lagè	minister of war
minis dinfomasyon	minister of information
jeneral	general
kolonèl	colonel
dezyèm kolonèl	second colonel
kapitèn	captain
majò	major
majò jon	baton major
wa	king
premye renn	first queen
dezyèm renn	second queen
renn lagè	queen of war
renn kòbèy	queen of the basket
sekretè	secretary

trezorye	treasurer
minis finans	minister of finance
minis enteryè	minister of the interior
laryè gad	rear guard

The order of procession is a performance of military ethos. The *pòt drapo* walks a considerable distance in front of the band to scout for friends and foes. After him is the *kolonèl,* who directs the band with his whistle and whip. Usually he has several officers flanking him, making up the *avan gad. Majò jon,* dancers, and musicians follow, with the queens and women's chorus toward the rear of the band, protected from attack.

Sometimes within the orchestra itself there is a hierarchy, with a president who leads the band with the *manman* drum, and various vice-presidents who play behind him. Likewise, the women's chorus may include queens of various ranks, or officers of the band. After the musicians and the chorus come the rank-and-file Rara fans, who walk and sing with the band. Last but not least, individual *machann* (market women) affiliate themselves with specific Raras and walk with the band, selling liquor, cigarettes, and small foodstuffs. As vendors, these women too hold a recognized rank in the band. They provide service and maintain their loyalty to the group, and in return they are given "security" and protected by the rear guard.

In spite of the religious and magical practices of Rara, and even the participation of entire religious houses, the *grad* (ranks) in Rara are military and official in nature and do not indicate religious authority. Raras are modeled not on an imagined theocracy, but rather on an imagined military government. In some cases there is more at stake in Rara leadership than merely the band. I came across one Rara that owns land. Members of the family cultivate it and give a portion of the harvest to the Rara president.[6] These kinds of Raras exist as an imagined state with a territory and a population, and thus possess the means to produce and reproduce.

In order to analyze the royal, military, and state titles in Rara, we must understand the Raras as historically and structurally related to other popular societies also ranked into military hierarchies. These groups include Chanpwèl, Carnival bands, and various kinds of *sosyete travay* (work cooperatives): *konbit, èskwad, kòdon, konvre* (in the south), *mazinga* (in the northwest), *ranpono* (in the north), and *kounabe* (in the Petit-Goâve region). These various work cooperatives often organize themselves into guards, squads, battalions, and so on.[7]

In some cases, the Rara is conceived as the army for a higher governing body such as a Chanpwèl society. According to Michel Laguerre, "The societies, comprised of mountain dwellers, retain a governmental structure with a military parallel with the structure of the army and the civil government of the country."[8] Rara band names are created to inspire fear, with groups like Ti Rayè (from *tirailleurs,* the artillery in the French army) and Chien Mechant (Angry Dog).

Rara ranks may correspond with, or may be distinct from, a sponsoring Vodou, Chanpwèl, or work society. In 1961 Paul Moral observed that work societies sometimes turn into Rara bands or engage in mass demonstrations to create political agitation.[9] In 1987 Rachel Beauvoir and Didier Dominique noted a similar line of transformation: "[B]etween January and April, many work societies transform into Rara bands; these groups dress in colored costumes and dance during the day, and punish people at night. The Society's money pays for the costumes, drinks and all the other necessary expenses."[10] Thus the president of a Chanpwèl may also be the president of a Rara band, or an *oungan* might be a *kolonèl* who leads the Rara. Often the Rara queens are women who have attained the rank of queen in a Chanpwèl society. However, Rara is its own enterprise, and those involved jockey for positions using their roles in other areas to obtain positions of power or prestige in the band, and vice versa. A Rara member who attains the rank of general is addressed as such, and as a decision-maker for several hundred people, he is in a true position of leadership.[11]

Rara's symbols and social organization reveal it to be one of the most militarized arenas of popular religious culture. At the absolute top of its hierarchies one finds the *lwa,* along with any *zonbi* that may have been captured and *mete sou bann nan* (put on the band). Together these form an invisible military force that helps the band vanquish its competitors. The true owner of the Rara called Mande Gran Moun, I was told, was the *lwa* Kouzen Azaka. Azaka "walked with" the band under the title of prime minister, and it was he who was ultimately in charge.[12] Laguerre writes about the militarizing of the *lwa* in Afro-Haitian Vodou:

> Since the colonial era, Voodooists have developed their own theological view of the supernatural world, which they see in terms of a complex politico-military structure that operates on a spiritual as well as a human level. The major spirits are known to have a specific function in this government, and

each one has a military or political title. General Clermeil is believed to be in charge of springs and rivers, General Brisé is supposed to protect the trees of Chardette, Baron Samedi is a senator and a diplomat. *Zaka* is minister of agriculture and *Loko* is minister of public health while *Danbala* is minister of finance.[13]

The militarization of Haitian culture in general and of these local societies in particular is the result of a long-standing historical process: colonial Haiti was controlled and maintained by the French army, and the nation won its independence only after the bloody armed resistance that Haitians launched in the late eighteenth century. Haitian political history since that time has been a long series of military coups d'état; the last one at this writing was the ousting of President Aristide in 1991. In their recent study on militarism in Haitian music, Gage Averill and David Yih argue that the Haitian war of independence was the pivotal moment that crystallized Haitian identity and that Haitians responded by "embracing a deep cultural metaphor of the people as an army." When the indigenous army won its independence from the French, the idea of the army came to have a positive value and an association with victory.[14] Throughout the nineteenth century, the country was regionalized into diverse centers of power, and each region created its own army, capable of defending its own territory. Militarism thus became a generative scheme of social organization in the peasantry, each social group always reserving the potential to become an actual fighting force.[15] Michel-Rolph Trouillot writes that in the nineteenth century, "Retired or ousted officers, political leaders and local landlords . . . put together small armed bands that were effective in their limited regional spheres and that sometimes gave critical support to rebelling regular troops."[16]

There is historical evidence that peasant armies incorporated music into the work of fighting. Haiti's former rulers, the colonists of Saint-Domingue, had maintained regimental music corps called *corps de musique,* which were attached to various divisions such as the *chasseurs* (light infantrymen), *grenadiers* (grenade-throwers), *tirailleurs* (artillery), and *garde du palais* (palace guard). At one point there were sixteen *corps de musique* in Port-au-Prince and more in the provinces.[17] The colonial army also established various drum corps called *batteries sonores,* which the Independent Haitian armies maintained. Averill and Yih argue convincingly that the musical style of Rara *ochan* musical salutes derives from French military drumming. The word *ochan* probably derives from the French *aux champs* (to forward march; literally, "to the fields"). It is likely that postcolonial popular armies also made use of drums and other instruments as communication tools in symbolic displays, maneuvers, and possibly battle.[18]

It is probable that processional activity like Rara even had its origins in the colonial era. Thomas Madiou writes of maroon armies throughout the colony. He notes that a man named Halaou was a leader in the Port-au-Prince region who walked with drums, trumpets, and sorcerers: "The Cul-de-Sac insurgents (an army of two thousand maroons) had at their head an African priest of great height and Herculean strength. He . . . always [carried] under his arm a large white cock which, he pretended, transmitted to him orders from heaven. He *marched preceded by the music of drums, lambis [conch shells], trumpets and sorcerers*" (emphasis added).[19]

But militarism in Haiti was consolidated and bolstered throughout the country's history, as peasants organized themselves into armed groups to defend their interests. In the south these were known as Piquets du Sud and in the north as Cacos du Nord. Throughout the nineteenth century, generals would march with these "armies" to overthrow the Port-au-Prince state, promising peasants they would effect their demands. A few years later, another peasant army would overthrow the state. The first *piquets* mobilized under a peasant leader known as Goman, claiming their right to cultivate land. Another southern peasant rebel, Jean-Jacques Accaau, led the same *piquets* against President Jean-Pierre Boyer (1822–1844) because of his abandonment of peasant interests. In the late 1860s, the *cacos* helped Sylvain Salnave overthrow Nicolas Geffrard. When he did not move to change their conditions, they overthrew Salnave himself.

In January 1915, General Vilbrun Guillaume Sam led a *cacos* army to Port-au-Prince and named himself president. Six months later that same army killed Sam after he ordered the execution of political prisoners allied to the *cacos*.[20] This incident was the catalyst for the U.S. invasion of that year. The killing of Sam, who was "ripped apart" by a "mob," has stayed in the middle-class and foreign imagination as the shadow side of popular gatherings, including Rara.

The United States Marines, during their 1915–1934 occupation of the country, centralized, trained, equipped, and funded the Haitian military. According to one source, the title of *kolonèl* became the highest rank in Rara during the American occupation: "The title *le kolonèl* refers to the chief of the rural police. In the past, he was called 'general' because that was the highest grade in the army. Since the time of the

American occupation of Haiti (1915–1934), he has been known as *kolonèl,* since this was the highest rank in the American Army represented in Haiti."[21] It was during the marine occupation that one of the best-known Rara bands in Haiti was formed, making it eighty years old at the present writing. Peasant communities during the U.S. occupation transformed themselves into armed fighting *cacos* units and launched a guerrilla resistance against the marines.[22] In 1957 Duvalier rose, and there was increased U.S. support to the Haitian army during the Cold War. (Until the Duvalier era, Rara bands were not allowed into Port-au-Prince; they were held at bay in the outskirts of the city.)[23]

After the fall of Jean-Claude Duvalier in 1986, six military juntas forced successive coups d'état, increasing the power of the army to an extreme. In 1995, for the first time in Haitian history, President Jean-Bertrand Aristide dissolved the army and replaced it with a police force. This move was engineered, however, under the greater supervision of the occupying United Nations troops after a 1995 U.S. military "intervasion."

Haitian militarism on the national and the local level has thus been the idiom through which hierarchies channel power to the absolute leadership of one man. Trouillot has outlined the historical pattern through which the executive branch effects the total usurping of state power. The logical culmination of this process was the totalitarianism of François Duvalier's presidency. In this politics of "big man-ism," all citizens were forced to identify their position in relation to the president, either proclaiming themselves pro-Duvalier or anti-Duvalier. Polarized and terrorized, each person learned to construct relationships of patronage and subservience with pro-Duvalierists in order to dodge the brutal repression that was sure to follow resistance or even ambivalence. "In the course of daily life anyone could claim a relationship, even fictitious, to the sole center and source of power in order to ensure a place on the side of the survivors."[24] With the construction of this shape of power relations, political patronage became the only way to survive and succeed.[25]

Local "big man-ism" is a mirror image of the national model in Haitian politics and is possibly derived in part from African roots. As Karin Barber reports of the Yoruba, "[T]he dynamic impulse in political life is the rise of self-made men. Individuals compete to make a position for themselves by recruiting supporters willing to acknowledge their greatness."[26] In Haiti, the powerful man who carries political weight is called a *gwo nèg.* The status of a "big man" derives to some extent from his performance abilities as a man-of-words. More than that, it is his every-day style and charisma, his personal power, that attracts followers. Writing on the Kono in Africa, Kris Hardin ties leadership to style, raising interesting questions about the relationship of aesthetics to power. "These aspects of social life also rely on questions of charisma, personal style, and the ability to demonstrate power, authority, and knowledge in credible ways."[27]

The ethos of *gwo nèg* leadership in Haiti is permeated with the imagery of ownership, evidenced in the phrase *moun pa'm* (my person). The Rara presidents are local *gwo nèg* who actively attract *moun pa'l* (literally, "their people") into relationships of reciprocity wherein they offer protection from other powerful people, potential access to resources, and relationships with other *moun pa'l*. The follower in return offers up his or her loyalty and services. In extreme cases, to resist alliance with the *gwo nèg* threatens one's very survival. Thus the power of the *gwo nèg* in Haiti operates through his many dependents. Again, this is parallel to the situation among the Yoruba, where "in a fairly flexible social structure where individuals could make their own position for themselves, attendant people were the index of how much support and acknowledgement the man commanded, and thus how important he was."[28]

Heading up a Rara in the Haitian political context confers on the president the multidirectional power of the *gwo nèg*. By bankrolling and organizing the band, he signals his power in the community. The *fanatik* that he attracts enhance his power as they perform their allegiance through their bodily presence and their singing. The Rara in turn performs for even "bigger men" through *ochan* and augments its collective association with these other powerful figures. Heading a Rara increases the sphere of one's local political reputation, and by the same token, receiving a Rara is a mark of power and wealth.

The president may not be involved with the weekly *sòti* of the group, but his identity is known in the community, and often the Rara will gather in his *lakou* for a weekly *balanse Rara* (playing without walking). It is the president who is held accountable for the security of the group. In the case of accidents or deaths in the Rara, the president can be brought before a tribunal (in the Chanpwèl system) or to district court.

A band may also be financed and governed by committee, as is the case often in Léogâne, where the Raras are particularly lavish and costly. More often, the president pays the costs of the band, which can include the purchase of instruments, costumes, food, and musicians' salaries.

The religious costs of Rara can also be high, and the *lwa* can demand all-night religious services, protective baths, animal sacrifices, or *wanga* made for the occasion. Also there are payments made to the police in the form of parade fees or bribes.

In more elaborate bands, each committee member has a title describing exactly what his position is to his comrades. Rara Mande Gran Moun (Ask the Elders) in Léogâne had a president, prime minister, second minister, and minister of information. In true bureaucratic style, none overstepped the bounds of another, and when I interviewed them, each carefully sent me to the next to answer questions which he deemed "out of his jurisdiction." The leadership committees in Léogâne often include absentee members of the Haitian diaspora living in Miami or New York, who send money to the group and join them during Holy Week. Financial patrons like these are sometimes given the honorary titles *parenn* (godfather) or *marenn* (godmother) in return for their support.

Rara members broadcast the reputation of the Rara leader *gwo nèg* and restate their political allegiances to him by performing praise songs in his honor. Many Rara songs are drawn from the vast repertoire of Afro-Haitian religious prayer songs, but each Rara usually has a few original songs created by its own *sanba* and *simidò*, and often these are advertisements for the leader. In 1992 La Belle Fraîcheur de l'Anglade sang that their president, Dieuvè, had all the money he needed and did not need to borrow from anybody. You can hear the song on tracks 8 and 9 of the CD that accompanies this book.

> Dieuvè isn't asking to borrow
> This year, Oh, They will need him
> Dieuvè isn't asking to borrow
> This year, Oh, They will need him, Papa
> He possesses all that he wants

> *Dieuvè p'ap mande prete*
> *Ane icit O, y'ap bezwen li*
> *Dieuvè p'ap mande prete*
> *Ane icit O, y'ap bezwen'l Papa*
> *Li posede sa'l vle*[29]

Delen, in contrast, was a Chanpwèl leader nearby with a notorious reputation for meanness, an ability and inclination to do sorcery against people, and ties with the *tonton makoutes*. La Belle Fraîcheur de l'Anglade made the decision to turn down a mountain path and avoid this Rara altogether. Staying behind to see them, I recorded their praise song to Delen. You can hear it on track 20 of the CD that accompanies this book.

> Let me go, Delen, Let me go, Let me go
> Delen has a Chanpwèl band
> I won't do that work anymore
> Let me go

> *Voye'm ale, voye'm ale Delen, Voye'm ale*
> *Delen gen on bann chanpwèl*
> *M' pa sa travay ankò*
> *Voye'm ale*

A very clear example of Rara patronage was evidenced in the Rara called Ya Sezi. They named their band "They'll Be Surprised" as a *pwen* (point), a message against all of their detractors who spread malicious gossip that they were too poor to form a Rara. When a local *gwo nèg* named Papa Dieupè heard them, he adopted them as his personal band. A Chanpwèl leader holding the highest rank of emperor, Papa Dieupè is rumored to be a multimillionaire with hundreds of acres under cultivation. He calls the Rara whenever he wants to augment celebrations at his compound for birthdays, weddings, and religious ceremonies. They made a special trip on Easter of 1993 to sing at his compound for him and his five wives:

> We're arriving in Our Father's *lakou*, Oh [Repeat]
> Ring the sacred rattle for me

> *Nan lakou lepè-a nou rive* Wo [Repeat]
> *Sonnen ason an pou mwen*[30]

In addition to promoting individual *gwo nèg*, Rara songs often boast about the Rara band itself. We encountered Bann Bourgeois de la Lwa outside of Saint Marc in 1993. They were a *charyio-pye*, a band without instruments that uses their stomping feet as percussion. Their trademark song was about singing itself. It was a rhythmic masterpiece, a fast call and response between the *sanba* and the chorus. You can hear it on track 12 of the CD that accompanies this book.

S: Oh, Look at a song   C: Ya!
S: Children, I'm going to sing   C: Ya!
S: Children, I'm going to talk   C: Ya!
S: Oh, *sanba,* I'm going to roll out a song   C: Ya!
S: Children, I'm going to sing   C: Ya!
S: Children, I'm going to talk   C: Ya!
S: Oh, *sanba,* I'm going to roll out a song   C: Ya!
S: Children, I'm going to talk   C: Ya!

S: O gade on konpa   C: Ya!
S: Ti moun yo m'pral chante   C: Ya!
S: Ti moun yo m'pral pale   C: Ya!
S: O sanba m pral roule   C: Ya!
S: O sanba m pral chante   C: Ya!
S: Ti moun yo m'pral pale   C: Ya!
S: O sanba m pral roule   C: Ya!
S: Ti moun yo m'pral pale   C: Ya!³¹

This following boasting song by Rara Mande Gran Moun in Léogâne brags that the *sanba* are so good people want to kill them.

Gonaïves, I'm not going to stop in Gonaïves
People want to kill us for our song [Repeat]
That's the maestro standing in front; he's the leader
He's the leader [Sing four times]

Let them talk
Mande Gran Moun is Number One
It cannot be stopped
That's why people want to kill me
People want to eat me for my song
That's the maestro standing in front; he's the leader

Gonaïves, mwen pa'p sa rete Gonaïves
Se pou Konpa sa moun yo vle touye nou [Repeat]
Se maestwo sa ki kanpe devan, se li ka'p kòmande
Se Li k'ap kòmande [Sing four times]

Kite yo pale
Mande Gran Moun ki Numbè One
Li p'ap ka rete
Se pou Konpa sa moun yo vle touye mwen
Pou Konpa sa moun yo vle manje mwen
*Se maestwo sa ki kanpe devan, se li ka'p kòmande*³²

Rara bands usually pay annual visits to selected patrons that they know will receive them, in addition to spontaneously performing for new people. In these relationships between local *gwo nèg*, diplomacy is an important activity. Yonker reports a ritualized invitation process: "In a custom known as 'bois drapeau' poles are distributed to potential patrons. If they agree to be patrons, they return the poles with a patterned cloth banner, such as those preceding this band in the Artibonite Valley. The number of such banners proclaims the popularity of the group."[33]

In Port-au-Prince, a word-of-mouth system lets *oungan* in the area know that a visit is planned to their *ounfò* so they can be prepared with a contribution. If they intend to be generous with their support, perhaps offering a meal to the musicians, or even a place to spend the night, they will arrange this ahead of time with the Rara leaders. For an *oungan* who serves a *lwa* who likes Rara, this is one way to please the *lwa*. Receiving an entire Rara band is also a way to broadcast one's wealth and enhance one's reputation. Gerard reported, "We mostly dance at *oungan* and *manbo*'s places. We don't dance for poor people."[34] In Port-au-Prince's cemetery neighborhood, one Rara band sent a series of typewritten letters of invitation, asking local *oungan* and *manbo* to receive the band. For a festival in which the majority of participants are non-literate, this display of literacy and formal diplomacy was a dramatic event.

Contrary to upper-class and American assumptions that Rara bands are unruly, undisciplined mobs, all bands have rules and regulations that members are penalized for breaking. One such set of rules and regulations for the Bizoton band Vapeur Vin Pou Wè was collected by Gerson Alexis in 1958. Among the stipulations are these:

> Article 1: The members of the Association must assemble on the proper days for processions before 8:00 at night, except Good Friday, Holy Saturday and Easter Sunday, when the meetings will be in the mornings: The first day before 8:00, the second day before 9:00, and the last days before 10:00. After these times, late members will pay a fine of 2 gourdes, except in case of illness or by previous arrangement.
>
> Article 6: All members of the band must wear a high hat with blue pants and a yellow shirt, or must pay a fine of 3 gourdes.[35]

Rara bands are organized local groups with formal ranks, costumes, and rituals, and they conceive of themselves as armies connected to imaginary states that move through territory, carry out armed maneuvers, and conduct diplomatic relations with other groups in the process of their musical celebrations. As local groups under the leadership of "big men," Rara bands mirror the politics of patronage that have characterized Haiti's national government. In their performances of maneuvers, diplomacy, and tribute to local notables, Rara bands distribute and redistribute prestige, reputation, and local resources.

THE ARMY FIGHTS: MUSICAL COMPETITION, MYSTICAL WEAPONS, AND ARMED WARFARE

Haiti is a populous country, so no Rara band is ever the sole performer in its locality. The wider an arc that a *kolonèl* decides to make with his Rara, the more likely it is that it will cross paths with other bands. Rara bands are always aware of each other and constantly compete to have a reputation for the "hottest" music, the best dancers, and the most *fanatik*. Each Rara band tries in different ways to destroy the others—to *kraze Rara* (literally, "crash the Rara"). *Kraze Rara* is signaled when a band's musicians stop playing and cannot get started again, or by a group disbanding altogether. The ultimate victory of one band over another is when the aggressors are able to capture the flag of the band they have "crashed."

Competition promotes virtuosity and inventiveness, though it is also potentially vicious. The public face of this competitive antagonism takes the form of performed polemics and rivalries. The most famous rivalry in the entire country is perhaps that between Ti-Malis and La Fleur de Rose in Léogâne, where to walk with one means you cannot safely walk in the other, and even Haitians living abroad form opinions about which band is best.[36] There are hidden competitions between bands as well, and these entail setting magical traps for one another in an elaborate series of war-game maneuvers. Occasionally the competition takes the form of sabotage such as kidnapping, stealing instruments, and jailing opponents. At the extreme, Rara bands enter into all-out physical battle, in which the strongest of the men fight one another with fists, rocks, clubs, and machetes. The Hôpital St. Croix in Léogâne assigns extra staff to treat the Rara wounded each year on Easter Week.[37]

Rara leaders may conduct spiritual or physical warfare for several reasons. They may be settling long-standing feuds, competing for

Raraman poses in distinct costume from the Artibonite (photo © Chantal Regnault)

followers, or be involved in complex local political dramas. The downward spiraling of the Haitian economy has pushed increasing numbers of people from the countryside into the capital city's slums. Many Rara bands come out of these slum neighborhoods and compete for resources, fans, and sheer reputation. Some of the most famous Raras come from Bel Air, a notorious slum that was historically the site of a maroon colony. Known for its fierce practice of the Kongo-based Petwo rites, these Raras are said to keep the slum-dwellers who are not members inside their homes at night.[38]

The goal of the Rara president, besides fulfilling his obligations to the *lwa,* is to attract the most followers. To be known as a Rara president is one way to perform one's status as a *gwo nèg* and garner its material benefits—more power and therefore more money—as well the religious benefit of being ritually remembered after one's death.

A very common Rara theme (and indeed a common theme in many Vodou songs) has to do with plots, conspiracies, and enemies waiting to entrap the singer. Rara Modèl in Léogâne sang about this plot against them:

> Plot, they're mounting a plot [Repeat]
> Danbala Wedo, they're mounting a plot
> They're mounting a plot, What will I say to them
> We can't see the people who crash a party
> Get away, Get away from them
>
> *Konplo, Yo monte konplo [Repeat]*
> *Danbala Wèdo, yo monte konplo-a*
> *Yo monte konplo sa m'a di avè yo*
> *Nou pa wè daso*
> *Dekole, Dekole sou yo*

David Yih perceptively relates these themes of mistrust to the history of Haitian slavery and exploitation:

> In the themes, attitudes, and emotional content of the songtexts we can read the response of Vodou to the circumstances under which it came forth. References to bondage, conflict, mistrust, betrayal, persecution, oppression, and war are frequent. These themes are often reflected in recurrent formulas—phrases encountered in several songs in the same or almost the same form.[39]

In the following Rara song, the threat of kidnapping and bondage is offset by the "talking bad" and bravado of the *sanba* who would lend his own rope to the kidnappers only to later escape:

They say they'll tie me up [Sing three times]
Here's the cord to tie me [Repeat]
When you hear midday ring, I'll throw down the cord and go

Yo di y'ap mare mwen [Sing three times]
Men kòd pou mare'm [Repeat]
Kan ou wè midi sonnen, m'ap lage kòd-la pou'm ale

In his work on the cultural patterns that inform the expressive talent and public performances of African-American men throughout the Caribbean, Roger D. Abrahams has found that verbal dexterity is a much cultivated and prized value and that men-of-words trade on oratory talent as a form of cultural capital as they compete to build reputations. Abrahams describes a multiplicity of West Indian performance troupes, often organized around a captain, who is usually the best performer. They put their talents in full view of the community during events such as Christmas serenading, Christmas mumming plays, Carnival, and Jonkonnu. "In those troupes that involve dancing, acrobatics, or fighting, [the man-of-words] has his equivalent, one we might call the man-of-action, the physically adept one who brings focus to the proceedings by his leadership and performance abilities."[40] Consider this description of the Trinidad Carnival Devil Band in 1956:

> There was a reigning beast, a man so dexterous and inventive in his dancing and portrayal of the beast as to be proclaimed best. Each year aspirants for his crown would "challenge him to combat." The challenge to combat occurred automatically when the two bands met for the first time. The combat took the form of the execution by the reigning beast of various dance steps which the challenger had to imitate. If he succeeded in imitating them he then executed steps of his own for the reigning beast to imitate. The beast who first failed to imitate the other's steps lost the contest.[41]

Similar competitions can be seen in African-American traditions in the United States today. The "Black Indians" of New Orleans Mardi Gras confront one another publicly each year and enter into intense symbolic battles, each man or woman ritually showing parts of their elaborately beaded costume, thereby challenging the opposing "Indian" to "go them one better." The winner is immediately apparent, judged on the spot by the reactions of onlookers and the demeanor of the two "Indians" themselves. It is not unheard of for the "Black Indian" gangs to fight one another with fists, knives, and guns, and more than one man has lost his life in these intensely competitive processions.[42] Break-dancing, capoeira, drag balls, and jazz improvisation are performed challenges within U.S. Black masculine cultures, just as graffiti writing is a visually performed challenge for urban "crews" or gangs.

Rara shares with all these practices a competitive spirit of artistic decoration and performance, but it is perhaps extreme in the way it spiritualizes landscape and uses mystical weapons (including poisons) and in the frequency with which bands fight one another, escalating the competition into violent and dangerous battles. Although it is a form of Black West Indian all-night reputation-enhancing performance associated with "play" values of "foolishness" and "nonsense," Rara bands are also committed to a level of battle over reputation and territory that marks it as a deadly serious event.

Poisons, Powders, and Magical Weapons

While the musicians and *fanatik* in Rara are singing their boasting and bragging songs, playing catchy melodies on the *banbou,* and drumming as hard as they can to create a carnivalesque atmosphere, the leaders are often competing against other bands in an inside world of secret politics. They hold nocturnal meetings and stage elaborate schemes involving espionage and magical warfare against other bands. The fears of Rara leaders about conspiracies against them are well-founded, because the magicians associated with Rara—*bòkò* and secret society leaders—perform rituals meant to weaken and *kraze* other Raras. In the first meeting of the Rara band of the season, the leaders of Rara La Belle Fraîcheur de l'Anglade got together and magically "tied up" an enemy Rara general and put him under a rock, weighing him down by magic to drain his power. General Kanep showed me a rock and a whip, explaining:

K: You call the names of all the Rara presidents that you are going up against, and you tie them up so they can't assault you. You put them underneath you. I named another general, I put him under this rock.

Q: How do you do that ceremony?

K: You name him, and you place him there, and he's now underneath you. You say, "All those who live, get beneath my feet."[43]

A similar practice was reported in the colonial period. In 1758 M. Courtain, judge at the Royal Seat in Cap Français, wrote that "They place the *makandal,* loaded with curses, under a large stone, and it is indubitable that this brings misfortune to whomever they wish it."[44] "Makandal" was also the name of a slave resistance leader who carried out mass poisonings and magical warfare against slaveowners in the late eighteenth century. His name became the designation for a sort of magic object.

During Rara season, band leaders send scouts to learn the plans of other *kolonèl* and may decide to avoid or encounter neighboring bands in their weekly *ekzèsis.* There are always possibilities for spontaneous encounters as well, because each band will stop and perform at such unplanned opportunities as approaching cars, in addition to performing for patrons scheduled in advance. Even in an unplanned encounter, the music has heralded a band's approach, and flag bearers who are vigilant have spotted the oncoming flag of the competitor.

The moment when two bands encounter and pass one another is called *mariaj Rara* (literally, "Rara marriage") and is an extremely dangerous and crucial point. Each band faces the challenge of continuing its musical beat and hopes to attract the fans of the other band. When relations are very good between groups, each will stop and perform an *ochan,* the musical salute reserved for patrons and contributors. If they are enemies, the bands use the moment as an opportunity to try to *kraze* one another and force the other band to stop playing and stop their walk.

Many Rara *kolonèl* are also *oungan* and *bòkò,* knowledgeable in *zam kongo* (Kongo weapons) that include *wanga,* botanical curatives, and toxins. They commonly manufacture *pwazon* (poisons) and *poud* (powders) and leave them in crossroads for other Raras to step on. These packages are meant to create "bad air" and confuse the other band, or else lead to sickness. In a skirmish, they administer the *poud* face-to-face, with a *kou'd poud* (literally, "hit of powder") when two bands meet. The aggressor will lift the powder to his lips and blow it into the faces of the men in the opposing Rara. *Poud* are made of diverse toxins: a variety of poison ivy called *pwa grate* (itching bean), *piman* (hot pepper), and other poisonous plants and herbs. It is to the advantage of the Rara leader to boast of having *poud,* to create a sense of awe in the community about his powers and his willingness to use them. General

Gerard enjoyed talking "bad" about his ability to *kraze* other Raras and attract their *fanatik:*

> Wherever it comes from, wherever it is, if there's a Rara in Bel Air I'll "crash" it. I'll make them carry their drums on their backs and go home. Any Rara I face. My Rara is the biggest Rara here.
>
> As soon as I give them a *kou'd poud,* they'll go home. Everybody will run. I'll turn that band around and everybody in it will follow me. My Rara will become the biggest Rara.[45]

Poud can reportedly cause burning and rashes on the skin, shortness of breath, blindness, paralysis, and even death. It is considered a serious weapon, and using it has historically been judged a crime.[46] The following account, reported to me by a schoolteacher in Beaufort in the Artibonite Valley, ascribes the death of a young man to powder, but a powder that was marked magically only for him:

> A: A young man fell in the Rara, and his parents said he had gotten hit with powder. He died. This was in 1981 in Beaufort, in section Jean Denis. The guy who got the *kou'd poud* was named Lucien. He went to an *oungan,* and the *oungan* analyzed it. He said it was powder that killed him.
>
> Q: How long did it take?
>
> A: It was very quick. The same day the guy got sick, he died. After about three hours.
>
> Q: How come only one person got hit?
>
> A: Well, it was a specific guy. He blew the powder in the name of that guy. You know powder is a magical thing. When you blow it in one person's name, other people aren't affected.[47]

To be known as a someone who can manufacture *poud* and use it in the Rara is to augment one's reputation as a magician and as a feared member of the community. Karin Barber notes that among the Yoruba, "The Big Man was pictured as rising above the malicious attacks of jealous rivals and at the same time getting away with any attacks he made on *them.*"[48] Surviving these attacks requires each Rara leader to carry antidotes to the powders of others. The members of Rara Brilliant Soleil in Léogâne explained:

> It's the *kolonèl* who knows what to do to go forward or to set traps. There are some Rara that go through a crossroads, and they put some "funny stuff" in the crossroads, to "crash" other Raras who come behind them. The col-

onel has to have a series of things with him, and he has to be smart enough to smash anything they leave for him, so he can get through.[49]

Rara leaders boasted about their ability to repair damage done by other Raras' powders. Gerard says, "If you encounter another Rara, they might blow [powder] on you. In order that your Rara doesn't 'crash,' you have to walk with your own equipment. Before you even face that Rara, if they know where you're going to pass, you can lift off anything [traps] they put down for you with your whip. So your Rara doesn't 'crash.' "[50]

In 1993 I was able to spend a few nights walking with La Belle Fraîcheur de l'Anglade, with whom I had spent two weeks in 1992. On the route from Tomasin to Kenskoff, high in the mountains above Port-au-Prince, the generals drew up elaborate battle plans, strategizing maneuvers with both friends and foes. Camping for a while with an allied band called Rara La Reine (The Queen's Rara) I heard them discussing an event that had taken place the night before. It seems that a spy sent from another Rara had walked with us and thrown powder on General Silvera's horse, trying to kill it. The horse had become sick with fever, but it had recovered, because, they said, the horse was actually mystically dedicated to a *lwa*.

Physical Fighting

In both Carnival and Rara, there is always the potential for violence that exists in large public crowds where young men are drinking. In Carnival a fairly serious physical competition called *gagann* finds two men hurling themselves at each other like roosters, bashing their upper chests together in an effort to knock each other down. *Gagann* can lead to *wozèt* (strangling; literally, "bow-tie") and end in outright fights. Other small-scale warfare goes on during Carnival; Mirville reports the use of slingshots as a weapon, and rocks are thrown from time to time.[51] Rara bands sometimes perform at the site of formal physical fighting. In the south of Haiti there are wrestling matches, and onlookers bet on the young men who fight while the Raras play. This goes on presently in Port-au-Prince in the neighborhood of Delmas 31, now called "Citè Jérémie" because five hundred migrants from Jérémie have settled there in the years since 1981.[52]

Violence in Rara can be devastating, especially if two groups plan to fight. Wade Davis describes meeting Andres Celestin, a *tonton makout* and Bizango president near Saint Marc. "Now he seemed a broken man, lying prostrate on a cot with much of his face swollen and distorted by a sharp blow received, as we would learn later, when two Rara bands had met and clashed several nights previously."[53] To avoid such violence, Raras' ministers of war will engage in diplomacy, as Beauvoir and Dominique note: "Often, for example, the groups enter a state of war when they encounter one another. They throw rocks, draw their machetes and fight. To avoid this, they must send a blue flag in front and the 'Minister of War' must go ahead and make peace."[54]

I never witnessed a violent encounter between two Rara bands, but rumors of aggressive incidents were common. On 25 January 1993, the newspaper *Le Nouvelliste* ran this headline: "Confrontation between 2 Foot Bands; Shots Fired in the Air." Apparently one Carnival band held hostage a musician from another band called Konbit Lakay. The incident was reported in the newspaper only because the military arrived and fired into the air to diffuse the situation. Later that season, two Raras in Pont Sonde came to blows and a man was decapitated by a machete.[55] Someone had died in Rara Saint Rose in a fight in the mountains between Léogâne and Jacmel the year before I arrived.[56] Over the months of my research, I was told many stories of legendary battles between bands involving death, jailings, and ongoing feuds. In 1986, for example, it seems that Rara Rosalie and Rara Rosignol planned a fight; as a result of the battle, two men died, one son of each president. They crossed the two bodies over one another in the street. Five years later the two bands reconciled and invited one another to feasts.[57] Myths spring up about people dying in Rara; more than one man swore to me that he had seen a man decapitated, then saw the body continue to dance as the head, fallen to the ground, kept blowing its trumpet.

This chapter has explored the overarching ethos of militarism that pervades the Rara festival, as bands construct themselves as popular armies and move into public space like battalions prepared for war. Rara bands imagine themselves to be self-organized popular armies, which may be ritualized performances of the peasant armies that played a central role in Haitian political history.

Rara hierarchy and organization reveal how the cultural practices of the Haitian popular classes display and draw attention to the local social order. Like many other popular groups, Raras are ranked in strict hierarchical relationships, displaying and performing the system of patronage that has fueled Haitian politics at all levels through the present day. As traditional peasant groups, Raras can be viewed as the prepolitical forerunners of the contemporary grassroots popular organizations that make up the democratic peasant movement.

An old-style *makout* and a coup-era military police (photo © Chantal Regnault)

Voices under Domination

Rara and the Politics of Insecurity

Several people were arrested and at least one person killed during pre-Easter rara celebrations. On March 12 in Carrefour Feuilles, police fired on a rara band *whose song they judged subversive.* On the same day on the Avenue John Brown, a youth called Noula was shot by an armed civilian. He was drunk and singing songs favorable to Aristide. [Emphasis added]

Haiti Insight, June 1994

On February 27, attaché Ti-Paul arrested two members of the rara band *Ti Malice Cachée.* Valval Augustin and Yayak were severely beaten in the Léogâne army post.

Haiti Insight, May 1994

The first half of the 1990s, during which this study was undertaken, marked a politically volatile and hitherto unprecedented period in Haitian history. The Rara festival, with its large gatherings of *pèp-la* (common people), interacted energetically with these historical events. The year 1990 saw the U.S.-sponsored, "first democratic elections" in Haiti. Elected by 67 percent of the vote, Jean-Bertrand Aristide's government marked the broadest involvement of the Haitian populace in the political process since the revolution of 1804. Ending six military juntas that had controlled Haiti since Jean-Claude Duvalier's fall from power, the elections ushered in a new period of hope among the Haitian majority. The coming to power of Aristide, a liberation theologian priest in favor of land reform and human rights, was a heady victory for Rara members. Aristide made Kreyòl the language of official discourse, becoming the first Haitian president to address the Haitian majority in their own language.

When Aristide was ousted in the 1991 coup d'état by top-ranking General Raoul Cedras, the country entered into a period of silent civil war between the army (and some capitalists) and the majority who had elected Aristide. This period was considered by longtime residents in Haiti to be worse even than the darkest repression of Duvalier.[1] From 1992 to 1994 the United States led an international embargo against Haiti, and during this time thousands of refugees escaping political violence were interned by the United States at the Guantanamo naval base. In 1995, Aristide was returned to power in a U.S.-led, U.N.-sponsored military action.

During the time of military rule—when the raised hopes of the Haitian majority turned to despair—the Raras in Port-au-Prince became politicized in complex and sometimes contradictory ways, some bands acting as followers (or paid mercenaries) of military "big men," and other bands engaging in outright resistance to the military. I am interested in both the explicit political interrelationships Rara bands created and the implicit class politics Rara underscored. Although this period in Haiti is historically singular in some ways, many other conditions are familiar: coup d'état, political instability, poverty, violent repression, and foreign domination have been features of Haitian life throughout its history. Rara bands have always acted in the face of these hardships; the nature of their expression responds precisely to these realities. The particularities of this political period provide an occasion to study how grassroots popular culture is produced under conditions of political insecurity.

Rara bands operate primarily within local power networks, performing religious work, yet there are times when the Rara festival intersects with state power in the arena of national politics. Rara members can become overtly political actors on the national stage and use their strength in numbers to minimize the risk of broadcasting political opinions they cannot otherwise voice. As stylized performances of the peasant armies of previous eras, Rara both creates popular solidarity and conveys cognitive messages to the dominant classes of the strength and power of the disenfranchised. Within this expressive politics, the significance and connotations of words and phrases are manipulated in a dialogic process of figurative change. Meanings and their referents can and do shift quickly and unpredictably.

When Rara bands move in large numbers through public thoroughfares singing *pwen* about current events, they open up a "social space" for popular expression. Rara creates a semiautonomous stage for discourse under conditions of insecurity. Insecurity here refers to "a state of apprehension that exists when people believe that their current condition is unstable or unclear." This term is useful because it applies to a range of social relations, from terror to other less dramatic factors such as political coercion, discrimination, or unemployment.[2] The conditions in Haiti during the twentieth century have occasioned multiple insecurities resulting from many causes: land erosion, massive migration, unemployment, poverty, famine, dictatorships, coups d'état, and foreign invasions. It is on a shifting and violent stage that Rara bands leave their home compounds and enter public space.

Although the entire Haitian population has felt the effects of insecurity, the experience of the poor majority is additionally troubled. A significant cause of their insecurity is the tenet of the enfranchised minority that the poor are not fully human and therefore their lives are of little worth. In the rhetoric of the dominant classes, "security" inevitably refers to issues of crowd control, defense of property, and aspects of physical repression of the poor. Insecurity for disempowered Haitians, then, takes the everyday form of poverty and diverse forms of repression. In the absence of freedom of speech (which exists in the Haitian constitution but which has rarely been practiced), actors in the Haitian majority deploy communication forms that are necessarily opaque and equivocal. James C. Scott reminds us that "The undeclared ideological guerrilla war that rages in this political space requires that we enter the world of rumor, gossip, disguises, linguistic tricks, metaphors, euphemisms, folktales, ritual gestures, anonymity."[3] Often it is the figurative and dialogic language of Vodou, Carnival, and Rara that makes speech possible among subordinate classes under conditions of domination. Through processes of coded, metaphoric speech, "readings" are constructed, political allegory is produced, and criticism is launched. Rara song lyrics and activities reveal the paradoxes and contradictions inherent in the "politics of insecurity" as Rara bands resisted military rule of the early 1990s at the same time they continued to coexist with established power.

When Rara groups launch song lyrics in the streets of Port-au-Prince that are barbed criticisms of political corruption, it is tempting to view Rara as a "form of peasant resistance" and ascribe to it the characteristics of a group fighting structural domination. To a certain extent this is the case, and I will examine moments of explicit political resistance here. However, there are deep problems with an understanding of Rara as resistance. For example, how do we analyze a Rara band whose musicians were pro-Aristide activists, but whose governing members were police from the "anti-gang" police squad, notorious for its human rights abuses? How do we understand Raras whose personnel were made up entirely of pro-Aristide people, but who were on the payroll of the coup d'état government city hall? Entire Rara bands under the dictatorship were even on the state payroll. The words *collaboration* and *accommodation* creep into the discussion. This problem perhaps is not so unusual. Achille Mbembe warns that "To account for both the imagery and efficacy of postcolonial relations of power, we must go beyond the binary categories used in standard interpretations of domination (resistance/passivity, subjection/autonomy, state/civil society, hegemony/counterhegemony, totalization/detotalization). These oppositions are not helpful; rather, they cloud our understanding of postcolonial relations."[4]

Popular politics in Haiti is only partially organized into self-conscious, goal-oriented groups. The peasant organizations that create platforms and make political demands are in the minority in Haiti. Scott reminds us that "most of the political life of subordinate groups is to be found neither in overt collective defiance of powerholders nor in complete hegemonic compliance, but in the vast territory between these two polar opposites."[5]

Perhaps argument about whether traditional culture is conservative or progressive, characterized by resistance or accommodation, misses the point. The relevant question may be: How does popular culture help people survive? An examination of the coded speech of Rara reveals that

Rara can be used as one of the tools in the struggle for existence among the popular classes.

HAITIAN POLITICAL INSECURITY AND THE CULTURAL SETTING

Popular culture in the turmoil of the post-Duvalier era can only be understood within the context of the workings of the dictatorship. Most of the logics and conditions of contemporary politics reveal the lasting effects of the U.S.-backed Duvalier regime. Michel-Rolph Trouillot has written a history of Haiti that begins with the question, "How could Duvalier have happened?" The book's answer is a careful historical argument that the power-heavy state devoured the nation in the absence of a developed civil society, aided and abetted by North American exploitation. Many of the coercive conditions of the Duvalier era were exaggerated but historically consistent with earlier moments. Trouillot thus understands Duvalierism as an extreme but logical result of the nation's history.

Because of the weakened condition of civil society in Haiti, hegemony there most often takes the form of direct dominance. The Duvalier method of rule was so absolutely totalitarian that it is no exaggeration to suggest that it permeated every single human interaction in Port-au-Prince society. At the apex of the state was the unchecked power of Duvalier himself. Those who held power enjoyed it only on the basis of a direct link to the chief of state. Indeed, any connection to Duvalier became a source of power, and the absurdities of this situation multiplied with the repression. Trouillot cites the case of a thief caught red-handed in the market. As the people began to chase after him, he shouted, "Long Live Duvalier!" They were forced to hesitate, to, as Trouillot puts it, "evaluate the implicit claim."[6] Invited to the home of a middle-class woman in 1984 (during Duvalier's rule), I was offered a cigarette and given a book of matches that bore the wedding inscription of Jean-Claude Duvalier and Michelle Bennett. Brandishing this book of wedding matches four years after the wedding was not only a gesture of social distinction but also an active claim to political security.

Professional norms under Duvalier were mediated, even generated, by the politics of dictatorship. All hirings and firings and evaluations of job performance were based on political ties, not ability. According to Trouillot, "Corruption became the raison d'être of the administrative machine."[7] The enforcement branch of the dictator was his private

A pro-Duvalier Rara demonstration (photo © Chantal Regnault)

paramilitary squad, named the VSN (Volontaire de la Securité Nationale) but called the *tonton makoutes*. This squad came to eclipse the
power of the national army, ruling out the possibility of a military coup
d'état.

In the post-Duvalier era, the *makoutes* disappeared as an organized
group, and the individual actors in the squad joined the private police
forces of military "big men" such as Henri Namphi, Prosper Avril, and
later Michel François and Phillipe Biamby. They vied for unregulated
power over various markets: foreign aid, arms, commodities, oil, and
most especially, cocaine. These forces were called *makoutes, atache,*
and, later, "Fraph" (literally, "to hit"), a right-wing group initially
funded by the United States' CIA that rapidly deteriorated into a co-
caine-trafficking network and death squad.[8]

Parasitic political classes in the capital developed under Duvalier, creating a culture that was shared by those empowered by the dictator. The
culture hinged on collaborating with Duvalier by maintaining an image
of civilized normalcy in the midst of great terror and violence. These
empowered classes performed the cultural work—television shows,
newspaper articles, press events, public parades, parties, fashion shows,
and Carnivals—producing images of normality and camouflaging the
grotesqueries of Papa Doc's manipulations.

Denial took on an intimacy and an absurdity in everyday life that
surfaced again during the rule of the junta immediately after Duvalier's
fall. I visited Port-au-Prince during this time in 1988, when a tanker of
contaminated gasoline had been sold to gas pumps all over the city.
Corrupt port officials directly allied with the junta had allowed the gas
to pass inspection, and the toxic gas began to make people ill, killing
several children living near gas stations. A European woman adopted
the strategy of driving with a scarf across her face to block the fumes.
Stopped by angry military men, she was told that to wear the scarf was
to object to the gas, which amounted to criticizing the government, and
if she were seen wearing it again she would be deported. Members of
the poor majority had learned that to protect themselves against gas
fumes was a subversive act in the logic of the state, although they learned
this through beatings with the *koko makak* (police baton).

The disenfranchised classes were less apt to work at covering up for
Duvalier (and the subsequent junta) and more likely to critique the rulers
when it was possible, though public dissent was clearly silenced. There
developed in Port-au-Prince two (at least) overlapping cultural spheres

structured by class and proximity to state power: the culture and society of Duvalierists, and the popular culture shared by the urban poor. Scott's remarks are true for Haiti:

> In extreme cases, certain facts, though widely known, may never be mentioned in public contexts . . . what may develop under such circumstances is virtually a dual culture; the official culture filled with bright euphemisms, silences, and platitudes and an unofficial culture that has its own history, its own literature and poetry, its own biting slangs, it own music, its own humor, its own knowledge of shortages, corruption, and inequalities that may, once again, be widely known but that may not be introduced into public discourse.[9]

It is for this "unofficial culture," the culture of the majority, the popular culture, that Rara became the public mouthpiece. If the enfranchised, Duvalierist classes performed the cultural work of maintaining the image of normalcy during repression, then the disenfranchised classes performed cultural work as well, work that took place in poor neighborhoods, Vodou temples, soccer teams, and other locations where the less powerful congregate. Much of this activity can be seen as making up the "hidden transcript": "discourse that takes place offstage, beyond direct observation by powerholders."[10]

During the repressive years of 1991–1995, the most basic aim of the discourse in the hidden transcript was to proclaim the existence and affirm the humanity of the people in the popular classes, whose everyday lives were threatened by rapes, murders, disappearances, and the belief on the part of the powerful that they were not fully human. "*Woy, men moun yo*" (Whoa, here are the people), refrain of the winning Carnival song by Boukman Eksperyans in 1991, was a seemingly simple-minded statement until it came to life in the voices of the people singing it in the streets. Facing police agents and the wealthy who sponsor Carnival each year, the crowd's roar of "Here are the people" became a challenge, a reminder that the majority was there, alive, and speaking in large numbers.[11]

Even as "*Woy, men moun yo*" affirmed the presence of the people, another song became a form of political commentary by referencing their absence. "Kote Moun Yo? Mwen Pa Wè Moun Yo" (Where are the people? I haven't seen the people) was a song that had been in the Haitian repertoire since before the 1950s, when the Voodoo Jazz group Jazz des Jeunes recorded it.[12] In 1992 it was incorporated into a refrain by RAM, one of the *rasin*, or "roots" bands. "Where Are the

People?" called into question the whereabouts of all the people who had left Haiti after the ousting of Aristide, many of them waiting in refugee camps at the Guantanamo naval base. The song also implicitly asked about the hundreds of people who "were disappeared" and killed by the army. "They're rounding up young kids in the neighborhood to take them off to disappear. So that they can go into the Cote Moun Yo category," said Richard Morse, the RAM band leader. He continued:

> "Where is everybody, I haven't seen them." Who am I talking about? Am I talking about Aristide? Am I talking about the thousand people who died and got buried out in Titanye? Am I talking about the people who got on boats and got the hell out the country and ended up in Guantanamo? Am I talking about in my hotel, the 50 percent of the staff who got fired? We are talking about a whole bunch of people who are no longer where you're used to seeing them. What causes that—military coup d'état?[13]

PWEN: INDIGENOUS THEORY OF MAGIC AND COMMUNICATION

"Whoa, Here Are the People" and "Where Are the People? I Haven't Seen the People" are two recurring themes in the Haitian popular repertoire. They are also examples of *pwen,* defined by Karen McCarthy Brown as "anything that captures the essence or pith of a complex situation" and presents it figuratively.[14] Included as *pwen* in Haitian culture are *pwovèb* (proverbs), *non pwen* (nicknames), and *chante pwen* (sung points). In Afro-Haitian religion, the stars and points in the *vèvè* (sacred cornmeal ground drawings) are called *pwen.* And *pwen cho* (hot points) are objects that are considered charms or magic "works," whose power is derived from spirits who are considered *lwa pwen* (bought spirits). Encompassing knowledge and power, *pwen* objects are aggressive forms of communication whose force depends on the capacity of the owner to direct his or her will onto a situation.[15] *Pwen,* then, are concerned with both the distillation of knowledge and the deployment of power.

Used as forms of verbal communication, *pwen* also involve knowledge, aggression, and directionality. Using *pwen* in Haitian Kreyòl is equivalent to the sophisticated, dialogic orality that in African-American speech is known as "signifying." Signifying, as elaborated by Henry Louis Gates Jr., "connotes the play of language—both spoken and body language—drawn to name something figuratively."[16] While all Rara texts can be described as signifying in this sense, the use of *pwen* that concerns us here is equivalent to what has been called "loud-talking" in the United States and what Gates calls "naming." *Pwen* involves a remark that on the surface is directed to no one in particular but that conveys an opinion or judgment.

In Haiti, *voye pwen* (sending a point) is effected when a proverb, image, or figure of speech is uttered by someone who is commenting on a particular situation or another person. Although there may be many people present, the utterance is metaphoric, forming a coded reference to knowledge that may or may not be shared by the others. Karen Richman has usefully analyzed the use of *pwen* as Kreyòl proverbs in political discourse. She points out that in the logic of *voye pwen,* the target of the proverb or phrase is identified as the *mèt* (owner). If the hearer identifies the *pwen* as "resembling" them, they "collect" it; this is called *ramase pwen* (literally, "gather the point"). "Thus, until a *pwen* is collected it lacks definition. The owner gathers it and thereby intends its meaning."[17] In this way, a critical statement can be made and the overhearing target may choose various options of response. Direct refutation of a *pwen* steps outside the bounds of the communication style and is considered clumsy; conversely, the sender may deny that a given statement was a *pwen* and therefore make the overhearer seem paranoid. The overhearer may choose to ignore the message, suspending conflict at the moment. The socially prized way to respond to *pwen* is to return it with another *pwen,* enlarging the frame of discourse by challenging or embellishing the utterance of the first communicator. *Voye pwen* is the logical form of speech for the hidden, private transcript that is offstage but nevertheless articulated in the presence of a cast of characters who may be accommodators, collaborators, and even spies for the repressive regime.

The use of *pwen* during Haiti's national elections from 1989 through 1991 has been well analyzed by Richman. An American ambassador who tried his hand at Kreyòl *pwen* warned in a press conference that Aristide was unqualified to run for president and that once the people were finished celebrating his election, they would be left with enormous problems: "*Apre bal la tanbou lou*" ("After the dance, the drum is heavy"), he stated. Aristide took ownership of the *pwen* and replied with another: "*Men anpil chay pa lou*" ("With many hands, the burden is not heavy").[18] These *pwen* were slogans that became household words in Port-au-Prince, and because they were uttered in the public transcript, they implicitly included and were meant to influence the Haitian people.

Political *pwen* as everyday passwords

The *pwen* that are "thrown" on the national stage are part of a second-ary dialogic discourse in Port-au-Prince whose vocabulary becomes a series of passwords in ordinary speech. Aristide's party, for example, was called "Lavalas" (the Flood). Aristide supporters before and after his election would say to one another, "*lavalas-ement*," turning it into an adverb meaning roughly, "*lavalas*-ly." It became an informal way to say, "I will cooperate, there is no problem," and to simultaneously iden-tify one's support of Aristide. After the coup d'état against Aristide, that word went immediately out of parlance, and to use the word in everyday speech was to expose oneself as a target for repression. I knew a family whose son Jean bore the nickname Lavalas. When they heard news of the coup against Aristide, the child's family began calling him Jean.

Studying what he terms "political derision" in Togo, C. Toulabor documents the way that people under one-party rule developed a system of separating words from their conventional meanings, creating an am-biguous vocabulary parallel to the official discourse.[19] The same pattern is part of vernacular political speech in Haiti. Some politicized *pwen* originate with ordinary citizens or with traditional Vodou or Rara song lyrics and go on to become political passwords within the hidden tran-script of street interactions. During the coup period, local youth formed vigilance brigades for community protection and referred to the military and their *ataches* as "Babylon." This biblical city carries symbolic mean-ing in various religions, but the closest source for Haitian youth was Rastafari, its vocabulary having reached Haiti's radio airwaves through the music of Bob Marley. Associated in Jamaica with European corrup-tion and the degradation of present conditions, the utterance of the word *Babylon* in Haiti informed the hearer that a police or *atache* was nearby.

This "poaching of meanings" became a way to employ coded speech with very practical purposes during the coup years.[20] First it enabled people to identify one another's sympathies early in a conversation and thereby avoid conflict. Second, small references to Aristide kept alive the hope that he would return. The following is but one example.

When Aristide, a Roman Catholic priest, was ousted, *père* (father) and its synonym *pè* (pair) became politically charged words. Vendors in the market might ask customers who were buying two items, "Ah, so you want a pair?" Given the vast popular support for Aristide, the an-swer was likely to be "Yes, that's right, it's the pair I want" ("*Se pè-a m vle*"). With a series of nods and smiles the two parties communicated their solidarity. In contrast, if the answer was "I want two, but I don't want a pair," the person was not an Aristide supporter. An argument might erupt in angry voices over whether the two items at hand were a pair, the imagery substituting for direct political debate. Given the power relations involved in the issue and the possibility that the buyer was an *atache,* the vendor could then retreat into the literal meaning of the phrase. Through a double vocabulary of political double-entendres, there are always two possible meanings for a given phrase, and one of them will always be innocuous.[21]

Although this form of public speech does not explicitly challenge regnant power, it does perform two kinds of cultural work for the dispossessed majority when it enables communication. For a population that lived in a daily condition of hunger under the U.S. embargo and who had lost young people to murder and exile, these small nods and smiles created through the practice of verbal signifying were both a profound source of encouragement and a way to effect popular organizing and networking. Thus, during the coup years, the Haitian people created areas of social discourse that eluded control by the military and created communication avenues in the public sphere through which to maneuver.

Rara and the Use of *Pwen*

During Rara season, the scope of "throwing *pwen*" is enlarged so that an entire community can *chante pwen* to various targets. These targets include other members of their community, "big men" in the locality, or figures on the national stage. A *pwen* may have several of these targets simultaneously, as does the following "scandal song," noted in chapter 1, about a woman who aborted a baby at seven months:

Talk about it, Oh, Talk about it, Oh
The family of Asefi will talk, Oh
Asefi who threw away a seven-month baby
Asefi who threw away a seven-month baby
Children are wealth, Oh, Talk about it, Oh

Pale O, Pale O
La fanmi Asefi a pale O
Asefi ki jete on pitit sèt mwa

Asefi ki jete on pitit sèt mwa
Pitit se byen O, pale O

Aristide was only able to fulfill seven months of his presidency before the coup, so this song could very well also have been a *pwen* suggesting that the "child" of democracy had been aborted. Aristide himself created familial images of his administration when, in an effort to contain the violent practices of the military, he presided over the "marriage" of the army and the people at his inauguration. As a *pwen* with multiple levels of allegory, this song is a paradigmatic example of Haitian popular cultural expression that has meaning on both local and national levels.

The presentation of new Rara songs is an exciting event for the community, and original songs are prized by Rara bands and their followers. Much more often, however, *pwen* songs are taken from a vast repertoire of proverbs and traditional songs and recycled to fit the present context. The singer Richard Morse said, "[I]n Vodou songs they don't say a lot of stuff. They just say a little phrase. And when your life crosses path with that song, you understand it very clearly."[22]

In his work on Vodou music, musicologist David Yih writes helpfully about recurring tropes in Vodou songs. Looking at the theme of the adversary in Vodou song, Yih argues that the history of oppression in Haiti has produced a sense of alienation and mistrust expressed in Vodou songs through the tension of "us against them." *Moun sa yo* (those people) are invoked often in warning songs. Yih notes that songs may also substitute *jouda yo* (gossipers; literally, "Judases"), *malpalan yo* (disparagers), *malfèktè yo* (evildoers), *malveyan yo* (malevolent ones), *medizan yo* (slanderers), and *fèzè yo* (wrongdoers).[23] Indeed, many recurring phrases in traditional Haitian music indicate a defensive, almost paranoid stance. Given that the repression under Duvalier partly depended on spies "fingering" their neighbors, this theme is understandable.

Yih presents evidence that at certain times the phrase *moun sa yo* has been used to refer to the Catholic activists of the *campagne des rejetés* (antisuperstition campaigns) who worked to destroy Vodou in the 1940s. This insight locates the lyrics in the religious history of Haitian power relations. Classifying the songs as "songs of resistance," Yih notes that they sometimes contain veiled threats:

Whoever speaks well—my eyes are here, my eyes are here
Whoever speaks ill—my eyes are here, my eyes are here

Agwe-Woyo, I'm in no hurry with those people
My eyes are here, my eyes are here
My eyes are here, watching them

Tout sa ki di byen je-m la je-m la
Tout sa ki di mal je-m la je-m la
Agwe-Woyo m pa prese avèk moun sa yo je-m la je-m la
Agwe-Woyo m pa prese avèk moun sa yo je-m la ap gade yo[24]

The antisuperstition campaigns of the early 1940s were launched by the Catholic Church to force the Vodou-practicing majority to renounce the *lwa*. At the height of the campaign, people's reputations were ruined, their livelihoods ended, their ritual houses burned, and sacred objects destroyed. These songs collectively acknowledge the anti-Vodou campaigns as the enemy and issue veiled threats. The tropes they use may have derived from even earlier songs, redeployed repeatedly. In addition to the phrase *moun sa yo*, the phases *kote moun yo* (where are the people), *je'm ap gade* (my eyes are watching), and *mwen pa moun isit* (I'm not from around here) are some that have been used throughout the generations in the production of *pwen*, signifying on conditions of adversity and repression.

One *pwen* that has probably long existed in traditional song resurfaced after the 1990 attempted coup against Aristide by Roger Lafontant before Aristide took office. The lyric was sung in spontaneous street demonstrations both in Haiti and in New York. After the ousting of Aristide, it was sung again by Raras in Haitian New York and in Miami (when to have sung it in Haiti would have been too direct a critique):

They hit us
The blow hurt us

Yo ba nou kou a
Kou a fè nou mal O

Turning on the pun of "blow" and "coup d'état," the song was a direct protest against the coup d'état and the military regime.

A song I recorded in 1993 in Bel Air (Port-au-Prince) used the metaphor of poisoned food along with *moun sa yo*:

My food was perfectly clean, they put poison in it
Avoid those people

Manje mwen la byen pwòp yo mete pwazon ladan'n
Evite moun sa yo

In the second verse, a person's wife was taken away. Perhaps she was seduced by another man; perhaps she was kidnapped and "disappeared," or maybe she was raped in the unprecedented intimidation campaigns of Fraph that used multiple rape as a primary tactic of terror:

My wife was there; they came
They took my wife
Avoid those people

Men madam mwen te la yo pase mwen
Yo pran madam mwen
Evite moun sa yo

These songs reveal the social creativity of the disenfranchised, who seize upon older social forms and change the allegories to fit current conditions. Gage Averill writes that "the pleasure that a group takes in singing along with a pwen is not in receiving a critique in its entirety but in deciphering the critique and combining it with the unspoken, shared community knowledge of what has transpired."[25]

After Aristide was ousted, the *mizik rasin* band RAM recorded a song that had long been in the traditional repertoire. The song was picked up by downtown Rara bands and reinserted into the Rara repertoire. Like the songs containing veiled threats from the antisuperstition era, the song was about hidden power in the face of apparent defeat. The central image is about a leaf falling from a tree, with the refrain "The day I fall is not the day I die":

Leaf, they see me on my branch
A bad time came along and I fell off
The day I fall is not the day I die
When they need me, where will they find me?

Fèy yo gade mwen nan branch mwen
Yon move tan pase, li voye m' jete
Jou ou wè m tonbe-a se pa jou m koule
Le y'a bezwen mwen kote y'a jwen mwen?

The next verse of the same song was borrowed from another traditional song. It was sung in the voice of a woman whose one son was forced to leave his home:

> Papa God, Oh
> Saint Nicolas, Eh
> My only son
> They made him leave the country

> *Papa bondye wo,*
> *Sen Nikola ye,*
> *Yon sèl pitit gason m wo,*
> *Yo fè'l kite peyi a l ale*

In the context of the coup period, the song became a parable for Aristide and all of his supporters. Everybody in Haiti understood the metaphoric implications of the lyrics: the leaf signified Aristide himself, or by extension, everybody sympathetic to the Lavalas movement, and Aristide was an "only," irreplaceable, beloved son whom "they" forced into exile. Because the song was in the first person, he belonged to everybody who sang it. When the official discourse of the period censored Aristide's name, photo, and political logo (the fighting cock), the song broke through the pregnant silence in the public space of Port-au-Prince. Radio stations played the song fervently, and the entire populace sang it in the corridors, Rara bands, Vodou ceremonies, and downtown market-places.

THE "BECOMING" OF *PWEN* WITHIN POLITICAL INSECURITY

During the volatile years of 1990–1995, meanings could shift dramatically in a very short time. The dialogic process of shifting meanings accelerated as layers of signification built up around one referent. Songs or phrases could become *pwen* by rapidly assuming new significations, creating additional tensions in public space. Nobody learned this better than a *machann* who sold medicinal leaves in the downtown business district. In the tradition of the street vendor, she was used to calling out her products and their price, and every day she sat and sang the litany of herbs and plants in her stock. When Marc Bazin was chosen as the de facto prime minister after the coup, she was arrested for shouting out the name of one of the plants. The herb *fo bazen* was the unfortunate homonym of "faux Bazin" (false Bazin). As with the little boy named Lavalas, words and even names can take on subversive connotations overnight in a shifting and repressive political landscape.

In the course of this argument I do not mean to present repression in Haiti as a force that popular classes bring on themselves through political agitation in the form of sending *pwen*. Military violence in Haiti has been shown by many analysts to be arbitrary: neighborhood raids, home invasions by police, and disappearances of youth are only sometimes linked to direct political activism. Arbitrary violence in poor neighborhoods is a tactic of terror that was perfected by the *tonton makout* squads under Duvalier.

In 1993, during some of the worst repression of the Cedras rule and at the height of the U.S. embargo and the refugee crisis, any song in Rara about leaving could serve as an excuse for the military to pressure a Rara. Given the reality that roughly seventy thousand Haitians fled by boat during the coup period, a song about leaving implied that people were fleeing to Guantanamo because the army was so repressive.[26] Seen another way, such a song meant that the singer wanted the army to leave. Or it suggested that people were dying. Traditional songs like "Sodo m'prale" (I'm going to the Vodou pilgrimage) were suddenly controversial:

> I'm going to Saut d'eau, really God, I'm going to Saut d'eau
> Light a lamp for me, I'm leaving
> Shake the rattle for me, I'm leaving
> Cecil, Oh, Virgin of Miracles, give me my wish, I'm leaving

> *Sodo m'prale, en verite bon dye sodo m'prale*
> *Limen limyè-a pou mwen prale*
> *Sonen ason-an pou mwen m'prale*
> *Sesil-O Vièj mirak-O banm demand m'prale*

During this particularly repressive period, any song for Ogou the warrior spirit was heard as a critique of the army. Within a two-week span in 1993 the army informally banned Ogou songs in the Raras. Perhaps the turning point came when one Rara danced past a police station singing for Ogou near the downtown market called Mache Solomon. Ironically, just after the Rara *kolonèl* administered protective baths to his followers and took to the streets, a policeman raised his gun and fired in the air. As the Rara scattered, he open-fired on the running crowd. In this case the protective baths apparently "worked": nobody was hurt.

In extremely charged political moments during this period, bands played the melody of a *pwen* song on the *banbou* without singing the lyrics. While this melody-without-words was played, Rara members in the streets and hearers in their homes mentally filled in the lyrics, and thus the sound of the *banbou* signified to the neighborhood the "political password" in the song.

One example of this musical signifying is the slogan popularized by Rara Nou Vodoule, a Rara band started by the members of *mizik rasin* groups Sanba Yo and Foula. The artists of these two groups formed their Rara in 1991 when Aristide was in power, calling their band Rara Nou (Our Rara).They intended it to be a Rara without a mystical *angajman* (contract), constructed as an intervention in cultural politics that would attract youth and reclaim the positive meaning of Rara. By the end of Rara season, their following reached at least three thousand young people, rivaling the large Raras in Léogâne. The signature melody of Rara Nou was a catchy ostinato that accompanied a song about a new type of violent criminal known as *zenglendo*.[27] In the history of Haitian crime, the head of state always held the monopoly on corruption and violence, and thus most murders during Duvalier's rule were carried out by *makoutes*. The fall of Duvalier broke up this monopoly and created new types of crimes and new perpetrators. Probably now-unemployed *makoutes* trained in terrorism, *zenglendo* robbed and killed their victims, who were typically members of the peasant and working classes that formed the bulk of President Aristide's popular support. At the time, Justice Minister Jean Joseph Exume considered the *zenglendo* "a criminal force tainted with politics."[28] In the minds of many Haitians, the *zenglendo* and their crimes were associated with the urban degradation of Miami and New York, and their advent in Port-au-Prince was extremely disturbing. The song sung by Rara Nou Vodoule—and other downtown Raras—was simple. You can hear the ostinato on track 13 of the CD that accompanies this book:

We don't want *zenglendo*
Arrest the *zenglendo*
Bar the *zenglendo*

Pa vle zenglendo
Arete zenglendo
Bare zenglendo

Though human rights abuse by the state was documented to have decreased during Aristide's presidency, the *zenglendo* seriously threatened the security of downtown Haitians. One leader of Rara Nou Vodoule described how the band tried to sanction suspected *zenglendo,* using the Rara's strength in numbers as a form of security. He said that as they walked by the homes of people known to be *zenglendo,* the Rara followers would often spontaneously "throw" the song as a *pwen.* Concerned that the former *makoutes* could have open-fired or thrown grenades at the crowd, the leader nevertheless calculated that the Rara followers would have considered him sympathetic to the criminals if he as a *kolonèl* had tried to control the singers.[29]

The year after Rara Nou Vodoule made its debut, Aristide was no longer in power. Nou Vodoule would not resume their activities en masse until the return of the president in 1995. In the interim, the musicians and singers joined other downtown bands. During this time, the *banbou* part to their *zenglendo* song was played, but the words were only sung in the minds of the hearers. Through the process of signifying, the music created a silent slogan. Opposition to terror and repression was thus wordlessly kept alive in the melodies of the Raras in Port-au-Prince.

SONGS OF WAR: RARA "ARMIES" AS "MOBS" AND THE MIDDLE-CLASS IMAGINATION

In spite of its frequent use of verbal indirection, Rara is not merely a symbolic performance. Rara can also be a potential weapon in peasants' ongoing power struggle against the elite and against other local groups. Locally, a Rara can use sheer strength in numbers to its advantage when members decide whether to let cars pass on the road. Scott reminds us that "Large, autonomous gatherings of subordinates are threatening to domination because of the licence they promote among normally disaggregated inferiors."[30] And as David Kertzer notes, "Political rites are effective when they inspire fear. The effectiveness of ritual also depends on the cognitive messages they so effectively convey."[31] Members of the classes I have termed "enfranchised," and in particular the literate bourgeoisie, displayed fear of Rara and often warned me that the bands were essentially "mobs" who were capable of killing me if they wished. Both bourgeois Haitians and Americans characterized Rara as "unruly crowds" and "killing mobs."

Many middle- and upper-class Haitians recited a common childhood story that I took to be a telling moment in class relations in the domestic sphere. They said that when a Rara passed by their houses, their maids or nannies rushed them to hiding places under beds or in cupboards. "The Rara is coming to eat you," the maids would say. In a small, everyday way, a maid could come to terrorize her charge on an evening, and in so doing contribute to the association of Rara with danger and physical threat.

Rara bands use music to extend the physicality of the group, a tactic that has proved useful elsewhere. Bernice Johnson Reagon recounts the ways African Americans used song to establish control over territory during Civil Rights demonstrations.

> Sound is a way to extend the territory you can affect. So people can walk into you way before they can get close to your body. And certainly the community singing that people do together is a way of announcing that we're here, that this is real, and so anybody who comes into that space, as long as you're singing, they cannot change the air in that space. The song will maintain the air as your territory.
>
> I've seen meetings where a sheriff has walked into a mass meeting and established the air. This is a sheriff everybody knows, and they're taking pictures or taking names, and you just know your job is in trouble. . . . The only way people could take the space back was by starting a song, and inevitably when police would walk into a mass meeting, somebody would start a song. And then people would join in, and as they joined in, the air would change.[32]

As large groups of lower-class people going down the roads making noise, Raras convey a message of sheer physicality, a reminder that the peasants are in the majority in Haiti. A crowd of hundreds of peasant-class or urban-poor bodies "unsupervised" by the ruling class, Rara is inherently threatening to dominant class sensibilities.

Interviews with members of the privileged classes of contemporary Haiti indicate that they were indeed intimidated by the formidable presence of Rara in public. Toward the end of Rara season, people planned trips to weekend houses in order to avoid Rara bands, and rumors circulated about violent incidents in Raras. In 1993 a group of missionaries driving too fast through a crowd was said to have been attacked by a Rara wielding machetes. In a similar vein, middle-class Haitians often instruct visiting North Americans that if they ever strike a pedestrian with a car, they should not stop but drive quickly away and report the accident. To stop to help the victim, some assured me, was dangerous because the crowd would turn on me and attack.

The supposed relation between Rara bands and "mob killing" was made explicit by the controversial American writer William Seabrook in his book on Haiti during the American occupation. While he observes the neighborhood *bwile Jwif* ritual when Judas is burned in effigy, his mind jumps to the story of President Guillaume Sam, whose dismemberment at the hands of a "mob" in 1915 was the catalyst for the American occupation of that year. He likens the Eastertime local communities "beating their drums" to the group who killed Sam:

> There in the sunshine before me stood the palace of the late Guillaume Sam; beside it stood the French legation in its walled garden; and there also in the sunshine, howling and dancing and brandishing their machetes, now ludicrous and harmless, was *the same identical crowd, the populace of Port-au-Prince*, which only in 1915 had invaded those buildings, shouting, "Qui bo' li? Where is he hiding?" just as they had shouted in search of these comic effigies of Judas, looking under beds, in closets, just as they had looked this morning for a straw-stuffed dummy; and finding President Guillaume Sam, the man of flesh and blood, had tossed him over the wall, torn him limb from limb, and dragged his mangled torso at the end of a rope through this same Champs de Mars, just as they were dragging the comic effigies of Judas now.[33] [Emphasis added]

Seabrook continues with a characterization of the Haitian poor that is consistent with dominant American portrayals of the "Negro" of the time: childlike, primitive, and humorous, but also savage. "The mass of the populace," he writes, "possessing childlike traits often naive and lovable as well as laughable, have also a powerful underlying streak of primitive, atavistic savagery."[34]

Sixty years later, American characterization of Haitian crowds in general and Rara in particular perpetuated the same fears. In a 1989 lecture to U.S. foreign service personnel (delivered by a Haitian speaker), the

United States Information Service characterized the Rara as an army capable of murder:

> When the Rara is in the middle of the crossroads, they're conducting a ceremony and it is dangerous to interrupt them. Don't join the party if you haven't been invited and never join them at night. If you're not strong enough they can hurt or even kill you.
>
> When driving through a Rara, wait until they ask you to pass. They will hurt you or beat you if you are aggressive. They are a solid unit like an army battalion.[35]

The lyrical strategies of Haitian Rara support observations that repressive contexts tend to generate double-voiced, allegorical, and parodic expression. Furthermore, these strategies support a theory of culture under domination that stresses the permeability of strict definitive categories like resistance versus collaboration and hegemony versus antihegemony. Political action and expression in nonliterate peasant societies will be generated out of traditional forms of social organization and will employ tactics cut and hewn by surviving generations of the disenfranchised population. This means that the political life of dominated groups will not consist of ongoing active opposition, but rather will be lived out along a broad continuum of political action and expression that spans open defiance and collaboration. Disenfranchised peasant groups will rarely create the organized political campaigns that are found in democratic and socialist worlds. Rather, they will find ways to survive on an everyday basis, while seizing opportunities to criticize, resist, or overthrow when the political climate affords.

I have argued that one of the ways that the popular classes of Haiti survive the political and economic insecurity they face is through a distinct politics of dialogic language that spans magic and communication. This politics depends on the metaphoric shifting and shiftable speech of Kreyòl. This figurative, lyrical language allows for multiple levels of meaning to inhere in a single phrase. Rara members deploy Kreyòl to create solidarity and political networks, to nurture hope, and sometimes to directly resist the military. The tropes and parables of Rara lyrics create social spaces in the public transcript in which the popular classes can maneuver. The dominant classes and the army, also Kreyòl speakers, are not far behind the populace in their decoding of Rara lyrics. The relatively powerless *ti nèg* uses Kreyòl Rara speech to fashion attacks and retreats, quickly shifting the referent to reveal new meanings and create new social spaces in which to survive. Popular speech thus matches the political reality of Haiti, which is constantly shifting and changing.

Rara feels like home in Prospect Park, Brooklyn (photo © Chantal Regnault)

Rara in New York City

Transnational Popular Culture

Woy Woy Woy
Why Why Why
That's right, That's right
The police can't stand to see Black
    [people]

Woy Woy Woy
Why Why Why
Se sa, se sa
La polis pa vle wè nwa

Rara Djakout, Prospect Park, Brooklyn,
August 1994

"Let's talk in Prospect Park, Ti-Madame," suggested Chiko, a Haitian
musician I wanted to interview on immigrant religion. That summer
of 1990 I was studying Afro-Haitian religious practice, analyzing
the ways that oungan *and* manbo *must reconfigure ritual to adapt to*
the commodification of space and time in the New York setting. When
we arrived in Brooklyn's largest park for the interview, we abruptly
came face to face with the slapping drum rhythms and loud songs
of hundreds of Haitian people dancing and singing. "This is Rara,"
shouted a pleased Chiko. I recognized some of the faces in the crowd
from Brooklyn's vibrant Vodou ceremonies. A flag bearer headed

183

the procession, followed by a line of drummers. Directly behind them was a row of young men blowing hocketed notes on banbou *and* klewon. *My tape recorder stayed inside my pack, and the interview was abandoned. What was this festival? Where did it come from? What was it doing here?*

The dancing crowds numbered in the hundreds. Young Haitian women stood by, wondering how far to get into singing the betiz *that were starting to fly. Older ladies wheeled babies in strollers alongside the parade. This event was free, outdoors, and easy to find. I could tell that for them it felt, smelled, and sounded like home.*

There was a lot going on—it looked like Carnival, but it also felt like Vodou. Speaking to the people present, I learned that many did not know a great deal about the history of this parade or its relationship to Vodou, but they nevertheless valued it enormously. The musicians were more knowledgeable—they told me it was a mystical festival, a dangerous festival, and, in Haiti, an old festival.

This encounter, minutes from my apartment in Brooklyn's Park Slope, was my first experience of Rara. Before that moment, I had barely heard of the festival. As I began to mill around and get a sense of the scene, I saw that this festival, and the experience of immersing themselves in it in New York, was a precious, emotionally charged celebration for the young men who were its performers. They were throwing themselves into the music and losing themselves, as in a Vodou dance. It seemed like a sense of community solidarity took form in the bodily experience of performing Rara in New York. Seeing all this led me to Haiti to research the present study on the meanings and uses of Rara.

Though there has been a significant Haitian population in New York for the last thirty years, an organized Rara had never been celebrated before 1990.[1] There had been moments of spontaneous Rara performance during political confrontations. Bursts of Rara singing and music erupted in Miami and New York at demonstrations against the Duvalier regime in the early 1980s and also during strikes involving Haitian labor groups. But the summer of 1990 saw something new: a full-blown Rara every Sunday, the same people returning each week to socialize, dance, and augment the singing. Only five years later, in 1995, four separate Rara bands assembled in Brooklyn's Prospect Park and Manhattan's

Central Park to play each summer weekend. Like the Raras in Haiti, the New York scene was dominated by men, but unlike Haiti, there were no queens, and the women on the scene were mostly relegated to the sidelines. Lifted from its Lenten context to fit the summer weather, Rara in the United States is a secular affair, and the *lwa* have not (yet) demanded libations, trips to the cemetery, or mystical seven-year contracts.

The people who gather each week have extended Haiti's grassroots popular culture onto their local U.S. terrain. The bands created entirely new lyrics to speak of the New York experience, and these new songs were carried to families and circulated in neighborhoods after the Rara. Today, Rara in New York has come to express a point of view about the Haitian immigrant predicament.

The Rara in New York is not a local phenomenon, however. The movements, ideologies, and economic transactions of Rara actors in the United States mirror the more complex realities of Haitian immigrants whom social scientists are now defining as "transmigrants." Transmigrants sustain social relations that link together their societies of origin and settlement. They may support houses in Haiti with jobs in New York. They may keep their children in Haiti. Transmigrants live, operate, and "develop subjectivities and identities embedded in networks of relationships that connect them simultaneously to two or more nation-states."[2] Indeed, when I began to walk in the Raras of Port-au-Prince, Léogâne, and even the more remote Artibonite Valley, I encountered young men from Brooklyn who were home for vacation or, more profoundly, who had returned to walk in pilgrimage in a family Rara.

Rara performance, with its roots firmly in Haiti, now has a role in a wider transnational Black Atlantic popular culture. Performance and attendance at Rara festivals took place as Haitian people moved back and forth between home villages in Haiti and points in the United States. A song created in Léogâne could be sung in Brooklyn a week later, creating a deterritorialized popular Haitian discourse that allowed traditional knowledge rooted in peasant culture, now inflected with the diaspora experience, to circulate internationally throughout many Haitian social spheres. Rara music and performance are in dialogue with the Haitian branches of dance-hall and hip-hop culture (that include Wyclef Jean, Bigga Haitian, King Posse, and Original Rap Stars). But as a particularly Haitian genre that large groups parade in public, Rara occupies a singular space that has unique possibilities for communication and performance.

Rara performance has been widely deployed as a political weapon in mass demonstrations. In Haiti, Raras protested the 1991 attempted coup d'état against Aristide by Roger Lafontant. One Rara member explained, "When they uprooted Lafontant that's what they used. They used *vaksin*, drums, and tree branches. Because when you beat the drums the spirits are ready to come. They know the call."[3] After Aristide was ousted later in 1991, musicians and their singing followers played for weeks on end at the United Nations and in rallies at Washington's Capitol Hill. Rara's combined religious and military ethos lent force to these moments, when the ritualized Rara "battalions" performed their opposition to the coup. Rara bands also gathered more recently in New York to sing and protest during demonstrations against the New York police's brutality in three cases involving African and Haitian men: Abner Louima, Amadou Diallo, and Patrick Dorismond.

Rara songs have made their way onto record albums by *mizik rasin* groups that have flourished since the fall of Duvalier, but the Rara activity I describe that is taking place throughout the diaspora consists of social organization, songwriting, and musical performances that are community-produced and noncommercial. The folk societies, "imagined governments" that dispatch Rara armies in Haiti, are replaced in New York by transmigrants who sculpt an imagined national terrain on the popular level in New York. Within this Brooklyn-based "nation-scape," Rara members in locations in the diaspora can *chante pwen* to the Haitian military, to Haitian presidential candidates, to the New York police force, and to other ethnic groups in Brooklyn.[4]

Though the literature on transnationalism has tended to focus on leaders and the politics of the nation-state, transmigrants at the grass-roots level use popular culture to reterritorialize both their practices and their identities. The weekend festivities in Brooklyn have made room for an unprecedented social sphere in which youth from a plurality of classes learn peasant culture in order to be viewed as authentic Haitians among their peers. In consciously performing peasant culture, Haitians are contesting both Haitian middle-class values and dominant Euro-American values. By rediscovering and embracing their African roots and their specific history through Rara, Haitians are privileging an identity that is distinct from whiteness yet is unique among other African-American groups. In creating this specific Haitian identity, Haitian transmigrants are rejecting U.S. racial categorizations.

TRANSNATIONALISM AND THE RARAMAN

Theoretical work by Linda Basch, Nina Glick Schiller, and Cristina Szanton Blanc that analyzes transnationalism builds on Immanuel Wallerstein's "world systems" framework, in which geographic regions perform different and unequal functions in a global division of labor. "Core" areas control and dominate production, while the natural resources and labor of the "periphery" are exploited.[5] Those who have augmented Wallerstein's work characterize the past several decades in terms of new levels of capital penetrations into "Third World" economies, the development of export processing, and the increased migration of people from the peripheries to the centers.[6] What is important for the discussion here is that economic conditions—the international division of labor and the new transnational forms of accumulation of capital—are affecting both the flows of transmigrant activities and "the manner in which they come to understand who they are and what they are doing."[7]

Transmigrants use their international ties to make strategic economic decisions in their best interests. Many people work in the United States but leave small children with family in Haiti, or collect rent on property in New York while retiring in Haiti. Basch, Glick Schiller, and Szanton Blanc see immigrants' building transnational social fields as a form of resistance against national hegemonies; however, they also see these strategies as paradoxically perpetuating their economic exploitation within the international division of labor.

My discussion of Rara as transnational popular culture focuses on theoretical inclusion of the social, cultural, and political dimensions of immigrant experiences. The Rara *ti nèg* who dances and sings in the street bands of New York may have migrated from Haiti to seek employment, or he may have been raised in New York. Most likely, however, the Rara *ti nèg* is carving out an identity as a "Raraman" in Prospect Park because of the time he has on his hands as a member of the classic "reserve army of labor," the sector of the working class that capital cannot employ—or the sector that is underemployed.

Migrant workers like the Raraman now form the basis of the modern industrial reserve army.[8] As Stuart Hall notes about Black people in Britain, the strategies for dealing with unemployment that these men develop must be seen as doubly positioned within their colonial history and their present underemployment.[9] Indeed, I suggest that the subjectivities of young Haitian men must be viewed as multiply positioned within their original colonial history, their class positions in contemporary Haitian society, and their newly found predicament as "racial minorities" in the United States.

This last point is particularly significant: racializations and racisms are processes in historical evolution and are both historically and culturally specific. The ways in which the Francophone and Anglophone West Indies developed racialized societies have resulted in particular configurations, ones that differ from contemporary U.S. racial codes.[10] Haitian-Americans' identity and subjective positions of racialization must be seen as being superimposed onto their new experience of U.S. constructions of race. Part of the challenge facing new Haitian immigrants is in assessing and renegotiating their newly found racial status in the United States.

One side of this strategy on the part of young Haitian men has been to cultivate styles and philosophies within a popular movement based on peasant tropes and quintessentially Haitian activities such as Rara. As a public, festive occasion when people can fashion and perform identities, exchange information, and create reputations, Rara has become a central form of activity in the emerging *rasin* movement.

Secular Raras in Diasporic *Rasin* Culture

The first Rara to form in New York in the summer of 1990 was created by musicians who were part of the recent *mizik rasin* movement that became viable in Haiti after the fall of Duvalier. Although there had been commercial music based on Vodou and Rara drumming in earlier periods of Haitian history—Voodoo Jazz of the 1940s and 1950s and the *kilti libète* (freedom culture) of the early 1970s—this music was thwarted by Haiti's Eurocentric codes and by the dictatorship itself.[11] In the late 1970s during the rule of Jean-Claude Duvalier, musical groups began to form that were influenced by the nationalisms of the U.S. Civil Rights struggle and Black Power movements, the rock music of Carlos Santana and Jimi Hendrix, the reggae of Bob Marley and the Wailers, and other musical styles of the African diaspora. Called Gwoup Sa, Moun Ife, then Sanba-Yo and Foula, these 1970s collectives developed musical styles that crossed the indigenous Vodou and Rara-based music with the codes of commercial pop music.[12] The groups were formed and re-formed by young men—and fewer women—who desired to be known as professional *sanba*.

After the dictatorship collapsed in 1986, a small cultural space opened up allowing this traditionalized music to emerge in the public sphere. Musicians were able to rehearse, carry their instruments in pub-lic, and book time in recording studios. *Mizik rasin* groups Sanba-Yo and Foula performed at the Port-au-Prince Rex Theatre and even Haiti's space for high culture, the Institute Française. The group Sanba-Yo re-corded a song called "Vaksinen" (Vaccinate) as a radio public service announcement encouraging parents to vaccinate their children. Its catchy, upbeat melody broadcasting its lively message was sung on the breath of anyone with a radio—the majority of people in Port-au-Prince.[13]

Duvalier's *makoutes* had responded to long hair on men with arrests and beatings. After Duvalier, the musicians in these groups began to wear their hair in long locks and to self-consciously adopt peasant styles of dress—straw *djakout* shoulder-bags, leather sandals, and pants rolled up at the cuffs (signifying fieldwork and also, in a second sense, spirit possession). By embracing the negative connotations of Rara, the *ti nèg* transformed himself into a stylish "drummer-hero," the Raraman who, by spinning traditional lyrics into new, politically relevant music, ex-pressed his verbal exhibitionism as a classic man-of-words.[14]

A group of men who had been involved in these early bands were now transmigrants. Some of these *rasin* musicians were funded by white, Black, and Japanese-American women whom they had married or lived with in New York. Using their charisma as *sanba* and artists, some left their Haitian wives for American women. In so doing they attained the prized "green card," or permanent resident status; this crucial legal standing allowed them to travel back to Haiti. In some cases, the men had public relationships with American women but maintained hidden relationships with their Haitian wives, who were often the mothers of their children. Haitian women lost relationships, resources, and status in this equation, which shows how sexuality, race, and national status are interrelated within issues of migration and this Caribbean popular movement.

Part of the *rasin* musicians' impetus for forming the Rara in New York was a perceived snub they received from other local drummers. During a particularly bad heat wave in 1990, they were escaping their apartments in Prospect Park, listening to the rhythms emanating from a large drumming collective of African-American and West Indian peo-ple near the Parkside entrance. According to Fito Vivien, "I saw a bunch of Jamaicans or Africans who were playing drums. We asked if we could play their drums and they said no—they looked at us funny for asking. I said to myself, OK, I'll come back and show you!"[15] The *rasin* musicians disappeared into the home of a friend they knew who had drums, then came back the next day playing Rara and walked past the stationary drumming circle. Soon enough, the forces of *teledjòl* (word of mouth; literally, "tele-mouth") brought out hundreds of other young people with free time and the inclination to sing. These other Haitians joined in the Rara and walked, danced, and "threw" songs, making each Sunday evening a community event.[16]

After spending the summer documenting the emergence of Rara in New York, I decided to visit Haiti during the next Lenten Rara season to trace the "historical source" of the New York Rara. I was operating under a premise that in tracing the festival back to Haiti I would find a more archaic, original practice. However, the currents of transnational popular culture had short-circuited my assumption. When I arrived in Port-au-Prince, the best-attended Rara was founded by some of the very same people who had formed Rara Djakout in New York.

Rara Nou Vodoule was a Rara whose headquarters near the main cemetery in Port-au-Prince became a gathering place for thousands of urban youth. Their song "Pa Vle Zenglendo" (Don't want criminals) was well-known by most downtown residents. It was a secular Rara, unsanctioned by the *lwa,* that took advantage of the decrease in violence under Aristide to dance in the streets and *pran plezi* (have fun). It was founded by members of Sanba-Yo and Foula, some of whom were raised in Protestant (Baptist and Seventh-Day Adventist) churches. The connection to literacy and the church gave these men's families an upwardly mobile status. They were now "returning to roots" and engaging in the project of consciously traditionalizing their own musical practice. Forming a Rara and taking it to the streets in direct competition with other Rara bands in the neighborhoods headed by sorcerers and Vodou societies was a way to popularize their own music, establish reputations as *gwo nèg,* and interact directly with the *pèp-la* (common people).

Just as Haitian transmigrants move back and forth from Haiti to New York, creating a continuous sphere of social relations, so they have created a single popular culture in both countries through Rara music and performance. People in both the Rara Djakout in New York and Rara Nou Vodoule in Port-au-Prince spoke to me about what they called the *mouvman Rara* (Rara movement). Said one man called Yanba Ye, "The real revolution is our culture. This is the only solution possible for us, in the situation we're living in. It's a roots revolution."

The leaders of this *rasin* movement are the *sanba* who use their personal charisma, songwriting talent, and roles in *mizik rasin* bands to enhance their reputations and move into *gwo nèg* status. In the Rara movement, the role of the *sanba* becomes enlarged into a role of moral leadership. Said Yanba, "You can't do things that are not good for society and call yourself a *sanba*. You have to be straight." One of the ways a *sanba* is recognizable to others is through a system of style-signs with which he dresses. This is a style Haitians call "roots," and it is constructed with elements of Haitian peasant dress adopted in a direct refutation of European styles. Leather sandals are worn instead of tennis shoes; leather or seashell jewelry is worn instead of gold. Some people wear their hair locked, making a double religious and political statement. Not called dreadlocks as in the tradition of Rastafari, their locked hair is called *cheve Simbi* (Simbi's hair) and refers to its wearer's identification with the *lwa* called Simbi who is associated with water and sometimes snakes. Politically, long locks celebrate the newly won freedom from the Duvalier regime, when men with hair longer than a few inches were arrested. Some women cut their hair short or lock it in opposition to the ubiquitous permanent waves most Haitian women wear in order to achieve French hairstyles. Some men wear Haitian straw hats and burlap shirts.

Style is a form of cultural bricolage, the reordering of objects to create fresh meanings within a total system of significances.[17] *Rasin* stylistic commentary contests the rigid, French-identified codes of Haitian society. In this sense Haitian men and women use bodily adornment to announce their politics with respect to French cultural hegemony, their own African histories, and their pro-peasant positions within Haitian cultural politics. People responding to the *rasin* movement wear these styles in the Haitian provinces, in the streets of Port-au-Prince, and in southern Florida, Miami, New York, Boston, Chicago, Canada, and Paris. They mix *rasin* styles with local fashion and with the ever-changing styles of hip-hop culture.

The Haitian bourgeoisie has cultivated its French Creole national culture and French-based style partly in response to their wish to establish their equality with white people and to distance themselves from the international image of Haiti as a subordinate, primitive culture.[18] *Rasin* movement members, though some are from the bourgeoisie, wish to turn that image on its head and embrace it for its positive wisdom and history. The values of "acting bad" and "acting African," which in Haiti are associated with the "play" values of Rara, with Kreyòl, and with the popular classes, are reworked in this second diaspora. African values are enacted in a positive way, where they are validated and privileged.

A parallel process occurs among Jamaican young people who leave the island for school. "In Jamaica the middle class is increasingly being used as a negative referent. It is a move on the part of young persons . . . to adopt a more folksy working-class orientation."[19] They, too, sometimes cultivate a more obviously "natural" African image.[20] In fact, Haitian *rasin* styles have been developed through a broad cultural conversation with the Jamaican Rastafari movement, which made its way to Haiti through the reggae on the radio and through the interactions between Haitian and Jamaican migrant workers in southern Florida.

RASIN AND RASTAFARI: TRANSNATIONAL YOUTH ROOTS CULTURE

The ideologies and styles of the Haitian *rasin* movement have without a doubt been influenced by the reggae music and the religiosity of Jamaica's Rastafari movement. Rastafari is the Jamaican religious movement whose members interpret the Bible to cast African people as the true Israelites who must return to Zion. The goal of the members of this millenarian movement is to be repatriated to Ethiopia, the nation that was ruled earlier in this century by the man they believe to be the second incarnation of Christ, Emperor Haile Selassie I. It is his precoronation name that the movement takes as its own: Raṣ Tafari.[21]

Although most Haitians have not embraced the worship of Haile Selassie as the messiah, some Haitian men have been influenced by Rasta "reasoning," the talent of oral philosophizing and debate. Haitian men appreciate Rastas' casting African people as central historical actors, their creative reinterpretations of biblical scripture, and their ideology of male supremacy. It is important to remember that Rastafari is not a fixed culture but rather a cultural constellation that has moved through several stages; it is a social movement in historical process. By the same token, individuals move through Rasta "careers" and take different positions to the movement. The point here is that Haitians have encountered and befriended Rastas of various stripes and have embraced many of the fundamental tenets of what has itself become a transnational Rasta culture. Haitian women may be sympathetic to Rastafari, though for a variety of reasons fewer women lock their hair and adopt explicit Rasta-affiliated identities.

Some Haitians, especially those who have lived in Florida, wear locked hair under Rasta tams woven in the combined colors of the Ethiopian and Garveyite nationalist flags: red, gold, green, and black. They share Rasta values of simple, nonviolent living and the Ital vegetarian diet. The English they learned in Florida is Jamaican English. *Roots* is a word in Iyaric (Dread Talk), the Rasta inner-language, connoting that which is chemical-free and natural, African-based, or nonexploitative.[22] Although it is impossible to document, the term *rasin* probably originated with this Rasta usage.

An early grassroots band that formed in Miami in the late 1970s was called Rasta Sanba Ginen. Mixing Rasta styles with Vodou references, the band members played Vodou rhythms along with the *nyahbinghi* drumming of Rasta meditative music and called their gatherings *binghis*, the Jamaican term for an all-night ritual drumming and chanting circle. The group was a cultural beacon for youth interested in the communal values of Haitian country living, formed by men who were political exiles and could not return to Haiti.[23]

When Duvalier fell in 1986 and a cultural space opened up for the emergence of the *rasin* movement, some of these young men and their wives moved from Florida to Haiti or to New York and refashioned their cultural identities. They abandoned part of their Rasta ideology and reformed their thinking based on the symbols and rituals of Vodou. One example of this rethinking involves the use of salt: the Ital diet of the Rasta excludes salt, but the figure who does not eat salt in Haiti is the *zonbi*, the person whose soul has been stolen. Haitians shifting from Rasta to *rasin* moved to reincorporate salt and meat into their diets. Similarly, they had grown long hair that they called dreadlocks in South Florida. In New York they began calling their hair *cheve Simbi* and referred to themselves as *zing*.[24] In rural Haiti, when children are born with locked hair (or a caul over their face) they are considered to be under the special protection of the *lwa* Simbi. A *zing* is a person who wears locked hair from birth and cannot bathe in rivers and streams for fear of being swallowed up by the spirit. Haitians who had organized their diet and grown their hair in the context of Rastafari philosophy moved to traditionalize their practices in the context of this new Haitian *rasin* movement.[25] Their movement away from Rasta and into *rasin* coincides with the right-leaning political shifts in Jamaica that accompanied the ouster of Manley by Seaga. This period of Reaganism and Thatcherism was a difficult time for Rastas. Reggae culture itself shifted at this time toward "slackness," or sexualizing vulgarity.

On 11 May 1995, the fourteen-year anniversary of the death of reggae superstar Bob Marley, an organization was founded in Haiti called Mouvman Rasta Faray Ayisyen (Haitian Rastafari Movement). This was a group of young men who had made their way back from Florida to Haiti in the years following Duvalier. "The Fari movement has already taken hold. There can be no democracy without the Rastafarians. We walk to the rhythm of love, justice, freedom and equality for every person," said their spokesperson to the Haitian press.[26] Being Rasta within Haiti becomes a mark of distinction, another position from which to make vocal demands of the present government.

Both Rara and the Jamaican reggae music enjoyed by Haitians is rivaled and cross-fertilized by the growing diasporic hip-hop and dance-hall cultures. Haitians in Haiti and its outpost in New York have been involved in hip-hop culture from early on, and young Haitians were part of the earliest formulations of hip-hop that were produced by youth in the Bronx in the late 1970s. Haitian immigrants were among the "crews" of young African American, Latino, and Caribbean artists who threw outdoor competitions of break-dancing, DJ-ing and rapping. While Jean-Michel Basquiat (the graffiti artist of Haitian descent) rose to fame in fine art circles, young Haitian rappers like "Jamerican and Sha" and DJ Frankie spun records in Roberto Clemente Park in the Bronx. They looked up to the more successful Bigga Haitian, who made LPs in which he rapped and toasted in both Jamaican English and Kreyòl.[27]

In the early 1990s, groups in Haiti like King Posse and Original Raps Stars made albums and music videos that combined dance-hall ragga-muffin and hip-hop styles, and their songs and their accompanying dances made their way into Carnival and Rara performance.[28] Wyclef Jean, himself a Haitian immigrant, rose to stardom with the group The Fugees and began recording raps in Kreyòl, which he released independently to Haitian radio in Port-au-Prince. He performed in Haiti several times, both with The Fugees and solo, as part of the Bouyon Rasin music festival in 1995. When he released his 1997 solo album, *Wyclef Jean Presents the Carnival,* he used Kreyòl in several songs, announcing and displaying his Haitian identity. The critical acclaim and high sales of the album gave Kreyòl language and Haitian participation in hip-hop new visibility. A track on his next album, *The Eclectic,* featured the well-known slogan constantly recycled in Carnival and Rara (and recorded in Boukman Eksperyans' best-known Carnival song, *"Kè'm Pa Sote"* (My heart doesn't leap / I am not afraid): "Grenn zaboka sevi zòriye anba l'acha'w—aswè-a m'p'ap dòmi—Yas!—yas Maman!" (A rough translation of this slogan would be: An avocado seed will be your pillow tonight—I won't be sleeping—Hey—Hey Mama!) This clear sonic *pwen* signaled to Haitian fans throughout hip-hop culture that the Haitian popular culture of Carnival and Rara was indeed part of hip-hop.[29]

Apart from the strong political and aesthetic influence that Rastafari and hip-hop have had on *rasin* culture, the profound effects of zouk music on all Haitian music, including *rasin* music, should not be underestimated. The mid-eighties saw the spectacular rise of zouk with the band Kassav, comprised of members from Guadeloupe and Martinique who now live in Paris. Kassav made over twenty albums from 1985 to 1990, some of which went gold. Their music was imported and consumed enthusiastically by transnational Francophone youth culture in Dominica, Saint Lucia, Haiti, the United States, Canada, Paris, Belgium, Switzerland, and West Africa.

The heavy use of brass instruments and the dance-hall quality of zouk gave it an association with *konpa dirèk,* the Haitian dance music based on merengue rhythms. However, zouk lyrics were more politically substantive, preaching messages of emancipation, social harmony, and cultural consciousness. In addition zouk is sung in Creole, giving voice to the tribulations and celebrations of Creole West Indian identity and implicitly resisting French cultural hegemony still active in the island *départments* of France.[30]

While zouk music buttressed *rasin* music in certain ways, the influences of zouk on *rasin* are limited. Zouk musicians, from the relatively prosperous French islands, have not cultivated a "rootsy" style of adornment, or an engaged activism. In many ways, the classic image of the "downpressed" Rasta with long dreadlocks and a walking staff who calls thunder and brimstone down on Jamaican society as he negotiates the slums of Kingston is a more powerful source of identification for the Haitian Raraman.

RARA AND *RASIN* AS CULTURAL CREOLIZATIONS

Both Rastafari and *rasin* are marginalized, poor people's movements led by Third World men who build community in performative gatherings called *binghis* and Raras; these performances give way to the commodified forms of Reggae music and *mizik rasin*. We can place the emergence of these various roots movements in broad historical context. As Hall notes in his essay on Black popular culture, three factors contribute to the emergence of contemporary constellations of Black popular expressions and the current scholarly work around them. First is the displacement of European models of culture and of Europeans as universal subjects. Second is the present dominance of the United States as the center of global cultural production and circulation. Third is the decolonization of the Third World and the construction of decolonized sensibilities and subjectivities.[31] These factors are giving way not only to forms of Black grassroots popular culture (which, of course, have existed since Black peoples arrived in the Atlantic world) but also to a new kind of self-consciousness about this culture on the part of its makers and its audiences.

In the New York setting, Rara gatherings create an in-between world that is not the Haitian countryside but is also not typical of metropolitan New York. The gatherings are not quite traditional, though they are not wholesale inventions. In seeking to establish social cohesion through reference to tradition in the midst of rapid social change, Rara in New York displays many of the characteristics of "invented tradition" in the way E. J. Hobsbawm and T. O. Ranger define them: "a set of practices, normally governed by overtly or tacitly accepted rules and of a ritual or symbolic nature, which seek to inculcate certain values and norms of behavior by repetition, which automatically implies continuity with the past."[32] But in a real way, Rara was not absent from people's lives long enough to be "invented" or revived. Writing on similar issues in the history of Yoruba religion in Cuba, David H. Brown maintains that "the issue of self-conscious rediscovery of 'African roots' encourages a more open and responsive notion of 'tradition,' one in which 'reafricanization' is as sensible as 'African survivals.'"[33] Rara in New York is a conscious and cooperative project that occurs as a process of change, with continuities and discontinuities.

When young Raramen make circular journeys playing Rara in a home village in February and in Brooklyn in June, new cultural relationships are created out of old "center" and "periphery" arenas. Ulf Hannerz has stressed that with respect to the domains of popular culture, center-periphery relationships must be seen as a continuously emergent historical structure, with a new kind of polycentricity in this transnational era. It is true that Haitians still travel to the French centers of Paris and Belgium for education in the centers of previous empires, or, more commonly, to the current centers of the United States and Francophone Canada for school and work. But the popular interest in Rara has altered the logic of the center-periphery flow. Roots-identified Haitian New

Rara *kolonèl* directs the band with whip and whistle (photo © Chantal Regnault)

Yorkers turn their gaze to Port-au-Prince and the *moun deyò* (people outside) in the rural provinces, often to the consternation of their parents. What is more, their attraction to Rastafari has given Haitians another cultural center—Kingston and its countryside. With little direct movement between Port-au-Prince and Kingston, these two peripheries have become centers of popular culture bridged by the original centers of New York and Miami. Likewise, in the case of zouk music, Haitians in Port-au-Prince sing along with Martiniquain in Fort-de-France via the connecting center of Paris. Thus the traditional center is still important to "structure access to the global cultural inventory," as culture tends not to flow straight from one periphery to another. These peripheries are themselves centers of knowledge and cultural activity.[34] The spatialization of cross-dialogue within populations in the African diaspora helps form an understanding of the patterns of creolization that are taking place among diverse and sometimes far-flung groups in the Black diaspora.

It is only by shifting our perspective that we can understand the ways in which "minority" cultures are formed and influenced by one another. Diasporic groups construct themselves not only with reference to the dominant culture of their own nation-state, but also with respect to other Black groups both near and far. It thus becomes clear that the process of identity building is coproduced with other minority communities, and not just against hegemonic groups. Identities are influenced in their processes of formation and redefinition by both local and distant forces.

THE CULTURAL POLITICS OF TRANSNATIONALISM: ROOTS IDENTITY IN NEW YORK CITY

Rara Nou Vodoule *ekzèsis* in Port-au-Prince, Rara Djakout gatherings in New York, and the Rasta Sanba Ginen Bingis in Miami carve out an alternative social space for Haitians to develop new peasant-identified, re-Africanized identities. Because the spaces are linked by continuous interactions of people traveling back and forth within them, the forces of transnational migration have generated *rasin* culture, like its Rasta counterpart, as a deterritorialized popular culture. No longer linked just to Port-au-Prince, this space is created anyplace in the Haitian diaspora that a *sanba* manifests his or her philosophy and style.

As I have mentioned, the Haitian roots identity is produced out of earlier *indègenisme* and *négritude* movements within Haiti, as well as U.S. Black Power ideologies and Jamaican Rastafari. In a sense, then, the philosophical base of the movement was already transnationalized, with roots in both Pan-Caribbean and U.S. antiracist struggles. Being openly roots-identified, however, is a relatively new option for Haitians inside Haiti.

Theories of a fixed ethnic identity are now giving way to questions about the processes of identity formation, the manipulation of identity, and the situational variability of identity.[35] Fredrik Barth in 1969 was the first to argue that ethnicity is the product of social ascriptions, developed out of the view one has of oneself as well as the views held by others—the result of a dialectical process involving internal and external identifications and designations.[36] Current theoretical work explores the subjectivities and struggles that are now constituted around race, nationhood, gender, sexuality, and transnational political economy. Gage Averill has noted that "the effort to create a roots music culture in Haiti after the fall of the dictatorship is a musical corollary to populist political movements and represents a musical discourse that has the potential to cross class and geographical lines in Haiti."[37] The social position of the roots-identified *sanba*, although it implies downward mobility, nonetheless gives Haitian youth a status based in distinctiveness and personal creativity; some have even parlayed this status into celebrity in *mizik rasin* bands. This identity, and the community it implies, is a unique product of the post-Duvalier era. Not only is it a new phenomenon in the Haitian community, but the "Haitian community" itself did not always exist in New York, despite a large Haitian population. Transnational politics and a revived Haitian nationalism all played a part in the construction of Haitian roots identity in the 1990s.

Glick Schiller and a team of social scientists have conducted extensive research on Haitian organizations to chart the emergence of the Haitian-American community and the construction of Haitian ethnicity in the United States.[38] Her convincing conclusion is that the concept of a Haitian ethnic community was taught by representatives of American institutions to members of the Haitian immigrant population. These institutions have included the Democratic Party, the Ford Foundation, the Center for Human Services, and various church groups. Glick Schiller sees the construction of Haitian-American ethnicity as a move on the part of hegemonic interests to create constituencies and interest groups that could be manipulated for various political reasons. Her work focuses mainly on Haitian leadership and the "higher" levels of Haitian politics. I suggest that the sense of ethnic community created by U.S. groups in turn spawned a public popular culture that has since leveled powerful and effective critiques at U.S. domestic and foreign policy and become a factor in U.S. policymaking decisions.

Although it is impossible here to present a detailed history of the Haitian population in New York and its construction as an ethnic community, it is necessary to stress several points about Haitian immigration to the northeastern United States. There has been a significant Haitian presence in New York since the 1950s. But a historic downward spiral of economic and political devastation in Haiti, added to the abuses of the Duvalier regime, forced hundreds of thousands of Haitians into exile, and huge Haitian enclaves grew outside Haiti. Now an estimated four hundred thousand Haitians live in the New York metropolitan area alone. These numbers are impossible to verify, both because the U.S. Census Bureau does not distinguish between African-American and West Indian ethnicities, and because many Haitian immigrants are undocumented.[39] In any case, estimates suggest that the Haitian presence is large and that it is growing: already Haitian Kreyòl is the second most common foreign language after Spanish in the New York City public schools.[40]

A common perception among North Americans is that Haitians are poor and uneducated. The reality is that most Haitians who immigrate are not from the lowest social classes. In fact, people of all class backgrounds have immigrated. Some 80 percent have had previous work experience, and 50 percent own their own homes in Haiti. Immigrating to New York eases the effect of poverty for the lower classes, but the upper classes experience a loss of status when they arrive in New York.[41]

Perhaps the most salient point about Haitian-American identity is the fact that the social cleavages that exist in Haiti are played out in the Haitian population in New York. Class, color, gender, religious, regional, and language differences have tended to divide Haitians and thwart their attempts at organization.[42] Despite this fact, outside events have forced to some extent the consolidation of a Haitian community and sense of Haitian ethnicity. During the tragedy of the *bòt pipol* (boat people) in the late 1970s, when many people lost their lives attempting to flee Duvalier, Haitians in the United States faced rejection based on associations with this stigmatized group. This stigma precipitated the construction of a Haitian community by Haitians themselves as they began organizing large political demonstrations against U.S. refugee policy.[43]

Then in 1990 the Food and Drug Administration (FDA) issued a ruling that banned Haitians from donating blood, declaring them transmitters of AIDS.[44] Again, Haitians held massive demonstrations in New York, Miami, Boston, Chicago, and even at the U.S. Embassy in Port-au-Prince.[45] Rara musicians played drums at the demonstrations, and songs were "thrown" critiquing the discriminatory practices of the FDA. In an event unprecedented in Haitian history, sixty thousand Haitians and their supporters walked across the Brooklyn Bridge in New York on 20 April 1990 and forced the entire city to become aware of the racism in the AIDS issue. Later that day Father Aristide delivered "electrical antiphonal oratory," casting the anger of the crowd into transnational perspective. Karen Richman writes that Aristide painted a picture in which Haitians'

> continued insecurity in the United States was an inevitable product of the unholy union between Home and Host states. Aristide's speech elaborated a triadic pun based on the rhyming Kreyòl words of SIDA (AIDS in French or Kreyòl) with siga, or cigar and the well-known idiom, *"men siga ou,"* literally, "here is your cigar," meaning, "surprise!" or "it will never happen the way you intended." . . . Haitians had become a bold cigar lit at both ends to resist the machinations of its imperialist smoker and the "pimps" and "house boys" campaigning in the upcoming elections back Home.[46]

With the entry of Aristide into the political arena, the popular classes in Haiti felt they had found a viable political representative. Aristide's use of Haitian Kreyòl and his policies for land reform and peasants' rights posed a real challenge to Euro-Haitian hegemony. These combined events in Haiti and the United States further opened the cultural space for the *rasin* movement.

Haitian Rara drummers were snubbed by Jamaican musicians in Prospect Park in 1990, just two months after they halted traffic in New York at the massive, exhilarating antiracism demonstration. Their creation of a parading Rara band was the moment in which Haitians girded themselves for an ongoing public display of their ethnic strength and national pride. Throughout that summer and each summer since, the Haitian Rara gatherings became an interpretive community that articulated a clear position with regard to the cultural politics in which they found themselves enmeshed. A popular politics emerged that was multiply positioned and that took a stance in relation to various historical processes.

The Raraman took up an ideological position with relationship to the War of Haitian Independence against the French (and by extension, all of Europe), the ruling Catholic Haitian elite, the hegemonic forces of "white" America, and other Black groups (Jamaicans, Trinidadians, and African Americans) in New York. The positions of the Raramen were often contradictory (or sometimes partial) truths and often obfuscated depressing realities, such as links between the *makoutes* and Vodou priests.

DEFINITIONS OF BLACKNESS IN HAITIAN *RASIN* CULTURE

Seen as a subculture, the Raras can be analyzed in terms of a double articulation of relationship—first to the "parent culture" (Haiti), and second to the dominant culture (the United States).[47] Opposition to dominant America was implicit in the "rootsy" peasant dress styles and the activity of public Rara parading itself. It took the same form of physicality that it took in Haiti: hundreds of Haitian people (Black bodies) walking along the park road and singing. The potential of the Rara for political disruption was not lost on the New York City Police Department. On several occasions they arrived in squad cars with their lights flashing and attempted to direct the Rara off the park road and onto the grass to let traffic through the park. The reaction of some young men in the crowd, although incomprehensible to the officers, was a show of performative opposition. They formed a ring and danced in a circle, singing an improvised song:

> Your mother's clitoris!
> The police have come to "crash" the Rara
>
> *Kou langet manman-ou—*
> *Polis vini pou kraze rara*

The police were perceived as an oppositional force that was inherently racist. The refrain of one of the original songs composed by Rara Neg Gran Bwa in Prospect Park was "*La polis pa vle wè nwa*" (The police can't stand to see Black [people]). This feeling grew from the group's experiences in Crown Heights and Bedford Styvesant neighborhoods, where community-police relations are marred by police corruption and brutality.

Yet as the work of Carolle Charles shows, Haitians in the United States have tended to disaffiliate with Black Americans. Haitian immigrants are aware that Black people represent "the bottom" of U.S. society. Haitians self-identify as Black, but they link their Blackness to Haitian history through Africa and not through the United States. Haitians reject U.S.-specific racializations, sometimes saying, "I don't want to be Black twice." Previously the most common Haitian-American tactic was to self-identify as French. People who were Kreyòl-speaking and fully Haitian would present themselves socially as French by speaking the French language. Charles writes of high-school children who camouflaged their identity as Jamaican so as not to be known as Haitian; she also notes others' willingness to be called "Frenchies" in their efforts to disaffiliate themselves with African Americans.[48]

The *sanbas* and Raramen of the Haitian *rasin* movement have created a second alternative to the dilemma of Black identity for Haitian Americans. Rather than playing on their French roots, they can perform, through style and bodily adornment, a specifically Afro-Haitian identity. In this way Haitians express solidarity with other Black groups while nevertheless maintaining and privileging their Haitianness. By virtue of the early independence revolution in Haiti, this construction of Haitianness is felt to be implicitly closer to Africa and more in touch with its Blackness than some other African American groups.

Social class and year of migration from Haiti affect people's relationship to the Rara gatherings in New York. For example, recent immigrants from the Port-au-Prince slums, having performed Rara in Haiti, arrived in Brooklyn in 1990 and found Rara waiting for them. They picked up where they left off, so to speak, and found that their "authentic" talent in "throwing" songs was prized by their Americanized colleagues. The older bourgeois gentleman who left Haiti thirty years ago and sees Rara for the first time in decades reacts to the scene with ambivalence: nationalist nostalgia mixed with class-based distaste. For the young Haitian American born and raised in New York, Rara may provide a key to the problem of identity and a milieu in which he can "learn" to be Haitian.

Tensions between the newly arrived Haitian and the established Haitian American play out in the Rara. The recent arrival, while most likely broke, not fluent in English, and possibly undocumented, may nevertheless be an accomplished drummer or a talented *sanba* who understands the process of songwriting and knows the codes of *voye pwen*. He can therefore present himself as the authentic Haitian, to the envy of the Haitian American raised in New York. The American Haitian, meanwhile, is envied by the new immigrant: he is literate, more likely to be established in a job, and able to navigate American culture. Rivalry and competition play out between the "Kongo" (someone who is too "country" or loud-talking) and the *biznisman* (an American Haitian who is too interested in money). At the same time, each desperately needs the other: the one for help in settling in as an immigrant, and the other to confirm a sense of Haitianness and culture.

HAITIAN NATIONALISM AND THE *RASIN* MOVEMENT

Haiti had the first and only successful slave revolution in Western history, a revolution fought by slaves with the inspiration of Vodou spirituality and magical weapons. Every Haitian is acutely aware of this chapter in history, citing the pivotal moment when Boukman, a maroon religious leader, held a ceremony in which he asked the Vodou *lwa* for assistance in the fight. This moment sealed the subsequent bond between religion and politics in Haiti. If Haitians have faced nothing but economic misery ever since, at least, they maintain, they have held their freedom. This has resulted in a fierce Haitian nationalism: a pride and an awareness that no other Afro-Atlantic country shares their achievement of revolutionary success. Haitians combat their status as one of the lowest groups on the economic ladder in New York by reiterating these symbols of independence.[49]

Nationalist tropes have assumed mythical status both in Haiti and in the diaspora, and early liberation fighters—Boukman, Makandal, and Dessalines—are constantly invoked in calls to unity among Haitians. But these same tropes also serve to distort other historical realities, like the continued downward spiral of the Haitian economy, the lack of a civil society that can support basic human needs like education and health care, and the dismal record of political despotism and foreign domination across Haitian history.

Because there are more economic opportunities in the United States than at home, Haitians in America can concentrate on working, on sending money back to Haiti, and on imagining a future where they will return to the island to live. They thus escape theorizing about U.S. racism because they consider themselves, as foreigners, outside racial conflicts.[50] By parading Rara—the strongly African, quintessential Haitian cultural form—they underscore to themselves and to other groups of African descent that their identity is fully realized through its own cultural roots. No longer one group against other Rara groups in local battle, the

Brooklyn celebrations are first and foremost conceptualized as Haitians against everybody else, a cultural show of Haitian nationalism with respect to both whites and Black people in America.

While the Brooklyn Rara is a statement of Haitian ethnic distinctiveness from all other groups, the Rara is also, paradoxically, an affirmation of Afrocentric identity and Pan-Africanism. Because the celebration takes place in a country where Haitians become part of a Black minority, Rara members see links between themselves and other African peoples. One strong indication of this general African nationalism is in the style of dress of Rara members. In addition to traditional Haitian peasant clothing, Rara members sport Malcolm X shirts, Nelson Mandela buttons, leather medallions of Africa, kente cloth articles, and Spike Lee t-shirts.

Paul Gilroy draws attention to the way that "Africanness," signaled by such things as Malcolm X shirts, "operates transnationally and interculturally through the symbolic projection of 'race' as kinship."[51] The discourse of Black brotherhood and sisterhood, which of course stems from the Black Protestant tradition of seeing all people as "God's children," was perhaps strongest during the Black Power era but still operates in arenas as varied as the Nation of Islam and the voguing balls of Black gay culture.

Haitian tropes of nationalism centered on the concept of the people as army operate quite differently from the rhetoric of the family. A central concept in *rasin* culture currently is the aspiration to continue the "revolution" that Aristide's Lavalas movement began and, by extension, to continue the original slave revolt against Europe. Says Djames, a leader of Rara Nèg Gran Bwa in Brooklyn: "You take Rara, you take your drum, you go outside, and you start to make your revolution. Even if you only have a machete in your hand, the other guy has guns, you feel like you are ten thousand men. That's the kind of feeling that comes over us even though the struggle against the high classes has not yet been won."[52]

This militarized sense of Haitian nationalism came vividly to life in the events surrounding the coup d'état against President Aristide. Some of the Raramen in Brooklyn had appointed themselves Aristide's unofficial musical entourage, acting as a kind of signal drumming corps for his public speaking engagements in the United States. They welcomed him with the hocketing tones of the *banbou* at Kennedy Airport when he visited New York in October 1991, and they embellished his arrival and departure at the Cathedral of Saint John the Divine when he spoke there. When the coup d'état against Aristide was announced, they mobilized immediately to become a presence in the subsequent vigils and marches. With the active participation of the crowds that gathered around them, the Rara and demonstrators created new songs to express their political voice. The core members of Nèg Gran Bwa Rara played at the rallies at the United Nations, in Washington, and in the large New York demonstrations that outnumbered even the famous anti-FDA demonstration. Gone were the summer's songs, "*La Polis pa vle wè nwa*" (The police don't want to see Black [people]). New songs instead expressed the Rara's collective sentiment regarding the Cedras coup.

During these Rara protest demonstrations, Rara bands took on the militarized identity of an army of invasion, and members spoke of forming a Haitian "Bay of Pigs" force to restore Aristide. The songs at the protest Raras after the coup did not follow the same logic as the statements given by Wilson Desir, the Haitian consul to New York, or even the statements given by Aristide himself. For example, many of the songs made reference to *Pè Lebrun* (necklacing) in a supportive light. "*Brule yo, brule yo*" (Burn them, burn them) were,the lyrics of one of the more popular songs. Some Vodou songs were sung, substituting Aristide's name for the *lwa*.

Most people in the demonstrations seemed to support the presence of the Rara, despite a wide variety of class backgrounds. Even those people who informed me that they were unaccustomed to going to Rara in Haiti were supportive. They were of the opinion that, because this was a Haitian political demonstration, the Rara was appropriate and not a spiritual or political threat. I was told by many that plenty of the people dancing in the Rara would not have been doing so if they had been in Haiti. Their original class affiliations had become modified by their status in New York and by their solidarity with Lavalas.

The Rara gatherings in New York and elsewhere in the United States did not form an official organization. But Rara gatherings became a place where popular Haitian culture was enacted and a poly-vocal politics emerged, based on Rara performance principles of *voye pwen*, personal charisma, and songwriting talent. Rara can be seen as an attempt to solve problems in the social structure that are created by contradictions and tensions in the larger society. The Rara solves, in an imaginary way, problems that at the material level remain unresolved.[53]

Haitian people performing Rara in New York are continuing an old historical tradition in order to consolidate their community, solidify their vision of ethnic identity, and further a political movement. The

Rara wins symbolic and actual space for the Haitian community in the United States. It wins real time for Haitians to enter a liminal, healing mode of performance and to experience—or create—the form in which they traditionally take pleasure in their culture, to be in their "deep skin."[54] In this sense, Rara is an answer to the alienation and oppression many Haitians face in U.S. culture.

Rara in New York maintains its basic spiritual principles, but it is also a new entity with a new vocabulary and philosophy of progressive Haitian politics, a position allied with Pan-Africanism, with peasants' rights in Haiti, and against dominant America and the Haitian elite. Through the Rara, members of the Haitian community are choosing values of community, resistance, nationalist and ethnic pride, and racial solidarity in the performative mode of song, dance, and celebration.

Chronology of Political Events, 1990–1995

ANNOTATED WITH TRANSNATIONAL
RARA BAND ACTIVITY

1986

FEBRUARY 7
Jean-Claude Duvalier leaves Haiti.[1]
Three-month period of intense public celebration; Rara bands reign in the streets.

1990

FEBRUARY
Boukman Eksperyans is the first roots band to win Carnival with song "Kè'm Pa Sote" (My heart doesn't leap).[2]

FALL
Father Jean-Bertrand Aristide announces presidential candidacy.

SUMMER
Rara Djakout is founded in Brooklyn, New York.

DECEMBER 16
Jean-Bertrand Aristide wins presidential election by 67 percent of the vote.
Colonel Raoul Cedras is chief of security for the election.
Rara Nou Vodoule launches massive Rara downtown.
Song "Pa Vle Zenglendo" (Don't want criminals) sings out against criminal activity by former makoutes.

1991

JANUARY 7
Former head of *tonton makoutes* Roger Lafontant attempts a coup against interim president Ertha Pascal-Trouillot to prevent Aristide's taking power; Lafontant arrested by Haitian military.
In three days of looting 125 people are killed and sixty-five million dollars' worth of damage is done to Port-au-Prince business district.
Rara bands take to the street to protest Lafontant and celebrate the failure of his coup.

FEBRUARY 7
Aristide is inaugurated president of Haiti.
Carnival season is launched.
Koudjay's Carnival song "Manman Poul La Trouillot" (Chicken mama Trouillot) satirizes interim president Ertha Pascal-Trouillot.[3]
Boukman Eksperyans's Carnival song "Gran Bwa Kriminel" criticizes the attempted coup by Lafontant against Aristide.
Boukan Ginen sings "Pale Pale Ou" (You can talk), celebrating the new climate of free speech under Aristide.[4]

JUNE
Rara Nèg Gran Bwa founded in Brooklyn, New York.

SEPTEMBER 25
Members of New York Raras play for Aristide upon his arrival at the airport in New York and in front of the United Nations when he speaks there.

SEPTEMBER 27

Aristide returns to Haiti from United Nations visit and delivers speech on National Palace steps that some charge advocates necklacing.

SEPTEMBER 30

Aristide is ousted from power by Haitian military and goes to Venezuela.

Sylvio Claude, who ran against Aristide in the presidential campaign, is necklaced in Les Cayes. Roger Lafontant is murdered in jail.

New York Raras mobilize and play in emotional pro-Aristide protest demonstrations outside the United Nations for weeks.

OCTOBER 3

The Organization of American States (OAS) adopts resolution calling on member nations to suspend economic activities with Haiti. Aristide visits United Nations security council.

New York Raras demonstrate at Freedom Plaza outside the United Nations; Mayor Dinkens addresses the crowd.

OCTOBER 4

Aristide goes to Washington, D.C., and forges alliance with Congressional Black Caucus.

New York Rara members go to Washington and play outside Capitol Hill.

In Brooklyn, crowds try to burn down Le Manoir Nightclub, reputed to be a makout *headquarters.*

1992

FEBRUARY: CARNIVAL

Carnival and Rara season begin under General Cedras's military coup government.

Roots band RAM releases hit song "Anbago" (Embargo) about the international embargo on Haiti.[5]

Boukman Eksperyans releases song "Kalfou Danjere" (Dangerous crossroads), whose coded lyrics decry the dishonesty of foreign diplomats and the Haitian military.[6]

FEBRUARY 23

The Washington accord is signed, calling for a new prime minister. Aristide is acknowledged as president, but no date is set for his return to Haiti.

APRIL

Mass exodus of Haitian refugees occurs.

MAY 24

The Bush administration announces that all Haitian refugees picked up at sea will be forcibly returned to Haiti.

JUNE 9

Presidential candidate Bill Clinton declares unacceptable the Bush administration's Haitian refugee repatriation policy.

JUNE 19

Marc Bazin is installed as de facto prime minister.

Léogâne Raras sing pwen *declaring Bazin fake and illegitimate.*

NOVEMBER 3

Bill Clinton wins U.S. presidential election.

1993

JANUARY 14

President-elect Clinton announces he will continue Bush policy of forcible repatriation.

Rara Inorab Kapab members are caught at Guantanamo and returned; they compose a song about their plight.[7]

FEBRUARY: CARNIVAL

Carnival and Rara season take place under extremely repressive military rule.

Boukman Eksperyans's Carnival song "Jou Malè" (Day of the shock), sung in the voices of military lwa *Ogou Badagri and Simbi Ganga, declares that Uzis and batons don't scare them.*[8]

RAM launches Carnival song "Agwe Toyowo," whose refrain, "la mè-a tèrib" is creolized to "l'ame-a terib." ("La mer est terrible" [the sea is ter-

rible] becomes *"l'armee est terrible"* [the army is terrible].*)*

JUNE 4

United States imposes new sanctions on Haiti.

JUNE 23

United Nations oil embargo and freeze of Haitian leaders' assets goes into effect.

Gas shortage causes miles-long lines at gas stations; violence and rampant black market gas profiteering occurs for the rest of the summer and autumn.

JULY 3

Governor's Island agreement signed by Cedras and Aristide, calling for new prime minister, general amnesty law, resignation of military leaders, a UN-mandated military and police training mission in Haiti, and Aristide's return to Haiti by October 30.

RAM's song "Fey" (Leaf) talks in metaphor about the strength of the popular classes despite the coup.[9]

AUGUST 27

Haitian parliament confirms Robert Malval as prime minister and approves a new government. International embargo against Haiti is suspended.

SEPTEMBER 11

Antoine Izmery, wealthy merchant and Aristide supporter, is assassinated during a memorial service at the Sacre Coeur Cathedral for the massacre at the Cathedral of Saint Jean Bosco.

EARLY OCTOBER

Mutilated Caucasian U.S. soldier is dragged through streets of Mogadishu and film is broadcast on international television.

OCTOBER 11

USS Harlan County, carrying a military training mission, is turned back from landing at the Port-au-Prince dock by crowd of *makoutes.*

OCTOBER 13

United Nations reimposes oil and other economic sanctions against Haiti.

U.S. Navy goes into Haitian waters to enforce the embargo.

OCTOBER 30

Date for Aristide's return passes.

1994

JANUARY–MARCH

Various diplomatic initiatives to return Aristide fail.

FEBRUARY: CARNIVAL

Fraph, the paramilitary death squad, launches a pro-military Rara band.

Boukman Eksperyans's Carnival song "Peye Pou Peye" (You must pay) speaks of the need to be held accountable for criminal actions.[10]

APRIL 12

Randall Robinson of TransAfrica begins hunger strike to protest Clinton administration's refugee repatriation policy.

APRIL 21

U.S. administration moves to sanction Haiti with complete economic embargo; closure of Dominican border.

MAY 6

United Nations announces complete economic embargo against Haiti.

MAY 8

Clinton administration announces new procedures for handling Haitian refugees and names William Gray III special advisor on Haiti. Randall Robinson ends twenty-seven-day hunger strike.

JUNE 16

Clinton administration announces new procedures for handling refugees. Refugee crisis deepens.

JUNE 22

United States freezes Haitian assets and suspends air traffic to Haiti.

Summer Raras in New York become a meeting ground for people unable to return to Haiti.

JUNE 29

United States revokes all nonimmigrant Haitian visas and reopens Guantanamo to process Haitian refugees.

Morale is low in summer Raras in New York because of deepening crisis in Haiti.

JULY 11
Haitian coup government expels UN/OAS human rights observers.

JULY 31
United Nations approves resolution authorizing the formation of a multinational coalition and authorizing the use of force to restore democracy to Haiti.

SEPTEMBER 15
Clinton addresses the United States to prepare the country for possible invasion of Haiti.
Opinion in Haitian-American population is divided. Many support the invasion. Raras are silent on the subject but continue to support Aristide.

SEPTEMBER 17
Delegation of former president Jimmy Carter, Senator Sam Nunn, and General Colin Powell arrives in Haiti for last-minute effort to peacefully resolve the Haitian crisis.

SEPTEMBER 18
Cedras agrees to step down by October 15. Clinton informs the U.S. nation in televised address that the Carter delegation has successfully negotiated a peaceful resolution to the crisis.
Cedras is given passage to Spain and considerable financial compensation.
At a private Vodou service in Brooklyn, the congregation holds Catholic prayer service to pray for Haiti.

SEPTEMBER 19
U.S. military peacefully enters Port-au-Prince with considerable African-American and Haitian-American personnel.

OCTOBER 10
Cedras submits his resignation.

OCTOBER 15
Aristide returns to Haiti to resume power.
Rara bands attend public events en masse outside National Palace.

1995

FEBRUARY: CARNIVAL
New rasin band Kanpesh wins Carnival with "Pale Yo" (Tell them) about the end of the coup period and the difficulties of the past three years.[11]
Boukman Eksperyans's song "Bawon" (Baron) criticizes International Monetary Fund privitization plan.[12]
Koudjay's song coins new dance called "zopope" depicting makoutes and atachés *as thin and powerless.*
RAM's Carnival song "Sa'n Pa We Yo" (Those we can't see) speaks of the missing, disappeared, killed, and exiled.
Manno Charlemagne releases Carnival song "Bo Tab La" (At the table), whose central imagery is of sitting together around a table.[13]
Rara Nou Vodoule resumes activities as biggest Rara in Port-au-Prince during Carnival and Rara seasons.
Manno Charlemagne elected mayor of Port-au-Prince.
Charlemagne takes up residence at Hotel Oloffson, run by *rasin* band leader from RAM.

JULY 29
Bouyon Rasin festival is held in Port-au-Prince, the first music festival to feature rasin *bands, organized by Haitians in the diaspora.*[14]

Glossary

angaje Under contract

atache Auxiliary military guards

avan gad Front guard

banbou, or *vaksin* The instruments most immediately associated with Rara music: hollowed-out bamboo tubes with a mouthpiece fashioned at one end

banda A rhythm that features fast slaps and rolls; the distinctive rhythm and dance of the Gede spirits

bann a pye A band on foot (as opposed to a band on a Carnival float)

bas A handheld round wooden frame with goatskin stretched across the top and interlacing tuning cords creating a web along the inside of the drum

Bawon The spirit who rules the cemetery

benyen Protective baths

betiz Obscenities; vulgar jokes or slogans

Bizango The term referring to the religious rite of a secret society

blan White, also foreigner

bòkò Sorcerer

bounda "Butt"

bouzen Prostitute, or loose woman

bwile Jwif Literally, "Jew burning"

Chanpwèl Secret societies

chante pwen To sing "points" or messages

charyio-pye A style of Rara band without instruments that uses foot stomping as percussion

chawonj Something smelly and nasty, or someone who will have sex with anyone, any place

dezòd Unruly; literally, "disorder"

djakout A type of straw shoulder-bag

ekzèsis Exercises; see also *repetisyon*

fanatik People who are not dressed up and in the Rara's chorus, but who dance in the crowd; fans

fete To party

foul Big crowd

Fraph The name of a paramilitary death squad; literally, "to hit"

fwomaj A vernacular usage for the symptoms of sexually transmitted disease; literally, "cheese"

Gede The deity associated with the ancestors, healing, sex, death, and hard work

Ginen A term meaning "Ancestral Africa"; also signifying moral living and proper use of spirituality

gouyad A dance in which the chin is tilted to the side, knees are bent, and the hips roll in circles

graj Aluminum scrapers that are twelve to twenty-four inches long, used as percussion instruments

Gran Mèt God; literally, "Great Master"

gwo bon anj   Part of the soul; literally, "good big angel"

gwo nèg   "Big man"

kay   House

kès   Portable drum used in Rara

kilòt   Women's underpants

kleren   Pure cane liquor that keeps Rara bands fueled with calories for much of their journey

klewon   Handmade metal trumpets with a yard-long tube and a flared horn at the end

koko   Vagina

kolonèl   Colonel

konbit   Work squad

konè   Trumpet; see *klewon*

konpa   Haitian popular couples dance music

kou'd leè   "Hit of bad air"

kou'd poud   "Hit of powder"

kraze   To crash, ruin

kraze Rara   "Crash the Rara"

krèk   Clitoris; sometimes used to refer to the vagina

lakou   An extended family compound

lanbi   Conch shells

langèt   Clitoris

Lavalas   Aristide's party, or "the flood"

lese frape   Let go; literally, "let hit"

lòt bò dlo   The other side of the water

lwa   The deities or spirits of Afro-Haitian religion

lwa pwen   A spirit that is purchased instead of inherited

machann   Market women

madivin   Lesbian

maji   Literally, "magic"; can refer to a mode of spirit work, or an object

majò jon   Baton major

manbo   Priestess

manman   Mother; also refers to the "mother drum"

Mardi Gras   "Fat Tuesday," one of the three important days of Carnival

marenn   Godmother

mariaj Rara   "Rara marriage" that occurs when two Raras meet and pass one another

masisi   Gay man

mayombero   A priest of Kongo-Cuban religion

mèt   Owner; literally "master"

mizik rasin   Roots music

mouvman Rara   Rara movement

Nago   Historically Yoruba nation in Vodou

nèg   (Black) man

non pwen   Nickname

ochan   Musical salute

ogan   A hoe-blade beaten with a piece of metal, also an important instrument in a religious ritual

Ogou   The deity of ironwork, warfare, and discipline

ounfò   Religious house

oungan   Vodou priest

ounsi   Religious society members

parenn   Godfather

peristil   Religious dance space

Petwo   Branch of Afro-Haitian religion, music, and dance, considered "hot" and "fierce"

peye sòti   "Pay to go"

pòt drapo   Flag-bearer

poto mitan   Ritual centerpost

pou plezi   For pleasure

pwèl   Pubic hair

pwen   A figurative word, song, proverb, slogan, or object that conveys a hidden meaning; literally, "point"

rasin   Roots

regleman   The "rule," the proper order of a religious ritual

reklamasyon   Literally, "reclaiming"

renn   Queen

repetisyon   Rehearsal

sanba   Songwriter

segon   Second drum

simidò   Songwriter; see also *sanba*

Sodo   A nationally known event at a mountain waterfall that draws crowds of pilgrims from all over Haiti and the diaspora

sosyete The religious society that forms Rara under the specific instructions of a *lwa,* for a set number of years and for distinct reasons; members of a Vodou congregation or Chanpwèl group

sòti Outing

tanbou a liy A metal mass-produced *timbale* drum used as a *kès*

tcha-tcha Small gourds filled with seeds

teledjòl Word of mouth; literally, "tele-mouth"

ti bon anj Part of the soul; literally, "good little angel"

timbale Metal mass-produced drum with sharp sound, played with two sticks

ti nèg "Small man"

tonton makout The secret police begun by dictator François Duvalier

travay maji Magic work

vakabondaj "Vagabondage"

vaksin Hollowed-out bamboo instrument; see *banbou*

vèvè Sacred cornmeal ground drawings

Vodou A rite, rhythm, and dance within Afro-Haitian religion; used as a gloss for the many branches and regional variations of the religion

Vodouisant Vodou practitioner

voye pwen To speak or sing figuratively to convey hidden meaning; literally, "send points"

wa King

wanga Magical work

zam kongo "Kongo weapons"

zenglendo A brand of violent criminal relatively new to Haiti

zonbi A spirit of the recently dead, captured and made to serve the capturer; also a metaphoric reference to the condition of servitude that is central to the Haitian historical experience

zouk Popular music from Martinique

zozo Penis

Notes

INTRODUCING RARA

1. Lolo Beaubrun of Boukman Eksperyans, interview, Port-au-Prince, March 1993. See their song "Jou Male" on the album *Libète Pran Pou Pran'l/Freedom Let's Grab It,* Mango 162-539946-2 (1995).

2. This Vodou song is usually played to the Nago rhythm. Boukman Eksperyans incorporated it into their 1993 Carnival song to a Petwo/Rara rhythm. It urged the public to put themselves on guard and prepare for the battle (against the military junta). It then became popular among street Raras. See Boukman Eksperyans, *Libète Pran Pou Pran'l/ Freedom Let's Grab It.*

3. See Michel-Rolph Trouillot, *Silencing the Past: Power and the Production of History* (Boston, Mass.: Beacon Press, 1995).

4. Bartolomé de las Casas, *History of the Indies* (New York: Harper and Row, 1971). Cited in Catherine Keller, "The Breast, the Apocalypse, and the Colonial Journey," in *The Year 2000: Essays on the End,* ed. Charles B. Strozier and Michael Flynn (New York: NYU Press, 1997). Haiti has had various names: The Amerindian "Aiyti-Kiskeya" was changed by Columbus to "Hispaniola" (Little Spain). In 1697, the French named their colony Saint Domingue, and in 1804, newly independent slaves and people of color returned the land to its original name of Haiti.

5. The original definition of the word *Creole* meant American, as in "born in the colony" (as opposed to the "mother" country).

6. Joseph R. Roach, *Cities of the Dead: Circum-Atlantic Performance* (New York: Columbia University Press, 1996); Paul Gilroy, *The Black Atlantic: Modernity and Double Consciousness* (Cambridge, Mass.: Harvard University Press, 1993).

7. Linda G. Basch, Nina Glick Schiller, and Cristina Szanton Blanc, *Nations Unbound: Transnational Projects, Postcolonial Predicaments, and Deterritorialized Nation-States* (Langhorne, Pa.: Gordon and Breach, 1994).

8. For a helpful analysis of Haiti in the hemispheric political economy of this period, see Alex Dupuy, *Haiti in the New World Order: The Limits of the Democratic Revolution* (Boulder, Colo.: Westview Press, 1997).

9. Many people recount stories of children who "take a ride" in a Rara only to find themselves far from home and lost when they are ready to return. The children's story *Market Day for Ti André* tells such a tale. Maia Wojciechowska and Wilson Bigaud, *Market Day for Ti André* (New York: Viking Press, 1952).

10. Claire Cesareo and Steven Rubenstein, "Prospectus for a Workshop: The Politics of Insecurity" (paper presented at the Workshop at the Social Science Research Center, New York, 1995).

11. See Leslie G. Desmangles, *The Faces of the Gods: Vodou and Roman Catholicism* (Chapel Hill: University of North Carolina Press, 1992).

12. Michel-Rolph Trouillot, *Haiti, State against Nation: The Origins and Legacy of Duvalierism* (New York: Monthly Review Press, 1990).

13. Human Rights Watch/Americas, National Coalition for Haitian Refugees, *Silencing a People* (New York: Human Rights Watch, 1993).

14. See interview with Antoine Izmery, "A Fake Kind of Development," in *The Haiti Files: Decoding the Crisis,* ed. James Ridgeway (Washington, D.C.: Essential Books, 1994).

15. Human Rights Watch/Americas, *Silencing a People.* Human Rights Watch/Americas, National Coalition for Haitian Refugees, *Rape in Haiti: A Weapon of Terror* (New York: Human Rights Watch, 1994). Human Rights Watch/Americas, National Coalition for Haitian Refugees, *Security Compromised: Recycled Haitian Soldiers on the Police Front Line* (New York: Human Rights Watch, 1995).

16. Natalie Zemon Davis, *Society and Culture in Early Modern France: Eight Essays* (Stanford, Calif.: Stanford University Press, 1975), xvi.

17. My thanks to Bernice Johnson Reagon for encouraging me to see contemporary song as potential historical text and for encouraging me to make field recordings as documentary. Also see Bernice Johnson Reagon, "The Lined Hymn as a Song of Freedom," *Black Music Research Bulletin* (Columbia College, Chicago) 12, no. 1 (1990). You can hear Reagon's music on the many albums of Sweet Honey in the Rock.

18. Peter Stallybrass and Allon White, *The Politics and Poetics of Transgression* (Ithaca, N.Y.: Cornell University Press, 1986). Achille Mbembe, "The Banality of Power and the Aesthetics of Vulgarity in the Postcolony," *Public Culture* 4, no. 3 (1992).

19. Stallybrass and White, *The Politics and Poetics of Transgression,* 5.

20. Roger D. Abrahams, *The Man-of-Words in the West Indies: Performance and the Emergence of Creole Culture* (Baltimore: Johns Hopkins University Press, 1983).

21. James C. Scott, *Domination and the Arts of Resistance: Hidden Transcripts* (New Haven: Yale University Press, 1990), 2.

22. Nina Glick Schiller, Linda G. Basch, and Cristina Szanton Blanc, *Towards a Transnational Perspective on Migration: Race, Class, Ethnicity, and Nationalism Reconsidered,* Annals of the New York Academy of Sciences 645 (New York: New York Academy of Sciences, 1992). Basch, Glick Schiller, and Szanton Blanc, *Nations Unbound,* 7.

23. Lois Wilcken, "Music Folklore among Haitians in New York: Staged Representations and the Negotiations of Identity" (Ph.D. dissertation, Columbia University, 1991). Elizabeth McAlister, "'Men Moun Yo; Here Are the People': Rara Festivals and Transnational Popular Culture in Haiti and New York City" (Ph.D. dissertation, Yale University, 1995). On the pilgrimage for Our Lady of Mount Carmel, see Elizabeth McAlister, "Vodou and Catholicism in the Age of Transnationalism: The Madonna of 115th Street Revisited," in *Gatherings in Diaspora: Religious Communities and the New Immigration,* ed. Stephen Warner, 123–60 (Philadelphia: Temple University Press, 1998).

24. *The Drums of Vodou featuring Frisner Augustin* (Tempe, Ariz.: White Cliffs Media Company, 1994). *Rhythms of Rapture: Sacred Musics of Haitian Vodou* (Washington, D.C.: Smithsonian/Folkways 40464, 1995). *Angels in the Mirror: Vodou Music of Haiti* (Roslyn, N.Y.: Ellipsis Arts, 1997).

25. Paul Farmer, *The Uses of Haiti* (Monroe, Maine: Common Courage Press, 1994).

26. My daughter and I wrote an essay about our meeting in Haiti, called "The Lucky

Ones: A Mother-Daughter Story of Love and War." It is published on the internet at http: //www.wesleyan.edu/religion/Lucky_Ones.pdf

27. I worked with a Marantz PMD 430 and Sony ECM 909 stereo microphone. We mixed and mastered the recordings on a Macintosh computer using Soundedit software.

28. This film can be viewed on the internet at http://condor.wesleyan.edu/emcalister/ rara/index.html. It is also available on video by writing to Ms. Verna Gillis, Soundscape, P.O. Box 70, Accord, NY 12404, email: gillis@ulster.net.

29. Anna Lowenhaupt Tsing, *In the Realm of the Diamond Queen: Marginality in an Out-of-the-Way Place* (Princeton: Princeton University Press, 1993), xv.

30. Abrahams, *The Man-of-Words in the West Indies.*

31. Mr. Moris Moriset, interview, Léogâne, March 1991.

CHAPTER 1. WORK AND PLAY, PLEASURE AND PERFORMANCE

1. Two gourdes was only worth about twelve cents; it was really only a token amount, but it added up when many cars contributed.

2. You can hear this performance on track 15 of the CD that accompanies this book.

3. You can hear this performance on track 3 of the CD that accompanies this book.

4. Harold Courlander, *The Drum and the Hoe: Life and Lore of the Haitian People* (Berkeley: University of California Press, 1973), 109.

5. "Le RARA est une association publique dont le but est d'égayer la section rurale et ses environs." Gerson Alexis, "Les Danses Rara," *Bulletin du Bureau d'Ethnologie* 3, nos. 17, 18, 19 (1959): 45.

6. Verna Gillis, "Rara in Haiti, Gaga in the Dominican Republic," liner notes to *Caribbean Revels: Haitian Rara and Dominican Gaga,* Folkways Records Album No. FE 4531, 1978.

7. This definition is biased toward a normative male experience, because European-American women, of course, worked in the home until very recently. Roger D. Abrahams and John F. Szwed, *After Africa : Extracts from British Travel Accounts and Journals of the Seventeenth, Eighteenth, and Nineteenth Centuries Concerning the Slaves, Their Manners, and Customs in the British West Indies* (New Haven: Yale University Press, 1983), 32.

8. Ibid.

9. Ibid.

10. H. T. De La Beche, *Notes on the Present Conditions of the Negroes in Jamaica* (London, 1825), 40. Cited in ibid., 33.

11. Jerome C. Handler and Charlotte J. Frisbie, "Aspects of Slave Life in Barbados: Music and Its Cultural Context," *Caribbean Quarterly* 11 (1972): 14. Cited in Abrahams and Szwed, *After Africa,* 33.

12. Abrahams and Szwed, *After Africa,* 34.

13. The lexeme "play" does not have an equivalent in Kreyòl. "Play" may have been picked up more easily by whites in the Anglophone colonies because it was so different from their notions of play. There is evidence that the English-speaking West Indians spoke also of "dances." While *travay* (work) is a fundamental category in Haitian Kreyòl, *fete* (to party) or *dans* (a dance) are its opposites. A religious ceremony is often called a *dans* (dance), or a *fèt* (party). By the same token, wherever there is music, revelry and socializing, it is a *fèt,* even in the case of wakes, where there is all-night joke-telling and card-playing at the house of the deceased. See Abrahams, *The Man-of-Words in the West Indies,* 52.

14. Médéric-Louis-Elie Moreau de Saint Mery, *Description topographique, physique, civile, politique et historique de la partie française de l'île S. Dominque,* nouvelle edition, ed. Blanche Maurel and Etienne Taillemitte (Paris: Société de l'histoire de la Colonie Française, 1958), 23–25.

15. Pierre Isnard Roman, "Recherche sur un rara Appelé la Màprise é l'arcahaie (Merlotte)," in *Faculty of Ethnology* (Port-au-Prince: N.p., 1993).

16. See Elizabeth McAlister, "Sacred Stories from the Haitian Diaspora: A Collective Biography of Seven Vodou Priestesses in New York City," *Journal of Caribbean Studies* 9, nos. 1–2 (1993): 10–27.

17. Sovè St. Cyr, interview, Port-au-Prince, April 1993.

18. *Oungan* Simeon, interview, Port-au-Prince, 30 March 1993.

19. Michael Largey, personal communication, 23 August 2000. See also Michael Largey, "Politics on the Pavement: Haitian Rara as a Traditionalizing Process," *Journal of American Folklore* 113, no. 449 (2000).

20. While Rara members use the word *kontra-a* (a contract), June Rosenberg reports that in the Dominican Republic Gaga festival they make "promises" to the spirits for seven years. A *promesa* is a private deal made with the saints in Latin American Catholicism; interestingly, the Dominican Gaga members also use this terminology. June C. Rosenberg, *Gaga: Religion Y Sociedad De Un Culto Dominicano* (Santo Domingo: USAD, 1979), 69.

21. Gabrielle R., interview, Léogâne, 1991. The word he uses is *djab,* from *djabolik* (diabolical). It is used to mean *lwa* in some parts of Haiti, or Petwo/Bizango *lwa,* or, metaphorically, any problem troubling someone. See Mimerose Beaubrun's notes to tracks 14 and 15 of the album *Rhythms of Rapture: Sacred Musics of Haitian Vodou,* CD on Smithsonian Folkways, SF 40464, 1995.

22. Similyen family, interview, Léogâne, 26 March 1991.

23. General Kanep of Rara La Belle Fraîcheur de l'Anglade, interview, Fermathe, April 1992.

24. *Oungan* Simeon, interview, Bel Air, Port-au-Prince, 31 March 1993.

25. Rara Inorab Kapab, Cité Soleil, 1 April 1993.

26. It is also on track 6 of *Rhythms of Rapture: Sacred Musics of Haitian Vodou,* CD on Smithsonian Folkways, SF 40464, 1995.

27. Dolores Yonker identified *charyio-pye,* or "chairo-pie or charges-au-pieds," as the dance with the "constant halt-run movement." Dolores Yonker, "Rara in Haiti," in *Caribbean Festival Arts: Each and Every Bit of Difference,* ed. John W. Nunley and Judith Bettelheim (Seattle: University of Washington, 1988), 154. My sources identified *charyio-pye* as the stomping of one foot after another to create a rhythmic basis for song, like a march in place. You can hear an example on track 12 of the CD that accompanies this book.

28. Gage Averill and Yuen Ming David Yih, "Militarism in Haitian Music," in *The African Diaspora: A Musical Perspective,* ed. Ingrid Monson (New York: Garland, 2000).

29. Aboudja Derencourt, musician, personal communication, Port-au-Prince, April 1993.

30. Katherine Dunham calls this instrument *granboe,* a term I have not encountered otherwise, except in Lisa Lekis's 1956 work. Katherine Dunham, *Dances of Haiti* (Los Angeles: Center for Afro-American Studies, University of California, Los Angeles, 1983), 16. Lisa Lekis, "The Origin and Development of Ethnic Caribbean Dance and Music" (Ph.D. dissertation, University of Florida, 1956), 200.

31. Jean Bernard, director of the Faculté d'ethnologie, Port-au-Prince, personal communication, Port-au-Prince, 1993.

32. Robert Farris Thompson, personal communication, New Haven, Conn., 1989.

33. Verna Gillis, "Rara in Haiti, Gaga in the Dominican Republic," liner notes to the album of the same name, Folkways Records Album No. FE 4531, 1978, p. 5.

34. Vaksineur Ti-Malis, interview, Léogâne, Holy Saturday 1991.

35. Gage Averill, "Thinking Rara: Roots Grafts in Haitian Popular Music" (paper presented at the International Association for the Study of Popular Music, New Orleans, 1990).

36. You can hear this on track 11 of the CD that accompanies this book and on track 19 of *Rhythms of Rapture*.

37. Averill, "Thinking Rara." Also see the section on Rara musical notation in Gage Averill, "Caribbean Musics: Haiti and Trinidad and Tobago," in *Music in Latin American Culture: Regional Traditions,* ed. John M. Schechter (New York: Schirmer, 1999).

38. Gage Averill, *A Day for the Hunter, a Day for the Prey: Popular Music and Power in Haiti,* Chicago Studies in Ethnomusicology (Chicago: University of Chicago Press, 1997), 20.

39. Within the Rada rite they include *yanvalou, mayi zepòl, nago gwan kou, nago cho, mazoun, twa rigòl, kongo-rada,* and *dyouba-matinik.* Dances for Petwo rites are various forms of *petwo;* for Banda the dance is likewise *banda.* Each of these dances features variations with different names.

40. Also see this author's essay "Vodou Music as Ritual Work" in the liner notes of *Rhythms of Rapture.*

41. Rachel Beauvoir and Didier Dominique, "Savalou E" (Port-au-Prince: N.p., 1987), 94.

42. Gage Averill, "Haitian Dance Band Music: The Political Economy of Exuberance" (Ph.D. dissertation, University of Washington, 1989), 24.

43. Ibid., 26.

44. Y.-M. David Yih, "Music and Dance of Haitian Vodou: Diversity and Unity in Regional Repertoires" (Ph.D. dissertation, Wesleyan University, 1995), 661.

45. *Ochan* from Cayes; Yih, "Music and Dance of Haitian Vodou," 662.

46. Susan Tselos, personal communication, San Francisco, 1991. Also see Susan Elizabeth Tselos, "Threads of Reflection: Costumes of Haitian Rara," *African Arts* 29, no. 2 (1996).

47. It is likely that American baton twirling derives from the Rara festival and was carried to the United States by Haitian refugees of the independence war of 1804; this warrants future research.

48. Dolores Yonker, "Haiti after the Fall: The Politics of Rara" (N.p., 1989). I thank Professor Yonker, one of the few researchers of the festival, for generously sharing with me all of her unpublished work on Rara.

49. J. G. F. Wurdemann, *Notes on Cuba,* 83–84, cited in David H. Brown, "Garden in the Machine: Afro-Cuban Sacred Art and Performance in Urban New Jersey and New York" (Ph.D. dissertation, Yale University, 1989), 46.

50. John W. Nunley and Judith Bettelheim, eds., *Caribbean Festival Arts: Each and Every Bit of Difference* (Seattle: University of Washington, 1988), 35.

51. Ibid.

52. Verna Gillis, "Rara in Haiti, Gaga in the Dominican Republic," liner notes to Folkways Records Album No. FE 4531, 1978, 4.

53. Morton Marks, "Uncovering Ritual Structures in Afro-American Music," in *Religious Movements in Contemporary America,* ed. Irving I. Zaretsky and Mark P. Leone (Princeton: Princeton University Press, 1974), 110.

54. Abrahams and Szwed, *After Africa.* Marks, "Uncovering Ritual Structures in Afro-

American Music." Karl Reisman, "Cultural and Linguistic Ambiguity in a West Indian Village," in *Afro-American Anthropology: Contemporary Perspectives*, ed. John F. Szwed and Norman E. Whitten (New York: Free Press, 1970).

55. D. Brown, "Garden in the Machine," 47.

56. Abrahams and Szwed, *After Africa,* 37.

CHAPTER 2. VULGARITY AND THE POLITICS OF THE SMALL MAN

1. See Andrew Parker, *Nationalisms and Sexualities* (New York: Routledge, 1992).

2. Evelyn Blackwood and Saskia E. Wieringa, *Same Sex Relationships and Female Desires: Transgender Practices across Cultures* (New York: Columbia University Press, 1999).

3. Mbembe, "The Banality of Power and the Aesthetics of Vulgarity in the Postcolony," 4.

4. "Love, Sex and Gender Embodied: The Spirits of Haitian Vodou," in *Love, Gender, and Sexuality in the World Religions,* ed. Nancy Martin and Joseph Runzo, 128–45 (Oxford: Oxford Oneworld Press, 2000).

5. Scott, *Domination and the Arts of Resistance,* 2.

6. Ibid., 175.

7. Boby Denis, record producer, interview, Port-au-Prince, 1993. For an extended work on *konpa,* see Averill, *A Day for the Hunter, a Day for the Prey.*

8. Rara Baby Cool, Port-au-Prince, 1993.

9. Ibid.

10. Peter Burke, *Popular Culture in Early Modern Europe* (New York: New York University Press, 1978), 123.

11. Rara Baby Fresh, Port-au-Prince, 1993.

12. Carolyn Cooper, "Erotic Play in the Dancehall: Slackness Hiding from Culture" (paper presented at the Women in Dance Hall conference, Kingston, Jamaica, University of the West Indies, Mona Campus, 1990). See also Carolyn Cooper, *Noises in the Blood: Orality, Gender, and the "Vulgar" Body of Jamaican Popular Culture* (Durham: Duke University Press, 1995).

13. Anonymous Rara, 1993.

14. Rara La Belle Fraîcheur de l'Anglade, 1992. *Ago* is an exclamation word in the ritual language (*langaj*) of Vodou.

15. Carolle Charles, "A Transnational Dialectic of Race, Class, and Ethnicity: Patterns of Identities and Forms of Consciousness among Haitian Migrants in New York City" (Ph.D. dissertation, SUNY Binghamton, 1990).

16. See for example Tricia Rose, *Black Noise: Rap Music and Black Music in Contemporary America* (Hanover, N.H.: University Press of New England, 1994). Cooper, *Noises in the Blood.*

17. Cooper, "Erotic Play in the Dancehall."

18. Sexual unions in Haiti are considerably more complicated than the "marriage" or "nonmarriage" model that most Eurocentric (i.e., Catholic) models presuppose. In Haiti there are at least five categories: *renmen* (in love), *fianse* (engaged), and *viv avèk* (together), where there is no cohabitation and little financial support, then *plase* (living together) and *marye* (marriage), which are stronger unions where partners live together and garner economic support. All of these unions are sanctioned socially by the poor. Also see J. Allman, "Sexual Unions in Rural Haiti," *International Journal of Sociology and the Family* 10 (1980).

19. Cathy Maternowska, personal communication, 1995. See M. Catherine Maternowska, "Coups d'État and Contraceptives: A Political Economy Analysis of Family Planning in Haiti" (Ph.D. dissertation, Columbia University, 1996).

20. Karen McCarthy Brown, *Mama Lola: A Vodou Priestess in Brooklyn* (Berkeley: University of California Press, 1991).

21. Cooper, "Erotic Play in the Dancehall." See also Cooper, *Noises in the Blood.*

22. See Norma McLeod and Marcia Herdon, "The Bormliza: Maltese Folksong Style and Women," in *Women and Folklore,* ed. Claire B. Ferrer (Austin: University of Texas Press, 1975). Cited in Ellen Koskoff, *Women and Music in Cross-Cultural Perspective* (New York: Greenwood Press, 1987).

23. Rara Modèl, Port-au-Prince, 1993.

24. Rara Baby Cool, Port-au-Prince, 1992.

25. Cooper, "Erotic Play in the Dancehall."

26. A fourth version of the song said "*Sez Desanm m'ap mande* [The 16th of December I'm asking]," referring to the date when Aristide was elected and insisting that he be brought back from exile.

27. Rara Modèl, Port-au-Prince, 1993.

28. Rara La Belle Fraîcheur de l'Anglade, 1992.

29. You can hear this song on track 14 of the CD that accompanies this book and also on track 4, *Caribbean Revels: Haitian Rara and Dominican Gaga,* Smithsonian Folkways SF 40402, 1991.

30. Cathy Maternowska, personal communication, July 1995.

31. Rara La Belle Fraîcheur de l'Anglade, 1992.

32. Judith Bettelheim, "Deconstructing the Mythologies: From Priestess to 'Red Hot Mama' in African and African American/Caribbean Performances" (paper presented at the Program of African Studies, Northwestern University, 17 February 1992).

33. Rose, *Black Noise,* 168.

34. Bettelheim, "Deconstructing the Mythologies."

35. Recorded in Andres Boca Chica in 1976 by Verna Gillis. On the recording *Caribbean Revels: Haitian Rara and Dominican Gaga.*

36. An exception is Paul Farmer, *Aids and Accusation: Haiti and the Geography of Blame* (Berkeley: University of California Press, 1992).

37. Although I targeted transvestitism in the Rara as an aspect of my research, I did not find the opportunity to interview any cross-dressers, because I could only identify them as transvestites when they cross-dressed during Holy Week, at which point they were too engaged in performance to talk. Cross-dressing is part of other West Indian festivals and is a topic that merits further research. See the Rara band comprised of men dressed as women in Dolores Yonker's photograph on the cover of the recording produced by *Caribbean Revels: Haitian Rara and Dominican Gaga.*

38. Anonymous, personal communication, Port-au-Prince, 1995.

39. Rara La Belle Fraîcheur de l'Anglade, Easter Sunday 1992.

40. Rara Relax Band, Port-au-Prince, 1993.

41. M. M. Bakhtin, *Rabelais and His World,* 1st Midland book ed. (Bloomington: Indiana University Press, 1984).

42. Mbembe, "The Banality of Power and the Aesthetics of Vulgarity in the Postcolony," 5 and 29.

43. Ibid., 12.

44. M. Trouillot, *Haiti, State against Nation.*

45. Scott, *Domination and the Arts of Resistance.*

46. M. Trouillot, *Haiti, State against Nation,* 218.

47. It read "Our Doc, who art in the National Palace." See Elizabeth Abbott, *Haiti: The Duvaliers and Their Legacy* (New York: McGraw-Hill, 1988).

48. General Cedras's household consumed in this way, according to journalist visitors, and the major Haitian hotels like the Plaza and Oloffson likewise feature "buffets" as a special weekly culinary event.

49. Mbembe, "The Banality of Power and the Aesthetics of Vulgarity in the Post-colony," 9.

50. Donald Cosentino, "Vodou Carnival," *Aperture* 126 (1992): 26.

51. Americas Watch, Physicians for Human Rights, National Coalition for Haitian Refugees, *Return to the Darkest Days: Human Rights in Haiti since the Coup* (New York, 1991).

CHAPTER 3. MYSTICAL WORK

1. D. Brown, "Garden in the Machine."

2. Maya Deren. *Divine Horsemen: The Living Gods of Haiti* (New York: Chelsea House, 1953), 62.

3. Elizabeth McAlister, "A Sorcerer's Bottle: The Art of Magic in Haiti," in *The Sacred Arts of Haitian Vodou,* ed. Donald Cosentino, 302–21 (Los Angeles: Fowler Museum of Cultural History, 1995). See Robert Farris Thompson, Joseph Cornet, and National Gallery of Art (U.S.), *The Four Moments of the Sun: Kongo Art in Two Worlds* (Washington, D.C.: National Gallery of Art, 1981). See also John M. Janzen, *Lemba, 1650–1930: A Drum of Affliction in Africa and the New World* (New York: Garland Pub., 1982), Luc de Heusch, "Kongo in Haiti: A New Approach to Religious Syncretism," *Man* 24 (1989), and Lilas Desquiron, *Racines du vodou* (Port-au-Prince: Henri Deschamps, 1992).

4. Simbi Ganga told me this: a *lwa* who "dances in the head" of Alex, a *sèvitè* at Soukri, the *lakou* (familial compound) devoted to "royal Kongo" traditions. "Kongo" is, like Rada, Ibo, and Nago, a "nation" within the religion. Simbi Ganga is a militarized (Haitian) "Kongo" *lwa* who comes as a commander in chief. Etymologically, *simbi* (*basimbi,* plural) is a word in KiKongo for an entire class of ancestral spirits, whose attributes and symbols remain relatively consistent in Haiti. The word *nganga* means "healer-priest" in KiKongo.

5. See Serge Larose, "The Meaning of Africa in Haitian Voodoo," in *In Symbols and Sentiments: Cross-Cultural Studies in Symbolism,* ed. I. M. Lewis (London: Academic Press, 1977).

6. Both men and women work outside the *lakou* in gardens, roads, and at other public sites, but it is the general association of work with the values of seriousness and family that concerns us here.

7. Abrahams, *The Man-of-Words in the West Indies,* 35.

8. See the twelfth definition of *work* in *Webster's New World Dictionary* (New York: Simon and Schuster, 1988), 1538.

9. For a lengthy discussion of a *travay maji* (magic work), see McAlister, "A Sorcerer's Bottle." For an extended discussion of mystical "work" and metaphors of labor exploitation, see Karen E. Richman, "They Will Remember Me in the House: The Pwen of Haitian Transnational Migration" (Ph.D. dissertation, University of Virginia, 1992).

10. This last comment comes from an interview with a member of Rara Brilliant Soleil, Léogâne, 26 March 1991.

11. In many other cultures, links are made between singing in public and prostitution. McLeod and Herdon, "The Bormliza."

12. Koskoff, *Women and Music in Cross-Cultural Perspective.*

13. In the north, they say *"Si kalfou pa bay, simitye pa'p manje,"* meaning "If the crossroads doesn't give, the cemetery doesn't eat."

14. To hear Chanpwèl music, listen to track 19b of Artists, *Rhythms of Rapture.*

15. Mr. Moris Moriset, interview, Léogâne, March 1991.

16. Papa Mondy Jean, interview, Port-au-Prince, March 1992.

17. Boukman Eksperyans, *"Kalfou Danjere"*(Mango, 1992).

18. *Vèvè* are intricate cornmeal drawings usually done at the base of *poto mitan* (centerposts) inside the *peristil.* Each *lwa* is associated with a particular symbolic design, recognizable to anyone familiar with the sign system. The *vèvè* are said by practitioners to invoke the *lwa,* to "call them" from below the earth or through the centerpost. Karen McCarthy Brown, "The Veve of Haitian Vodou: A Structural Analysis of Visual Imagery" (Ph.D. dissertation, Temple University, 1976).

19. Stones were shaped and used by Taino or Arawak peoples in their religious practice. Many present-day *oungan* and *manbo* have them in their altars and use them to perform spiritual work. I observed such a stone used in making a *wanga,* a work of magic, in a bottle. McAlister, "A Sorcerer's Bottle."

20. The counterclockwise direction of many Afro-Atlantic religious rituals has been noted by Robert Farris Thompson in lectures at Yale University. For evidence of counterclockwise rituals in southern U.S. ring-shouts, see Sterling Stuckey, *Slave Culture: Nationalist Theory and the Foundations of Black America* (New York: Oxford University Press, 1987).

21. Rara Chien Méchant, Léogâne, *Rara in Léogâne* (Port-au-Prince: Arc-en-Ciel Video, 1993).

22. Kouzen Azaka's costume—blue denim pants and shirt, red neck scarf, and straw hat—was adopted by Duvalier's *tonton makoutes,* plus sunglasses and guns. These *oungan* in the Rara were presumably referencing Azaka primarily, with an inevitable but secondary association with the paramilitary force.

23. *Oungan* Simeon, interview, Port-au-Prince, 30 March 1993.

24. Ibid.

25. Ibid.

26. Simeon showed it to me, and indeed the bottle was very hot. A heated stone seemed to be lashed to its midsection.

27. *Oungan* Simeon, interview, Port-au-Prince, 30 July 1993.

28. Jose M., interview, Union City, New Jersey, 17 December 1987. Cited in D. Brown, "Garden in the Machine," 376.

29. It is I who use the term "recently dead" as a spiritual category; it best describes the concept, which some have called "living dead" (which to me sounds sensationalist) and others call "the ancestors." In Kreyòl these entities are called "dead," but they must be distinguished as "recently dead" from the Gede and other *lwa* who were living people once and who moved into a more abstract cosmic level.

30. Wade Davis, *Passage of Darkness: The Ethnobiology of the Haitian Zombie* (Chapel Hill: University of North Carolina Press, 1988).

31. Deren, *Divine Horsemen,* 35.

32. Papa Mondy Jean, interview, Port-au-Prince, May 1993. Although Maya Deren wrote a slightly different account, this is the belief explained to me by people at the time and place of my field research.

33. Sephiz, interview, Port-au-Prince, June 1993.

34. Master Drummer Fritznel, interview, Léogâne, March 1991. Although spirit pos-

session is a central part of Afro-Haitian religion, it occurs infrequently in Rara. I have several times seen people possessed during Rara, but mostly within the "private," or "home" space of the *peristil* before the band emerges into public space.

35. Papa Mondy Jean, interview, Port-au-Prince, 5 March 1993.

36. In 1993 it cost thirty Haitian dollars for a skull, roughly twelve U.S. dollars for a person without a reciprocal relationship with cemetery workers. Ibid.

37. Philip D. Curtin, *The Atlantic Slave Trade: A Census* (Madison: University of Wisconsin Press, 1969).

38. The word *fetish* comes from the Portuguese who colonized the Bakongo people. What the Bakongo called *minkisi* the Portuguese called *fetico*. Later the word was used a great deal by nineteenth-century anthropologists and subsequently by psychoanalysts and Marxian economists. Wyatt MacGaffey, "Fetishism Revisited: Kongo Nkisi in Sociological Perspective," *Africa* 47, no. 2 (1977): 172.

39. Thompson, Cornet, and National Gallery of Art (U.S.), *The Four Moments of the Sun*, 37.

40. Ibid. See also MacGaffey, "Fetishism Revisited," 173.

41. For an extended discussion of the Kongo sources of *zonbi* practices, see McAlister, "A Sorcerer's Bottle."

42. *Oungan* Simeon, interview, Port-au-Prince, 30 July 1993.

43. Papa Dieupè, interview, Artibonite, Easter Sunday 1993.

44. *Bòkò* St. Jean, interview, Port-au-Prince, 1988.

45. St. Jean, interview, Port-au-Prince, October 1988.

46. This is a common song that is sung in the *peristil* and in Rara. It was borrowed by Boukan Ginen for their Carnival song in 1995 called *"Rev Nou."*

47. For an excellent work on the ethos of "religion" versus sorcery in Haiti, see Larose, "The Meaning of Africa in Haitian Voodoo."

48. Boukman Eksperyans, *"Kalfou Danjere."*

49. For this insight about the middle passage, I thank and acknowledge Sean Harvey, e-mail communication, 22 March 2001.

50. Rene Depestre, "Change," *Violence* 2, no. 9 (Paris: Seiul, 1971). While foreigners have used "the zombie" as a way to exoticize the "dark, malevolent" aspects of Haiti, Haitian intellectuals have often used the image of the *zonbi* as a metaphor for the existential dilemmas of life under foreign-backed postcolonial dictatorships. Laënnec Hurbon, *Culture et dictature en Haïti: L'imaginaire sous contrôle* (Paris: L'Harmattan, 1979). See also Franketienne, *Dezafi* (Port-au-Prince, 1974) and Rene Depestre, *The Festival of the Greasy Pole* (Virginia: University of Virginia Press, 1990), originally published as *Le Mat de Cocagne* (Paris: Editions Gallimard, 1979).

51. Richman, "They Will Remember Me in the House," 159.

52. President Gerald of Etoile Salomon, interview, Port-au-Prince, April 1992.

53. Ibid.

CHAPTER 4. RARA AND "THE JEW"

1. This chapter is revised from Elizabeth McAlister, "'The Jew' in the Haitian Imagination: Pre-Modern Anti-Judaism in the Postmodern Caribbean," in *Black Zion: African American Religious Encounters with Judaism,* ed. Yvonne Chireau and Nathaniel Deutsch, 203–27 (New York: Oxford University Press, 2000). Christendom also links the Jews, the devil, and the peoples of the First Nations in New Spain and the United States.

See Fernando Cervantes, *The Devil in the New World: The Impact of Diabolism in New Spain* (New Haven: Yale University Press, 1994).

2. This is the time of Jesus' death noted in scripture.

3. Thérèse Roumer, interview, Petionville, 16 February 1993.

4. George Fouron, personal communication, New Haven, Conn., November 1997.

5. Thérèse Roumer, interview, Petionville, 16 February 1993.

6. W. B. Seabrook, *The Magic Island* (New York: Harcourt Brace and Company, 1929), 270–72. For work on American paternalistic writing on Haiti, see J. Michael Dash, *Haiti and the United States: National Stereotypes and the Literary Imagination,* 2d ed. (New York: St. Martin's Press, 1988).

7. See, for example, Muriel Thayer Painter, Edward H. Spicer, and Wilma Kaemlein, eds., *With Good Heart: Yaqui Beliefs and Ceremonies in Pascua Village* (Tucson: University of Arizona Press, 1986), and James S. Griffith, *Beliefs and Holy Places: A Spiritual Geography of the Primeria Alta* (Tucson: University of Arizona Press, 1992), 95.

8. See Marilyn Ekdahl Ravicz, *Early Colonial Religious Drama in Mexico: From Tzompantli to Golgotha* (Washington, D.C.: Catholic University of America Press, 1970). Richard Trexler, "We Think, They Act: Missionary Theatre in Sixteenth-Century New Spain," in *Understanding Popular Culture: Europe from the Middle Ages to the Nineteenth Century,* ed. Steven L. Kaplan (New York: Mouton, 1984).

9. Maccoby points out the consistent use of Judas by Christian myth as a symbol for all Jews. "Of all Jesus' twelve disciples, the one whom the Gospel story singles out as traitor bears the name of the Jewish people." Hyam Maccoby, *Judas Iscariot and the Myth of Jewish Evil* (New York: Free Press, 1992).

10. Sander Gilman, *The Jew's Body* (New York: Routledge, 1991), 18.

11. Joshua Trachtenberg, *The Devil and the Jews: The Medieval Conception of the Jew and Its Relation to Modern Antisemitism,* 2d paperback ed. (Philadelphia: Jewish Publication Society of America, 1983), 20.

12. Cecil Roth, *A History of the Marranos* (Philadelphia: Jewish Publication Society of America, 1932). *Anusim,* Hebrew for "forced ones," has now replaced the English "Crypto-Jews" or the Spanish *conversos* (converted Jews) and the more derogatory *marranos* (swine) in Jewish studies literature. See also David M. Gitlitz, *Secrecy and Deceit: The Religion of the Crypto-Jews* (Philadelphia: The Jewish Publication Society, 1996). For a critical historiography of Jews in the colonial Atlantic, see Jonathan Schorsch, "American Jewish Historians, Colonial Jews and Blacks, and the Limits of Wissenschaft: A Critical Review," *Jewish Social Studies* 6, no. 2 (2000).

13. Roth, *A History of the Marranos.*

14. Painter, Spicer, and Kaemlein, *With Good Heart,* 352.

15. Trachtenberg, *The Devil and the Jews,* 22.

16. Trexler, "We Think, They Act."

17. For a discussion of the conflation of British, Protestant, and civilized into one identity against Native American "heathens," see James Axtell, *The Invasion Within: The Contest of Cultures in Colonial North America* (New York: Oxford University Press, 1996).

18. See Roth, *A History of the Marranos.* The anti-Judaism taught by the Catholic clergy in Haiti bears the characteristics of a classically premodern Jew-hatred centering on the betrayal of Judas. In this logic, Jews are primarily polluters and traitors; there is little reference to the modern anti-Semitic tropes of a Jewish conspiracy of exploitation hinging on issues of capital or usury. See the chapter "From Anti-Judaism to Anti-

Semitism," in Gavin I. Langmuir, *History, Religion, and Antisemitism* (Berkeley: University of California Press, 1990), 275–305.

19. On the Inquisition and the Jews in Mexico, see Seymour B. Liebman, *The Jews in New Spain: Faith, Flame, and the Inquisition* (Coral Gables, Fla.: University of Miami Press, 1970).

20. Trachtenberg, *The Devil and the Jews*, 26.

21. See Marc Shell, "Marranos (Pigs), or from Coexistence to Toleration," *Critical Inquiry* 11, no. 2 (1991).

22. Carolyn E. Fick, *The Making of Haiti: The Saint Domingue Revolution from Below* (Knoxville: University of Tennessee Press, 1990), 278.

23. George Breathett, *The Catholic Church in Haiti (1704–1785): Selected Letters, Memoirs, and Documents* (Salisbury, N.C.: Documentation Publications, 1982), 4.

24. Anne Greene, *The Catholic Church in Haiti: Political and Social Change* (East Lansing: Michigan State University Press, 1993), 76.

25. G. Debien, "La Christianisation des esclaves des Antilles françaises aux xviie et xviiie siècles," *Revue d'histoire de l'Amérique française* 21 (1967): 99–113.

26. Ephesians 6:5.

27. See Trachtenberg, *The Devil and the Jews*.

28. Joan Dayan, *Haiti, History, and the Gods* (Berkeley: University of California Press, 1995), 252.

29. Ibid., 253.

30. Moreau de Saint Mery, *Description topographique, physique, civile, politique et historique de la partie française de l'île S. Dominque*, 55.

31. Dayan, *Haiti, History, and the Gods*, 252.

32. Ibid.

33. Cited in Laënnec Hurbon, *Dieu dans le vodou haitien* (Paris: Payot, 1972), 21. My translation.

34. D. Brown, "Garden in the Machine," 16.

35. Stallybrass and White, *The Politics and Poetics of Transgression*, 3.

36. The band Ya Seizi can be heard playing in Papa Dieupè's compound on track 11 of the CD that accompanies this book.

37. Another Rara tradition that is a form of spiritual work is called *Chay Rara* (burden of the Rara). In this kind of Rara, one man is chosen to "carry the mystical weight of the Rara." At certain crossroads, he is beaten with the whip. He is said to be heavily protected and charged with spiritual energy and feels nothing. This tradition is found in the Artibonite region and may have a symbolic connection to Jesus, or to *zonbi*, or to both. This practice of the Rara band is not a party occasion at all, but rather is using the Rara as an intense form of spiritual work.

38. Papa Mondy Jean, interview, Port-au-Prince, April 1992.

39. A few Rara presidents told me that there was a game, a noisemaker, that the Jews held in their hands and spun at the Crucifixion. This made a noise that came to be called "Rara." Papa Telemarque, interview, Darbonne, Léogâne, 6 March 1993. One notices a possible, if obscure, connection with the noisemakers of Purim.

40. Rara costumes are elaborately sequined in parts of Haiti. President Simeon, interview, Port-au-Prince, 30 July 1993.

41. President Simeon, interview, Port-au-Prince, 20 March 1993.

42. President Simeon, interview, Port-au-Prince, 30 July 1993.

43. Hurbon, *Culture et dictature en Haïti*, 43.

44. Alfred Métraux, *Voodoo in Haiti* (New York: Oxford University Press, 1959), 326.

45. Papa Dieupè, interview, Artibonite, Easter Sunday 1993.

46. McAlister, "A Sorcerer's Bottle."

47. A similar symbolics works in the Afro-Cuban religion Lukumi. Unbaptized ritual objects and "working" charms are called *judeo* (Jewish).

48. Mayard of Rara Mande Gran Moun, interview, Léogâne, 20 March 1993. David H. Brown reports an interesting parallel in the Kongo-derived Palo Monte practices in Cuba. As he constructs a *prenda,* a "working" object, on Good Friday, a Mayombero comments to Brown, "On the day of the week, the week of the year when they are quiet— Good Friday—we are doing our thing." Says Brown, "As spiritual opposites of Christ and the Saints of Olofi and the orichas, they are 'driving nails' on the day of the Crucifixion." D. Brown, "Garden in the Machine," 375.

49. See Hurbon, *Culture et dictature en Haïti,* 133.

50. Liebman, *The Jews in New Spain,* 31.

51. Clarence Henry Haring, *The Spanish Empire in America,* 1st Harbinger Books ed. (New York: Harcourt Brace and World, 1963), 29. Cited in Liebman, *The Jews in New Spain,* 42.

52. Liebman, *The Jews in New Spain,* 42.

53. Zvi Loker, "Were There Jewish Communities in Saint Domingue (Haiti)?," *Jewish Social Studies* 45, no. 2 (1983).

54. Ibid., 137.

55. Bernard Glassman, *Anti-Semitic Stereotypes without Jews: Images of the Jews in England, 1290–1700* (Detroit: Wayne State Press, 1975), 25.

CHAPTER 5. RARA AS POPULAR ARMY

1. You can hear the salute in the chapter epigraph on track 10 of the CD that accompanies this book.

2. Contemporary grassroots peasant organizations include Tèt Kole (Heads Together) founded in 1986, M.P.P. (Peasant Movement of Papay) founded in the 1970s, and Soley Leve (The Sun Is Rising) founded in 1990. These organizations represent powerful blocs on the national stage and regularly make headlines in the Haitian press.

3. Moreau de Saint Mery, *Description topographique, physique, civile, politique et historique de la partie française de l'île S. Dominque.*

4. Dolores Yonker, "Rara: A Lenten Festival," *Bulletin du Bureau National D'Ethnologie* 2 (1985).

5. D. Brown, "Garden in the Machine," 58.

6. Roman, "Recherche Sur Un Rara Appele La Meprise a L'arcahaie (Merlotte)."

7. Rénald Clerismé, "Organization: For Us, It Is Our Lives," *Crossroads: Contemporary Political Analysis and Left Dialogue* 47 (1995). See also Emmanuel Paul, "Folklore Du Militarism," *Optique* 6 (1954): 24–27. Cited in Y.-M. David Yih, "Music and Dance of Haitian Vodou: Diversity and Unity in Regional Repertoires" (Ph.D. dissertation, Wesleyan University, 1995), 121.

8. Michel S. Laguerre, *Les Associations traditionelles de travail dans la paysannerie haitienne* (Port-au-Prince: N.p., 1975), 4. Cited in Beauvoir and Dominique, "Savalou E," 105; my translation. Ranks in these hierarchies can include Prezidan Konsey, Vis Prezidan, Gouvene Pep, Gouvene Laplas, Dirije Laplas, Jeneral Laplas, Adjwen Laplas, Jeneral Dekouvet, Dirije, Ren Bayonet, Ren Drapo, Ren Dirije, Ren Kobey, and then Sekrete, Trezorye, Minis Lage, Minis de Finans, and Prezidan ak Ren Chita. Beauvoir and Dominique, "Savalou E," 106.

9. Paul Moral, *Le Paysan haitien* (Paris, 1961), 190. Cited in Beauvoir and Dominique, "Savalou E," 100. Emphasis added.

10. Beauvoir and Dominique, "Savalou E," 110.

11. In contrast, as in the *sosyete travay,* a member may possess an honorific title without participating in the band at all; in this case the member may be a financial supporter or a landowner who wishes to have a rank but no duties. This sometimes meets the resentment of other band members, who may have lowlier titles and perform more of the work of the band.

12. President of Mande Gran Moun, interview, March 1993.

13. Michel S. Laguerre, *Voodoo and Politics in Haiti* (New York: St. Martin's Press, 1989), 122. Many *lwa* are contemporarily depicted as military figures, including the entire "line" of Ogou, the "god of war." Not violent per se, these spirits impart military knowledge in general, including self-control, discipline, and fearlessness. For a feminist perspective on Ogou, see Karen McCarthy Brown, "Why Women Need the War God," in *Women's Spirit Bonding,* ed. Janet Kalven and Mary I. Buckley (New York: Pilgrim Press, 1984), and Karen McCarthy Brown, "Systematic Remembering, Systematic Forgetting: Ogou in Haiti," in *Africa's Ogun,* ed. Sandra T. Barnes (Bloomington: Indiana University Press, 1989).

14. Gage Averill and Yuen Ming David Yih, "Militarism in Haitian Music," in *The African Diaspora: A Musical Perspective,* ed. Ingrid Monson (New York: Garland, 2000).

15. Beauvoir and Dominique, "Savalou E,"95.

16. M. Trouillot, *Haiti, State against Nation,* 95.

17. Constantin Dumerve, "Musique et danse vaudouesques," *Les Griots* 3, no. 3. Cited in Averill and Yih, "Militarism in Haitian Music."

18. Yih, "Music and Dance of Haitian Vodou," 132.

19. Cited in Jean Fouchard, *The Haitian Maroons* (New York: Blyden Press, 1981), 346.

20. For this brief outline I owe thanks to my colleague at Yale, Rénald Clerismé, who shared with me his knowledge of traditional culture history and his experience with peasant organizations. This synopsis is borrowed from his article, Clerismé, "Organization," 8.

21. Verna Gillis, "Rara in Haiti, Gaga in the Dominican Republic," liner notes to the album of the same name, Folkways Records Album No. FE 4531, 1978, p. 4.

22. At the present writing, the public living-room area in the headquarters of the U.S. embassy marine guard displays a series of photographs of Americans leading captive Cacos out of the bush, thus visually reinscribing for newly arrived marines their roles as dominators of the Haitian popular classes. I saw the photos at one of their Friday "open-house" gatherings for expatriate Americans in 1993, before the 1995 U.S. inter-vasion.

23. Georges Corvington, personal communication, Port-au-Prince, 1993. Also see Tselos, "Threads of Reflection," note 4.

24. M. Trouillot, *Haiti, State against Nation,* 179. For theories on maximizing prestige, see Edmund Leach, *Political Systems in Highland Burma* (Cambridge: Harvard University Press, 1954).

25. Michel-Rolph Trouillot, personal communication, 1991.

26. Karin Barber, "How Man Makes God in West Africa: Yoruba Attitudes toward the Orisha," *Africa* 51, no. 3 (1981): 724.

27. Kris L. Hardin, *The Aesthetics of Action: Continuity and Change in a West African Town* (Washington, D.C.: Smithsonian Institution Press, 1993), 213.

28. Barber, "How Man Makes God in West Africa," 728.

29. La Belle Fraîcheur de l'Anglade, Easter 1992.

30. Recorded 11 April 1993, Verettes. Another song by Ya Seizi is on a recording compiled by this author; see Artists, *Rhythms of Rapture.*

31. You can hear this on track 12 of the CD that accompanies this book. Bann Bourgeois de la Lwa. Recorded 27 March 1993, Route Gonaives north of Saint Marc near Beaufort.

32. Mande Gran Moun, Léogâne, 1993. *Kolonèl* of Mande Gran Moun, interview, Léogâne, March 1993.

33. Yonker, "Haiti after the Fall."

34. President Gerard of Rara Etoile Salomon, interview, Port-au-Prince, 7 April 1992.

35. Alexis, "Les Danses Rara," 60.

36. Videotapes of Rara in Léogâne circulate throughout New York City and Miami, giving Haitians in those two U.S. cities the annual opportunity to hear the songs. Léogâne is the town best known for Rara in Haiti; each band sponsors a feast, called *cav,* during Lent and invites others. Then on Easter weekend bands all over the south converge between Carrefour du Fort and Léogâne for competition. Many Port-au-Prince youth and returning diaspora members go to Léogâne specially for Rara; it has become one of the cyclical tourist spots for the mobile Port-au-Prince dweller. The Rara scene in Léogâne is complex and populous and deserves a monograph on its own in the future. To hear Léogâne-style music, listen to track 18 of the CD that accompanies this book.

37. Dr. McCleary, personal communication, Hôpital St. Croix, Léogâne, 27 March 1991.

38. M. Alphonse, drummer, personal communication, Bel Air, Port-au-Prince, 18 March 1991.

39. Yih, "Music and Dance of Haitian Vodou," 473.

40. Abrahams, *The Man-of-Words in the West Indies,* xvi.

41. Cited in ibid. See also Nunley and Bettelheim, *Caribbean Festival Arts.*

42. Larry Bannock, chief of the Goldenstar Hunters, interview, New Orleans, Mardi Gras 1990.

43. General Kanep of Rara La Belle Fraîcheur de l'Anglade, interview, March 1992.

44. Courtain, "Mémoire sommaire sur les préteudues pratiques magiques et empoisonnements prouvés au proces instruit et jugé au Cap contre plusieurs negres et negresses dont le chef, F. Macandal, a été condamné au feu et executé le 20 janvier 1758." Presented by Franklin Midy, *Chemins critiques* 1, no. 1 (1989): 135–42. Cited in Yih, "Music and Dance of Haitian Vodou," 86.

45. President of Rara Etoile Salomon, interview, Port-au-Prince, 7 April 1992.

46. Moreau de Saint Mery, *Description topographique, physique, civile, politique et historique de la partie française de l'île S. Dominque.*

47. Beaufort schoolteacher, interview, 27 March 1993.

48. Barber, "How Man Makes God in West Africa," 729.

49. Similyen family, interview, Léogâne, 26 March 1991.

50. President of Rara Etoile Salomon, interview, Port-au-Prince, 7 April 1992.

51. Ernst Mirville, *Considerations ethno-psychoanalytiques sur le carnival haitien* (Port-au-Prince: Collection Coucouille, 1978), 80.

52. Wilfred, interview, Rue Xaragua, April 1993.

53. Wade Davis, *The Serpent and the Rainbow* (New York: Simon and Schuster, 1985), 258.

54. Beauvoir and Dominique, "Savalou E," 110.

55. Father Jean-Yves Urfie, editor of Newspaper *Libète,* personal communication, Pont-Sonde, April 1993.

56. President of Rara Saint Rose, interview, February 1993.
57. Master Drummer for Mande Gran Moun, interview, Léogâne, 25 March 1993.

CHAPTER 6. VOICES UNDER DOMINATION

1. Americas Watch, *Return to the Darkest Days.*
2. Cesareo and Rubenstein, "Prospectus for a Workshop."
3. Scott, *Domination and the Arts of Resistance,* 137.
4. Mbembe, "The Banality of Power," 3.
5. Scott, *Domination and the Arts of Resistance,* 136.
6. M. Trouillot, *Haiti, State against Nation,* 179.
7. Ibid., 173–76.
8. Fraph was meant to become a right-wing party alternative to Jean-Bertrand Aristide's party, and as such was given seed money by the United States Central Intelligence Agency. The group quickly became involved in cocaine trafficking, and its *ti nèg* foot soldiers—high on drugs and rich in dollars—carried out an unprecedented campaign of gang rape against poor women and children, often in front of family members, atrocities that will undoubtedly affect Haitian society for generations. See Human Rights Watch/Americas, "Rape in Haiti," and Terry Rey, "Junta, Rape, and Religion in Haiti, 1993–1994," *Journal of Feminist Studies in Religion* 15, no. 2 (1999).
9. Scott, *Domination and the Arts of Resistance,* 51.
10. Ibid., 4.
11. "Gran Bwa" by Boukman Eksperyans, Carnival 1992 (unreleased).
12. The album is *Jazz des Jeunes,* Ibo ILP 113. You can hear a related song, with the refrain "Where are the people," on track 21 of the CD that accompanies this book.
13. Richard Morse, interview, Port-au-Prince, April 1992.
14. Karen McCarthy Brown, "Alourdes: A Case Study of Moral Leadership in Haitian Voudou," in *Saints and Virtues,* ed. John Stratton Hawley (Berkeley: University of California Press, 1987), 151.
15. See McAlister, "A Sorcerer's Bottle."
16. Henry Louis Gates, *The Signifying Monkey: A Theory of Afro-American Literary Criticism* (New York: Oxford University Press, 1988), 69.
17. Karen E. Richman, "'With Many Hands, the Burden Isn't Heavy': Creole Proverbs and Political Rhetoric in Haiti's Presidential Elections," *Folklore Forum* 12, no. 1/2 (1990): 117–18.
18. Ibid. See also Richman's other works on Haitian political discourse, including "'A Lavalas at Home/a Lavalas for Home': Inflections of Transnationalism in the Discourse of Haitian President Aristide," in *Towards a Transnational Perspective on Migration: Race, Class, Ethnicity, and Nationalism Reconsidered,* ed. Nina Glick Schiller, Linda G. Basch, and Cristina Szanton Blanc (New York: New York Academy of Sciences, 1992).
19. C. Toulabor, "Jeu de mots, jeux de vilain. Lexique de la derision politique au Togo," *Politique Africaine* 3 (1981). Cited in Mbembe, "The Banality of Power and the Aesthetics of Vulgarity in the Postcolony," 6.
20. See Mbembe, "The Banality of Power and the Aesthetics of Vulgarity in the Postcolony."
21. Scott, *Domination and the Arts of Resistance,* 157.
22. Richard A. Morse, personal communication, Port-au-Prince, 1993.
23. Yih, "Music and Dance of Haitian Vodou," 474–75.

24. Ibid., 447.

25. Averill, *A Day for the Hunter, a Day for the Prey,* 32.

26. The statistic is from the National Coalition for Haitian Refugees, *Haiti, Darkness Remains: Critique of the State Department's Profile of Asylum Claims and Country Conditions* (New York: Americas Watch, 1995).

27. Emperor Soulouque, who ruled Haiti from 1847 to 1859, created a sort of paramilitary force called the Zenglens. Perhaps this is the source of the word, which literally means "shards of glass."

28. Human Rights Watch/Americas, "Security Compromised."

29. Anonymous leader, interview, Port-au-Prince, 22 March 1991.

30. Scott, *Domination and the Arts of Resistance,* 65.

31. David Kertzer, *Ritual, Politics, and Power* (New Haven: Yale University Press, 1988), 180.

32. Bernice Johnson Reagon, interview with Bill Moyers, Public Broadcasting System, 1989.

33. Seabrook, *The Magic Island,* 273.

34. Ibid., 276. Also see Melville J. Herskovits, *The Myth of the Negro Past* (Boston: Beacon Press, 1958).

35. USIS talk at USAID, Port-au-Prince, 1989.

CHAPTER 7. RARA IN NEW YORK CITY

1. Afro-Haitian religious rituals have been (and are) performed by Haitians in New York, but only in very private circles. See Karen McCarthy Brown, *Mama Lola.*

2. Basch, Glick Schiller, and Szanton Blanc, *Nations Unbound,* 7. See also Glick Schiller, Basch, and Szanton Blanc, *Towards a Transnational Perspective on Migration.*

3. Anderson, interview, Léogâne, 26 March 1991. Tree branches were carried by anti-Duvalier demonstrators as a visual pun on their intent to uproot him from Haitian soil.

4. See Benedict R. Anderson, *Imagined Communities: Reflections on the Origin and Spread of Nationalism,* rev. ed. (London: Verso, 1983).

5. Immanuel Maurice Wallerstein, *The Modern World-System* (New York: Academic Press, 1974), 229–31.

6. June Nash, "The Impact of the Changing International Division of Labor on Different Sectors of the Labor Force," in *Women, Men, and the International Division of Labor,* ed. June Nash and Patricia Fernandez-Kelly (Albany: SUNY Press, 1983). Also see Roy Bryce-Laporte, *Sourcebook on the New Immigrants* (New Jersey: Transaction Books, 1980).

7. Basch, Glick Schiller, and Szanton Blanc, *Nations Unbound,* 12.

8. See Richman, "They Will Remember Me in the House."

9. Stuart Hall, *Policing the Crisis: Mugging, the State, and Law and Order* (New York: Holmes and Meier, 1978), 381.

10. United States racial codes, also in process, are different from North to South: this work focuses on the particularities of New York in the 1990s.

11. The history of these groups is outside the scope of this discussion, but Gage Averill has outlined it well in Gage Averill, "'Se Kreyòl Nou Ye'/'We're Creole': Musical Discourse on Haitian Identities," in *Music and Black Ethnicity: The Caribbean and South America,* ed. Gerard Behague (New Jersey: Transaction Press, 1994).

12. These pioneers of *rasin* music included Sanba Zawo, Sanbaje, Azouke (Gregory

Sanon), Aiyzan (Harry Sanon), Godo (Patrick Pascale), Aboudja (Ronald Derencourt), Chiko (Yves Boyer), Tido (Wilfred Laveaud), Bonga (Gaston), Lòlò (Theodore Beaubrun, Jr.), and many others. Women in the movement include Manze (Mimerose Beaubrun) and Sò An (Annette August).

13. This song was chosen in 1989 by filmmaker Jonathan Demme for a compilation album of Haitian music on a major United States label: *Konbit: Burning Rhythms of Haiti,* A&M 75021–5281–2 (1989). You can hear a song of Foula called "Sovè" on *Global Gatherings: Authentic Music from Joyous Festivals around the World,* Roslyn, N.Y.: Ellipsis Arts, CD 3234.

14. Abrahams, *The Man-of-Words in the West Indies.*

15. Fito Vivien, interview, Brooklyn, 3 March 1991.

16. See Elizabeth McAlister, "Rara: Haitians Make Some Noise in Brooklyn," *The Beat Magazine* (summer 1991).

17. Claude Lévi-Strauss, *The Savage Mind* (Chicago: University of Chicago Press, 1966). Cited in Dick Hebdige, *Subculture, the Meaning of Style* (London: Methuen, 1979), 177.

18. Charles, "A Transnational Dialectic of Race, Class, and Ethnicity," 96.

19. Randal L. Hepner, "Chanting Down Babylon in the Belly of the Beast: The Rastafari Movement in Metropolitan U.S.A.," in *Chanting Down Babylon: A Rastafari Reader,* ed. Samuel Murrell (Philadelphia: Temple University Press).

20. Hebdige, *Subculture, the Meaning of Style,* 44–45.

21. For standard works on Rastafari in Jamaica, see Leonard E. Barrett, *The Rastafarians: Sounds of Cultural Dissonance,* rev. and updated ed. (Boston: Beacon Press, 1988). See also Barry Chevannes, *Rastafari: Roots and Ideology,* Utopianism and Communitarianism series (Syracuse, N.Y.: Syracuse University Press, 1995), and Horace Campbell, *Rasta and Resistance: From Marcus Garvey to Walter Rodney,* 1st American ed. (Trenton, N.J.: Africa World Press, 1987).

22. See Velma Pollard, "Dread Talk: The Speech of the Rastafarians in Jamaica," *Caribbean Quarterly* 26, no. 4, and Velma Pollard, "The Social History of Dread Talk," *Caribbean Quarterly* 28, no. 4.

23. *Sanba* Wowo, interview, New York, July 1995.

24. This information comes from interviews with Sanba Yanba Ye, Sanba Djames, and Sanba Wowo, New York City, 1993. For an informative discussion of the origin of dreadlocks among Jamaican Rastafarians, see Barry Chevannes, "The Origins of the Dreadlock," in *Institute of Social Studies* (The Hague: N.p., 1989).

25. See Paul Gilroy, *'There Ain't No Black in the Union Jack': The Cultural Politics of Race and Nation* (London: Routledge, 1992), 186.

26. Gerard Michel quoted in *Libète,* no. 138, 17 May 1995, p. 6.

27. DJ Frankie, interview, Bronx, 2000. Bigga Haitian, a.k.a. Charles Dorismond, is the son of Andre Dorismond, lead vocalist with the famous Webert Sico Group. Bigga Haitian is also the brother of Patrick Dorismond, who was tragically slain by police in Brooklyn in the notorious police brutality event of 2000. See Bigga Haitian, *I Am Back,* A Royal Productions/Jomino/Roots International, 1997.

28. King Posse, "Retounen" (Comeback), track on *Putomayo Presents: Carnival 2001,* New York: Putomayo Recordings, 2001; Original Rap Staff, *Kè Pò Pòz,* France: Declic AMCD 77120, 1996. Also see Various artists, *Haiti Rap and Ragga: Match la Red,* France: Declic Communications 319–2, 1994, and Black Leaders, *Tout Moun Jwen,* Krazy Staff Productions/Cross Over Records KS-BL001, 1997.

29. Various artists, *Bouyon Rasin: First International Haitian Roots Music Festival,* notes by Claus Schreiner and Gage Averill, Global Beat Records 9601, 1996; Wyclef Jean,

The Eclectic: 2 Sides II a Book, Sony Columbia, 2000; and Wyclef Jean, *Wyclef Jean Presents the Carnival,* Sony Columbia, 1997. *Mizik rasin,* ragga, and hip-hop artists are also in conversation, across national boundaries. For example, Boukman Eksperyans recorded most of their 1998 album, *Revolution,* in The Refugee Camp, The Fugees's original basement recording studio, in a home that Wyclef Jean owns. That album features Jerry du Plexis, The Fugees writer and bass player.

30. Jocelyne Guilbault, "On Interpreting Popular Music: Zouk in the West Indies," in *Caribbean Popular Culture,* ed. John A. Lent (Bowling Green, Ohio: Bowling Green State University Press, 1990), 93. See also Jocelyne Guilbault, *Zouk: World Music in the West Indies* (Chicago: University of Chicago Press, 1993).

31. Stuart Hall, "What Is This 'Black' in Black Popular Culture?" in *Black Popular Culture,* ed. Gina Dent (Seattle: Bay Press, 1992), 22.

32. E. J. Hobsbawm and T. O. Ranger, *The Invention of Tradition* (Cambridge: Cambridge University Press, 1983), 1.

33. D. Brown, "Garden in the Machine," 93.

34. Ulf Hannerz, "Cities, Culture and Center-Periphery Relationships" (paper presented at the American Anthropological Association, Atlanta, 1994). Hannerz speaks of Sansone's work on young Black Surinamese who move from Paramibo to the old metropole of Amsterdam, become Rasta, trade goods for *ganja* with other Rastas in London, and look to Kingston as a cultural center. Livio Sansone, "From Creole to Black: Leisure Time, Style and the New Ethnicity of Lower-Class Young Blacks of Surinamese Origin in Amsterdam: 1975–1991," unpublished manuscript, 1991.

35. For a literature review on ethnic identity, see Joane Nagel, "Constructing Ethnicity: Creating and Recreating Ethnic Identity and Culture," *Social Problems* 41, no. 1 (1994).

36. Fredrik Barth and Universitetet i Bergen, *Ethnic Groups and Boundaries: The Social Organization of Culture Difference* (Prospect Heights, Ill.: Waveland Press, 1998).

37. Averill, "'Se Kreyòl Nou Ye'/'We're Creole,'" 178.

38. For a recapitulation of her extensive research, see chapter 6 of Basch, Glick Schiller, and Szanton Blanc, *Nations Unbound,* 201–7.

39. As of 1980, the U.S. Bureau of the Census reported 92,400 Haitian-born persons in the United States, whereas the newspaper *Haiti Obsevateur* claimed an estimate of 400,000 in New York, based on circulation statistics of the paper. In Lois Wilcken, "Vodou Music among Haitian Living in New York" (master's thesis, Hunter College, 1986), 26.

40. Michel S. Laguerre, *American Odyssey: Haitians in New York City* (Ithaca, N.Y.: Cornell University Press, 1984), 30.

41. Carolle Charles, "Distinct Meanings of Blackness: Haitian Migrants in New York City," *Cimarron* 2, no. 3 (1990): 130.

42. Charles, "A Transnational Dialectic of Race, Class, and Ethnicity."

43. Nina Glick Schiller, "All in the Same Boat? Unity and Diversity in Haitian Organizing in New York," in *Caribbean Life in New York City: Sociocultural Dimensions,* ed. Constance Sutton and Elsa Chaney (New York: Center for Migration Studies, 1987), 193.

44. AIDS became known in Haitian circles as *les quatres H's:* Homosexuals, Hemophiliacs, Heroin addicts, and Haitians. For further analysis of the link between AIDS and Haiti, see Farmer, *Aids and Accusation.*

45. *Haiti Progrès* (April 25–May 1) 1990, cited in Richman, "'A Lavalas at Home/a Lavalas for Home.'"

46. Richman, "'A Lavalas at Home/a Lavalas for Home,'" 193.

47. Stuart Hall, Tony Jefferson, and University of Birmingham Center for Contemporary Cultural Studies, *Resistance through Rituals: Youth Subcultures in Post-War Britain* (London: Hutchinson, 1976).

48. Charles, "A Transnational Dialectic of Race, Class, and Ethnicity." David H. Brown reports that Haitians who fled to Cuba after the independence revolution also pretended to a socially superior rank by calling themselves "French." D. Brown, "Garden in the Machine," 33.

49. Charles, "A Transnational Dialectic of Race, Class, and Ethnicity," 243–44.

50. Ibid., 252–53.

51. Paul Gilroy, "It's a Family Affair," in *Black Popular Culture,* ed. Gina Dent (Seattle: Bay Press, 1995), 306.

52. Sanba James, interview, Brooklyn, 7 December 1991.

53. Hall, Jefferson, and University of Birmingham, *Resistance through Rituals,* 29–39.

54. Sanba Yanba, interview, New York, 1992.

APPENDIX: CHRONOLOGY OF POLITICAL EVENTS, 1990–1995

1. Much of the information about political events is derived from the chronology in Georges A. Fauriol, ed., *Haitian Frustrations: Dilemmas for U.S. Policy: A Report of the CSIS Americas Program* (Washington, D.C.: Center for Strategic and International Studies, 1995).

2. Recorded on Boukman Eksperyans, *Kanaval Rasin-Vodou Adjae,* Converge Ent/ Sumthing Distribution, 2000.

3. Track 4, Koudjay Banbou Nwa, *Sanba M'Dogwe,* CDP&P-113, n.d.

4. Track 5, Boukan Ginen, *Jou A Rive,* Danbury, Conn.: Xenophile 4024, 1995.

5. On RAM, *Aibobo,* Cave Wall Records, 1995.

6. Title track of Boukman Eksperyans, *Kalfou Danjere,* Mango 162–539 927-2, 1992.

7. This song is track 8 of *Rhythms of Rapture.*

8. On Boukman Eksperyans, *Libète Pran Pou Pran'l/Freedom Let's Grab It,* Mango 162–539946-2, 1995.

9. On RAM, *Aibobo.*

10. On Boukman Eksperyans, *Revolution,* Tuff Gong Records, 1998.

11. See Kanpèch, *Pale Yo,* Coconut Grove Recording Co., Inc., CGRC 8196-2, 1996.

12. Boukman Eksperyans, *Revolution.*

13. These songs can be heard on the Carnival issue I recorded and produced with Holly Nicolas for National Public Radio's Afropop Worldwide. "Carnival Update," April 1995.

14. Various artists, *Bouyon Rasin: First International Haitian Roots Music Festival,* notes by Claus Schreiner and Gage Averill, Global Beat Records 9601, 1996.

Sources

BIBLIOGRAPHY

Abbott, Elizabeth. *Haiti: The Duvaliers and Their Legacy*. New York: McGraw-Hill, 1988.

Abrahams, Roger D. *The Man-of-Words in the West Indies: Performance and the Emergence of Creole Culture*. Baltimore: Johns Hopkins University Press, 1983.

Abrahams, Roger D., and John F. Szwed. *After Africa: Extracts from British Travel Accounts and Journals of the Seventeenth, Eighteenth, and Nineteenth Centuries Concerning the Slaves, Their Manners, and Customs in the British West Indies*. New Haven: Yale University Press, 1983.

Alexis, Gerson. "Les Danses Rara." *Bulletin du Bureau d'Ethnologie* 3, no. 17, 18, 19 (1959): 41–62.

———. "Notes Sur Le Rara." *Bulletin du Bureau d'Ethnologie* 27 (1961): 42–45.

Allman, J. "Sexual Unions in Rural Haiti." *International Journal of Sociology and the Family* 10 (1980): 15–39.

Americas Watch, Physicians for Human Rights, National Coalition for Haitian Refugees. *Return to the Darkest Days: Human Rights in Haiti since the Coup*. New York, 1991.

Anderson, Benedict R. *Imagined Communities: Reflections on the Origin and Spread of Nationalism*. Rev. ed. London: Verso, 1983.

Appadurai, Arjun, and Carol Breckenridge. "Why Public Culture." *Public Culture* 1, no. 2 (1988): 5–9.

Aubin, Eugene. *En Haiti*. Paris: A. Colin, 1910.

Averill, Gage. "Caribbean Musics: Haiti and Trinidad and Tobago." In *Music in Latin American Culture: Regional Traditions*, ed. John M. Schechter, 126–91. New York: Schirmer, 1999.

———. *A Day for the Hunter, a Day for the Prey: Popular Music and Power in Haiti*. Chicago Studies in Ethnomusicology. Chicago: University of Chicago Press, 1997.

———. "Haitian Dance Band Music: The Political Economy of Exuberance." Ph.D. dissertation, University of Washington, 1989.

———. "'Se Kreyòl Nou Ye'/'We're Creole': Musical Discourse on Haitian Identities." In *Music and Black Ethnicity: The Caribbean and South America*, ed. Gerard Behague, 157–86. New Jersey: Transaction Press, 1994.

———. "Thinking Rara: Roots Grafts in Haitian Popular Music." Paper presented at the International Association for the Study of Popular Music, New Orleans, 1990.

Averill, Gage, and Verna Gillis. "Rara in Haiti—Gaga in the Dominican Republic." Liner notes to *Rara in Haiti—Gaga in the Dominican Republic.* Smithsonian Folkways, 1991.

Averill, Gage, and Yuen Ming David Yih. "Militarism in Haitian Music." In *The African Diaspora: A Musical Perspective,* ed. Ingrid Monson, 267–93. New York: Garland Publishing, 2000.

Axtell, James. *The Invasion Within: The Contest of Cultures in Colonial North America.* New York: Oxford University Press, 1996.

Bakhtin, M. M. *Rabelais and His World.* 1st Midland book ed. Bloomington: Indiana University Press, 1984.

Barber, Karin. "How Man Makes God in West Africa: Yoruba Attitudes toward the Orisha." *Africa* 51, no. 3 (1981): 724–45.

Barrett, Leonard E. *The Rastafarians: Sounds of Cultural Dissonance.* Rev. and updated ed. Boston: Beacon Press, 1988.

Barth, Fredrik, and Universitetet i Bergen. *Ethnic Groups and Boundaries: The Social Organization of Culture Difference.* Prospect Heights, Ill.: Waveland Press, 1998.

Basch, Linda G., Nina Glick Schiller, and Cristina Szanton Blanc. *Nations Unbound: Transnational Projects, Postcolonial Predicaments, and Deterritorialized Nation-States.* Langhorne, Pa.: Gordon and Breach, 1994.

Bastide, Roger. *African Civilizations in the New World.* Trans. Peter Green. New York: Torchbooks, 1971.

Beauvoir, Rachel. "Shanpwel: Structures and Functions of a Haitian Secret Society." Undergraduate thesis, Tufts University, 1984.

Beauvoir, Rachel, and Didier Dominique. "Savalou E." Port-au-Prince: N.p., 1987.

Beche, H. T. De La. *Notes on the Present Conditions of the Negroes in Jamaica.* London, 1825.

Bettelheim, Judith. "Deconstructing the Mythologies: From Priestess to 'Red Hot Mama' in African and African American/Caribbean Performances." Paper presented at the Program of African Studies, Northwestern University, 17 February 1992.

Blackwood, Evelyn, and Saskia E. Wieringa. *Same Sex Relationships and Female Desires: Transgender Practices across Cultures.* New York: Columbia University Press, 1999.

Bourguignon, Erika. "Syncretism and Ambivalence in Haiti: An Ethno-Historic Study." Ph.D. dissertation, Northwestern University, 1951.

Breathett, George. *The Catholic Church in Haiti (1704–1785): Selected Letters, Memoirs, and Documents.* Salisbury, N.C.: Documentation Publications, 1982.

Brodwin, Paul E. "Political Contests and Moral Claims: Religious Pluralism and Healing in a Haitian Village." Ph.D. dissertation, Harvard University, 1991.

Brown, David H. "Annotated Glossary for Fernando Ortiz's *The Afro-Cuban Festival.*" In *Cuban Festivals: An Illustrated Anthology,* ed. Judith Bettelheim, 49–98. New York: Garland, 1993.

———. "Garden in the Machine: Afro-Cuban Sacred Art and Performance in Urban New Jersey and New York." Ph.D. dissertation, Yale University, 1989.

Brown, Karen McCarthy. "Alourdes: A Case Study of Moral Leadership in Haitian Voudou." In *Saints and Virtues,* ed. John Stratton Hawley. Berkeley: University of California Press, 1987.

———. *Mama Lola: A Vodou Priestess in Brooklyn.* Berkeley: University of California Press, 1991.

———. "Systematic Remembering, Systematic Forgetting: Ogou in Haiti." In *Africa's Ogun,* ed. Sandra T. Barnes, 65–89. Bloomington: Indiana University Press, 1989.

———. "The Veve of Haitian Vodou: A Structural Analysis of Visual Imagery." Ph.D. dissertation, Temple University, 1976.

———. "Why Women Need the War God." In *Women's Spirit Bonding,* ed. Janet Kalven and Mary I. Buckley, 190–201. New York: Pilgrim Press, 1984.

Bryce-Laporte, Roy. *Sourcebook on the New Immigrants.* New Jersey: Transaction Books, 1980.

Burke, Peter. *Popular Culture in Early Modern Europe.* New York: New York University Press, 1978.

Campbell, Horace. *Rasta and Resistance: From Marcus Garvey to Walter Rodney.* 1st American ed. Trenton, N.J.: Africa World Press, 1987.

Carby, Hazel V. *Reconstructing Womanhood: The Emergence of the Afro-American Woman Novelist.* New York: Oxford University Press, 1987.

Casas, Bartolomé de las. *History of the Indies.* New York: Harper and Row, 1971.

Cervantes, Fernando. *The Devil in the New World: The Impact of Diabolism in New Spain.* New Haven: Yale University Press, 1994.

Cesareo, Claire, and Steven Rubenstein. "Prospectus for a Workshop: The Politics of Insecurity." Paper presented at the Workshop at the Social Science Research Center, New York, 1995.

Charles, Carolle. "Distinct Meanings of Blackness: Haitian Migrants in New York City." *Cimarron* 2, no. 3 (1990).

———. "A Transnational Dialectic of Race, Class, and Ethnicity: Patterns of Identities and Forms of Consciousness among Haitian Migrants in New York City." Ph.D. dissertation, SUNY Binghamton, 1990.

Chevannes, Barry. "The Origins of the Dreadlock." In *Institute of Social Studies.* The Hague: N.p., 1989.

———. *Rastafari: Roots and Ideology.* Utopianism and Communitarianism series. Syracuse, N.Y.: Syracuse University Press, 1995.

Clerismé, Rénald. "Organization: For Us, It Is Our Lives." *Crossroads: Contemporary Political Analysis and Left Dialogue* 47 (1995): 8–10.

Conway, Frederick. "Pentacostalism in the Context of Haitian Religion and Health Practice." Ph.D. dissertation, American University, 1978.

Cooper, Carolyn. "Erotic Play in the Dancehall: Slackness Hiding from Culture." Paper presented at the Women in Dance Hall conference, Kingston, Jamaica, University of the West Indies, Mona Campus, 1990.

———. *Noises in the Blood: Orality, Gender, and the "Vulgar" Body of Jamaican Popular Culture.* Durham: Duke University Press, 1995.

Cosentino, Donald. "Vodou Carnival." *Aperture* 126 (1992): 23–29.

Courlander, Harold. *The Drum and the Hoe: Life and Lore of the Haitian People.* Berkeley: University of California Press, 1973.

———. *Haiti Singing.* Chapel Hill: University of North Carolina Press, 1939.

Curtin, Philip D. *The Atlantic Slave Trade: A Census.* Madison: University of Wisconsin Press, 1969.

Dash, J. Michael. *Haiti and the United States: National Stereotypes and the Literary Imagination,* 2d ed. New York: St. Martin's Press, 1988.

Davis, Natalie Zemon. *Society and Culture in Early Modern France: Eight Essays.* Stanford, Calif.: Stanford University Press, 1975.

Davis, Wade. *Passage of Darkness: The Ethnobiology of the Haitian Zombie.* Chapel Hill: University of North Carolina Press, 1988.

———. *The Serpent and the Rainbow.* New York: Simon and Schuster, 1985.

Dayan, Joan. *Haiti, History, and the Gods.* Berkeley: University of California Press, 1995.

Debien, G. "La Christianisation des esclaves des Antilles françaises aux XVIIe et XVIIIe siècles." *Revue d'histoire de l'Amerique française* 21 (1967): 99–113.

Denis, Lorimer, and Emmanuel Paul. *Essai d'organographie haitienne.* Port-au-Prince: Bureau d'ethnologie, 1980.

Depestre, Rene. "Change." *Violence* 2, no. 9 (1971).

———. *The Festival of the Greasy Pole.* Virginia: University of Virginia Press, 1990.

Deren, Maya. *Divine Horsemen: The Living Gods of Haiti.* New York: Chelsea House, 1953.

Desmangles, Leslie Gérald. *The Faces of the Gods: Vodou and Roman Catholicism.* Chapel Hill, N.C.: University of North Carolina Press, 1992.

Desquiron, Lilas. *Racines du vodou.* Port-au-Prince: Henri Deschamps, 1992.

Dumerve, Constantin. "Musique et danse vaudouesques." *Les Griots* 3, no. 3 (1939): 411–14.

Dunham, Katherine. *Dances of Haiti.* [Los Angeles, Calif.]: Center for Afro-American Studies, University of California, Los Angeles, 1983.

Dupuy, Alex. *Haiti in the New World Order: The Limits of the Democratic Revolution.* Boulder, Colo.: Westview Press, 1997.

———. *Haiti in the World Economy: Class, Race, and Underdevelopment since 1700.* Boulder, Colo.: Westview Press, 1989.

Farmer, Paul. *Aids and Accusation: Haiti and the Geography of Blame.* Berkeley: University of California Press, 1992.

———. *The Uses of Haiti.* Monroe, Maine: Common Courage Press, 1994.

Fauriol, Georges A. *Haitian Frustrations: Dilemmas for U.S. Policy: A Report of the CSIS Americas Program.* Washington, D.C.: Center for Strategic and International Studies, 1995.

Fick, Carolyn E. *The Making of Haiti: The Saint Domingue Revolution from Below.* Knoxville: University of Tennessee Press, 1990.

Fleurant, Gerdès. *Dancing Spirits: Rhythms and Rituals of Haitian Vodun, the Rada Rite.* Westport, Conn.: Greenwood Press, 1996.

Fouchard, Jean. *The Haitian Maroons.* New York: Blyden Press, 1981.

Franketienne. *Dezafi.* Port-au-Prince: Farkin, 1975.

Frith, Simon. "Towards an Aesthetic of Popular Music." In *Music and Sociology,* ed. Richard Leppert and Susan McClary, 133–49. Cambridge: Cambridge University Press, 1987.

Gates, Henry Louis. *The Signifying Monkey: A Theory of Afro-American Literary Criticism.* New York: Oxford University Press, 1988.

Gilman, Sander. "Black Bodies, White Bodies: Toward an Iconography of Female Sexuality in Late Nineteenth-Century Art, Medicine, and Literature." In *'Race,' Writing, and Difference,* ed. Henry Louis Gates, 223–61. Chicago: University of Chicago Press, 1986.

———. *The Jew's Body.* New York: Routledge, 1991.

Gilroy, Paul. *The Black Atlantic: Modernity and Double Consciousness.* Cambridge: Harvard University Press, 1993.

———. "It's a Family Affair." In *Black Popular Culture,* ed. Gina Dent, 303–16. Seattle: Bay Press, 1995.

———. *'There Ain't No Black in the Union Jack': The Cultural Politics of Race and Nation.* London: Routledge, 1992.

Gitlitz, David M. *Secrecy and Deceit: The Religion of the Crypto-Jews.* Philadelphia: The Jewish Publication Society, 1996.

Glassman, Bernard. *Anti-Semitic Stereotypes without Jews: Images of the Jews in England, 1290–1700.* Detroit: Wayne State Press, 1975.

Glick Schiller, Nina. "All in the Same Boat? Unity and Diversity in Haitian Organizing in New York." In *Caribbean Life in New York City: Sociocultural Dimensions,* ed. Constance Sutton and Elsa Chaney. New York: Center for Migration Studies, 1987.

Glick Schiller, Nina, Linda G. Basch, and Cristina Szanton Blanc. *Towards a Transnational Perspective on Migration: Race, Class, Ethnicity, and Nationalism Reconsidered.* Annals of the New York Academy of Sciences 645. New York: New York Academy of Sciences, 1992.

Greene, Anne. *The Catholic Church in Haiti: Political and Social Change.* East Lansing: Michigan State University Press, 1993.

Griffith, James S. *Beliefs and Holy Places: A Spiritual Geography of the Primeria Alta.* Tucson: University of Arizona Press, 1992.

Guilbault, Jocelyne. "On Interpreting Popular Music: Zouk in the West Indies." In *Caribbean Popular Culture,* ed. John A. Lent, 79–97. Bowling Green, Ohio: Bowling Green State University Press, 1990.

————. *Zouk: World Music in the West Indies.* Chicago: University of Chicago Press, 1993.

Guss, D. M. "The Selling of San Juan: The Performance of History in an Afro-Venezuelan Community." *American Ethnologist* 20 (1993): 450–73.

Hall, Stuart. *Policing the Crisis: Mugging, the State, and Law and Order.* New York: Holmes and Meier, 1978.

————. "What Is This 'Black' in Black Popular Culture?" In *Black Popular Culture,* ed. Gina Dent, 21–37. Seattle: Bay Press, 1992.

Hall, Stuart, Tony Jefferson, and University of Birmingham Center for Contemporary Cultural Studies. *Resistance through Rituals: Youth Subcultures in Post-War Britain.* London: Hutchinson, 1976.

Handler, Jerome C., and Charlotte J. Frisbie. "Aspects of Slave Life in Barbados: Music and Its Cultural Context." *Caribbean Quarterly* 11 (1972).

Hannerz, Ulf. "Cities, Culture, and Center-Periphery Relationships." Paper presented at the American Anthropological Association, Atlanta, 1994.

————. "The Cultural Role of World Cities." In *Humanising the City,* ed. Anthony Cohen and Katsuyoshi Fukui. Edinburgh: Edinburgh University Press, 1993.

Hardin, Kris L. *The Aesthetics of Action: Continuity and Change in a West African Town.* Washington, D.C.: Smithsonian Institution Press, 1993.

Haring, Clarence Henry. *The Spanish Empire in America.* 1st Harbinger Books ed. New York: Harcourt Brace and World, 1963.

Hebdige, Dick. *Subculture, the Meaning of Style.* London: Methuen, 1979.

Hepner, Randal L. "Chanting Down Babylon in the Belly of the Beast: The Rastafari Movement in Metropolitan U.S.A." In *Chanting Down Babylon: A Rastafari Reader,* ed. Samuel Murrell. Philadelphia: Temple University Press.

Herskovits, Melville J. *The Myth of the Negro Past.* Boston: Beacon Press, 1958.

Heusch, Luc de. "Kongo in Haiti: A New Approach to Religious Syncretism." *Man* 24 (1989): 290–302.

Hill, Errol. *The Trinidad Carnival: Mandate for a National Theatre.* Austin: University of Texas Press, 1972.

Hobsbawm, E. J., and T. O. Ranger. *The Invention of Tradition.* Cambridge: Cambridge University Press, 1983.

Hoffman, François Leo. "Francophilia and Cultural Nationalism." In *Haiti, Today and Tomorrow,* ed. C. Foster and A. Valdman. New York: University of America Press, 1984.

Honorat, M. Lamartiniere. *Les Danses folklorique haitiennes.* Vol. 2 of *Imprimerie de l'état.* Port-au-Prince: Bureau d'ethnologie, 1955.

Huizinga, Johan. *Homo Ludens: A Study of the Play-Element in Culture.* First Beacon paperback ed. Boston: Beacon Press, 1955.

Human Rights Watch/Americas, National Coalition for Haitian Refugees. "Rape in Haiti: A Weapon of Terror." New York: Americas Watch, 1994.

———. "Security Compromised: Recycled Haitian Soldiers on the Police Front Line." New York: Americas Watch, 1995.

———. *Silencing a People.* New York: Human Rights Watch, 1993.

Hurbon, Laënnec. *Culture et dictature en Haïti: L'imaginaire sous contrôle.* Paris: L'Harmattan, 1979.

———. *Dieu dans le vodou haitien.* Paris: Payot, 1972.

Izmery, Antoine [an interview with]. "A Fake Kind of Development." In *The Haiti Files: Decoding the Crisis,* ed. James Ridgeway. Washington, D.C.: Essential Books, 1994.

Janzen, John M. *Lemba, 1650–1930: A Drum of Affliction in Africa and the New World.* New York: Garland Pub., 1982.

Kastner, Georges. *Manuel général de musique militaire à l'usage des armées françaises.* Paris: Typ. F. Didot frères, 1848.

Keller, Catherine. "The Breast, the Apocalypse, and the Colonial Journey." In *The Year 2000: Essays on the End,* ed. Charles B. Strozier and Michael Flynn, 42–58. New York: NYU Press, 1997.

Kertzer, David. *Ritual, Politics, and Power.* New Haven: Yale University Press, 1988.

Koskoff, Ellen. *Women and Music in Cross-Cultural Perspective.* New York: Greenwood Press, 1987.

Laguerre, Michel S. *American Odyssey: Haitians in New York City.* Ithaca, N.Y.: Cornell University Press, 1984.

———. "Les Associations traditionelles de travail dans la paysannerie haitienne." Port-au-Prince: N.p., 1975.

———. *Urban Life in the Caribbean: A Study of a Haitian Urban Community.* Cambridge, Mass.: Schenkman Publishing, 1982.

———. *Voodoo and Politics in Haiti.* New York: St. Martin's Press, 1989.

Lancaster, Roger N. *Life Is Hard: Machismo, Danger, and the Intimacy of Power in Nicaragua.* Berkeley: University of California Press, 1993.

Langmuir, Gavin I. *History, Religion, and Antisemitism.* Berkeley: University of California Press, 1990.

Largey, Michael. "Politics on the Pavement: Haitian Rara as a Traditionalizing Process." *Journal of American Folklore* 113, no. 449 (2000): 239–54.

Laroche, Maximilen. *L'image comme écho: Essais sur la littérature et la culture haitïennes.* Montreal: Les Editions Nouvelles Optiques, 1978.

Larose, Serge. "The Meaning of Africa in Haitian Voodoo." In *In Symbols and Sentiments: Cross-Cultural Studies in Symbolism,* ed. I. M. Lewis, 85–116. London: Academic Press, 1977.

Leach, Edmund. *Political Systems in Highland Burma.* Cambridge: Harvard University Press, 1954.

Leiris, Michel. "On the Use of Catholic Religious Prints by the Practitioners of Voodoo in Haiti." *Evergreen Review* 4, no. 13 (1960): 84–94.

Lekis, Lisa. "The Origin and Development of Ethnic Caribbean Dance and Music." Ph.D. dissertation, University of Florida, 1956.

Le Roy Ladurie, Emmanuel. *Carnival in Romans.* 1st ed. New York: G. Braziller, 1979.

Levine, Lawrence W. *Highbrow/Lowbrow: The Emergence of Cultural Hierarchy in America.* Cambridge: Harvard University Press, 1988.

Lévi-Strauss, Claude. *The Savage Mind.* [Chicago]: University of Chicago Press, 1966.

———. *Structural Anthropology.* Garden City, N.Y.: Anchor Books, 1967.

Liebman, Seymour B. *The Jews in New Spain: Faith, Flame, and the Inquisition.* Coral Gables, Fla.: University of Miami Press, 1970.

Lipsitz, George. *Dangerous Crossroads: Popular Music, Postmodernism, and the Poetics of Place.* London: Verso, 1994.

Loker, Zvi. "Were There Jewish Communities in Saint Domingue (Haiti)?" *Jewish Social Studies* 45, no. 2 (1983): 135–46.

Maccoby, Hyam. *Judas Iscariot and the Myth of Jewish Evil.* New York: The Free Press, 1992.

MacGaffey, Wyatt. "Fetishism Revisited: Kongo Nkisi in Sociological Perspective." *Africa* 47, no. 2 (1977).

MacGaffey, Wyatt, Michael D. Harris, Sylvia H. Williams, David C. Driskell, and National Museum of African Art (U.S.). *Astonishment and Power.* Washington, D.C.: Published for the National Museum of African Art by the Smithsonian Institution Press, 1993.

Marks, Morton. "Uncovering Ritual Structures in Afro-American Music." In *Religious Movements in Contemporary America,* ed. Irving I. Zaretsky and Mark P. Leone. Princeton: Princeton University Press, 1974.

Maternowska, M. Catherine. "Coups d'État and Contraceptives: A Political Economy Analysis of Family Planning in Haiti." Ph.D. dissertation, Columbia University, 1996.

Mayard, Yvonne. *Autrefois nan pays d'Haiti.* Port-au-Prince: Imprimerie Centrale, 1967.

Mbembe, Achille. "The Banality of Power and the Aesthetics of Vulgarity in the Postcolony." *Public Culture* 4, no. 3 (1992): 1–22.

McAlister, Elizabeth. "'The Jew' in the Haitian Imagination: Pre-Modern Anti-Judaism in the Postmodern Caribbean." In *Black Zion: African American Religious Encounters with Judaism,* ed. Yvonne Chireau and Nathanial Deutsch, 203–28. New York: Oxford University Press, 2000.

———. "Love, Sex, and Gender Embodied: The Spirits of Haitian Vodou." In *Love, Gender, and Sexuality in the World Religions,* ed. Nancy Martin and Joseph Runzo, 128–45. Oxford: Oxford Oneworld Press, 2000.

———. "'Men Moun Yo; Here Are the People': Rara Festivals and Transnational Popular Culture in Haiti and New York City." Ph.D. dissertation, Yale University, 1995.

———. "Rara: Haitians Make Some Noise in Brooklyn." *The Beat Magazine* (summer 1991): 28–29.

———. "The Rite of Baptism in Haitian Vodou." In *Religions of the United States in Practice,* ed. Colleen McDannell. Princeton: Princeton University Press, 2001.

———. "Sacred Stories from the Haitian Diaspora: A Collective Biography of Seven Vodou Priestesses in New York City." *Journal of Caribbean Studies* 9, no. 1 and 2 (1993): 10–27.

———. "A Sorcerer's Bottle: The Art of Magic in Haiti." In *The Sacred Arts of Haitian Vodou,* ed. Donald Cosentino, 302–21. Los Angeles: Fowler Museum of Cultural History, 1995.

———. "Vodou and Catholicism in the Age of Transnationalism: The Madonna of 115th Street Revisited." In *Gatherings in Diaspora: Religious Communities and the New Immigration,* ed. R. Stephen Warner, 123–60. Philadelphia: Temple University Press, 1998.

———. "Vodou Music and Ritual Work." In *Rhythms of Rapture: Sacred Musics of Haitian Vodou.* Smithsonian Folkways, 1995.

———, ed. "Angels in the Mirror: Vodou Music of Haiti." Roslyn, N.Y.: Ellipsis Arts, 1997.

McLane, Daisann. "The Haitian Beat Thrives in Times of Suffering." *New York Times,* 8 March 1992.

McLeod, Norma, and Marcia Herdon. "The Bormliza: Maltese Folksong Style and Women." In *Women and Folklore,* ed. Claire B. Ferrer. Austin: University of Texas Press, 1975.

Métraux, Alfred. *Voodoo in Haiti.* New York: Oxford University Press, 1959.

Midy, Franklin. "Mémoire" [by Courtain]. *Chemins Critiques* 1, no. 1 (1989): 135–42.

Mirville, Ernst. *Considerations Ethno-Psychoanalytiques Dur Le Carnival Haitian.* Port-au-Prince: Collection Coucouille, 1978.

Moral, Paul. *Le Paysan Haitien.* Paris, 1961.

Moreau de Saint Mery, Médéric-Louis-Elie. *Description topographique, physique, civile, politique et historique de la partie française de l'île S. Dominque.* Nouvelle ed. Ed. Blanche Maurel and Etienne Taillemitte. Paris: Société de l'histoire de la Colonie Français, 1958.

Murray, David. *Opacity: Sexuality, Masculinity, and Performances of Identity in Martinique.* New York: Lang, 2001.

Nagel, Joane. "Constructing Ethnicity: Creating and Recreating Ethnic Identity and Culture." *Social Problems* 41, no. 1 (1994).

Nagle, Robin. *Claiming the Virgin: The Broken Promise of Liberation Theology in Brazil.* New York: Routledge, 1997.

Nash, June. "The Impact of the Changing International Division of Labor on Different Sectors of the Labor Force." In *Women, Men, and the International Division of Labor,* ed. June Nash and Patricia Fernandez-Kelly, 3–69. Albany: SUNY Press, 1983.

National Coalition for Haitian Refugees. *Haiti, Darkness Remains: Critique of the State Department's Profile of Asylum Claims and Country Conditions.* New York, 1995.

Nicholls, David. *From Dessalines to Duvalier: Race, Colour, and National Independence in Haiti.* Cambridge, England: Cambridge University Press, 1979.

Nicolas, Lovely, and Liza McAlister. "The Lucky Ones: A Mother-Daughter Story of Love and War." Published online at Oxygen.com: http://womenshands.oxygen.com/artisans/haiti/lucky.html.

Nunley, John W., and Judith Bettelheim, eds. *Caribbean Festival Arts: Each and Every Bit of Difference.* Seattle: University of Washington, 1988.

Painter, Muriel Thayer, Edward H. Spicer, and Wilma Kaemlein, eds. *With Good Heart: Yaqui Beliefs and Ceremonies in Pascua Village.* Tucson: University of Arizona Press, 1986.

Parker, Andrew. *Nationalisms and Sexualities.* New York: Routledge, 1992.

Patterson, Charles. *Anti-Semitism: The Road to the Holocaust and Beyond.* New York: Walker, 1982.

Paul, Emmanuel. "Folklore Du Militarism." *Optique* 6 (1954): 24–27.

———. *Panorama Du Folklore Haitien.* Port-au-Prince: Imprimerie de l'Etat, 1962.

Pollard, Velma. "Dread Talk: The Speech of the Rastafarians in Jamaica." *Caribbean Quarterly* 26, no. 4 (1980): 32–41.

———. "The Social History of Dread Talk." *Caribbean Quarterly* 28, no. 4 (1982): 17–41.

Ravicz, Marilyn Ekdahl. *Early Colonial Religious Drama in Mexico: From Tzompantli to Golgotha.* Washington, D.C.: Catholic University of America Press, 1970.

Reagon, Bernice Johnson. *The Lined Hymn as a Song of Freedom.* Black Music Research Bulletin 12, no. 1. Chicago: Columbia College, 1990.

Reisman, Karl. "Cultural and Linguistic Ambiguity in a West Indian Village." In *Afro-American Anthropology: Contemporary Perspectives,* ed. John F. Szwed and Norman E. Whitten, 129–42. New York: The Free Press, 1970.

Rey, Terry. "Junta, Rape, and Religion in Haiti, 1993–1994." *Journal of Feminist Studies in Religion* 15, no. 2 (1999): 73–99.

Richman, Karen E. "'A Lavalas at Home/a Lavalas for Home': Inflections of Transnationalism in the Discourse of Haitian President Aristide." In *Towards a Transnational*

Perspective on Migration: Race, Class, Ethnicity, and Nationalism Reconsidered, ed. Nina Glick Schiller, Linda G. Basch, and Cristina Szanton Blanc, 189–200. New York: New York Academy of Sciences, 1992.

———. "They Will Remember Me in the House: The Pwen of Haitian Transnational Migration." Ph.D. dissertation, University of Virginia, 1992.

———. " 'With Many Hands, the Burden Isn't Heavy': Creole Proverbs and Political Rhetoric in Haiti's Presidential Elections." *Folklore Forum* 12, no. 1/2 (1990): 115–23.

Roach, Joseph R. *Cities of the Dead: Circum-Atlantic Performance.* The Social Foundations of Aesthetic Forms series. New York: Columbia University Press, 1996.

Romain, Jean-Baptiste. *Africanismes Haitiens.* Port-au-Prince: Imprimerie M. Rodriguez, 1978.

Roman, Pierre Isnard. "Recherche Sur Un Rara Appele La Meprise a L'arcahaie (Merlotte)." In *Faculty of Ethnology.* Port-au-Prince: N.p., 1993.

Rose, Tricia. *Black Noise: Rap Music and Black Music in Contemporary America.* Hanover, N.H.: University Press of New England, 1994.

Rosenberg, June C. *Gaga: Religion y Sociedad de un Culto Dominicano.* Santo Domingo: USAD, 1979.

Roth, Cecil. *A History of the Marranos.* Philadelphia: Jewish Publication Society of America, 1932.

Sansone, Livio. "From Creole to Black: Leisure Time, Style, and the New Ethnicity of Lower-Class Young Blacks of Surinamese Origin in Amsterdam: 1975–1991." Unpublished manuscript, 1991.

Schechter, John M., ed. *Music in Latin American Culture: Regional Traditions.* New York: Schirmer, 1999.

Schorsch, Jonathan. "American Jewish Historians, Colonial Jews and Blacks, and the Limits of Wissenschaft: A Critical Review." *Jewish Social Studies* 6, no. 2 (2000): 102–32.

Scott, James C. *Domination and the Arts of Resistance: Hidden Transcripts.* New Haven: Yale University Press, 1990.

———. *Weapons of the Weak: Everyday Forms of Peasant Resistance.* New Haven: Yale University Press, 1985.

Seabrook, W. B. *The Magic Island.* New York: Harcourt Brace, 1929.

Shell, Marc. "Marranos (Pigs), or from Coexistence to Toleration." *Critical Inquiry* 11, no. 2 (1991): 306–35.

Stallybrass, Peter, and Allon White. *The Politics and Poetics of Transgression.* Ithaca, N.Y.: Cornell University Press, 1986.

Stuckey, Sterling. *Slave Culture: Nationalist Theory and the Foundations of Black America.* New York: Oxford University Press, 1987.

Szwed, John F. *Black America.* New York: Basic Books, 1970.

Thompson, Robert Farris. "The Flash of the Spirit: Haiti's Africanizing Vodun Art." In *Haitian Art,* ed. Ute Stebich. New York: Brooklyn Museum of Art, 1978.

Thompson, Robert Farris, Joseph Cornet, and National Gallery of Art (U.S.). *The Four Moments of the Sun: Kongo Art in Two Worlds.* Washington, D.C.: National Gallery of Art, 1981.

Toulabor, C. "Jeu De Mots, Jeux De Vilain. Lexique De La Derision Politique Au Togo." *Politique Africaine* 3 (1981): 55–71.

Trachtenberg, Joshua. *The Devil and the Jews: The Medieval Conception of the Jew and Its Relation to Modern Antisemitism.* 2nd paperback ed. Philadelphia: Jewish Publication Society of America, 1983.

Trexler, Richard. "We Think, They Act: Missionary Theatre in Sixteenth-Century New Spain." In *Understanding Popular Culture: Europe from the Middle Ages to the Nineteenth Century,* ed. Steven L. Kaplan, 189–227. New York: Mouton Publishers, 1984.

Trouillot, Henock. *Introduction à une histoire de vaudou.* Port-au-Prince: Les Editions Fardion, 1983.

Trouillot, Michel-Rolph. *Haiti, State against Nation: The Origins and Legacy of Duvalierism.* New York: Monthly Review Press, 1990.

———. *Silencing the Past: Power and the Production of History.* Boston: Beacon Press, 1995.

Tselos, Susan Elizabeth. "Threads of Reflection: Costumes of Haitian Rara." *African Arts* 29, no. 2 (1996): 58–65.

Tsing, Anna Lowenhaupt. *In the Realm of the Diamond Queen: Marginality in an Out-of-the-Way Place.* Princeton, N.J.: Princeton University Press, 1993.

Turner, Victor Witter. "Carnival in Rio: Dionyssian Drama in an Industrializing Society." In *The Celebration of Society: Perspectives on Contemporary Cultural Performance,* ed. Frank E. Manning. Bowling Green, Ohio: University Popular Press, 1983.

———. *The Ritual Process: Structure and Anti-Structure.* Chicago: Aldine Pub. Co., 1969.

Wallerstein, Immanuel Maurice. *The Modern World-System.* New York: Academic Press, 1974.

Whitten, Norman E., and John F. Szwed. *Afro-American Anthropology: Contemporary Perspectives.* New York: Free Press, 1970.

Wilcken, Lois. *The Drums of Vodou, Featuring Frisner Augustin.* Tempe, Ariz.: White Cliffs Media Company, 1992.

———. "Music Folklore among Haitians in New York: Staged Representations and the Negotiations of Identity." Ph.D. dissertation, Columbia University, 1991.

———. "Vodou Music among Haitians Living in New York." Master's thesis, Hunter College, 1986.

Wojciechowska, Maia, and Wilson Bigaud. *Market Day for Ti André.* New York: Viking Press, 1952.

Wurdemann, J. G. F. *Notes on Cuba: Containing an Account of its Discovery and Early History; A Description of the Face of the Country, Its Population, Resources, and Wealth; Its Institutions, and the Manners and Customs of its Inhabitants, with Directions to Travellers Visiting the Island.* Boston: James Munroe and Company, 1844.

Yih, Y.-M. David. "Music and Dance of Haitian Vodou: Diversity and Unity in Regional Repertoires." Ph.D. dissertation, Wesleyan University, 1995.

Yonker, Dolores. "Haiti after the Fall: The Politics of Rara." N.p., 1989.

———. "Rara: A Lenten Festival." *Bulletin du Bureau National d'Ethnologie* 2 (1985): 63–71.

———. "Rara in Haiti." In *Caribbean Festival Arts: Each and Every Bit of Difference,* ed. John W. Nunley and Judith Bettelheim. Seattle: University of Washington, 1988.

DISCOGRAPHY

Artists, Various. *Africans in America: America's Journey through Slavery.* Rycodisc, RCD 90444/3, 1998. Four compact discs accompanying four-part television series for WGBH/Boston, produced by Bernice Johnson Reagon. One track, "Nago," is by *mizik rasin* musicians.

———. *Air Mail Music: Haiti.* Paris: Productions Sunset France, SA 141033, 1999. Selections of Troubadour and Rara music.

————. *Angels in the Mirror: Vodou Music of Haiti*. Produced by Elizabeth McAlister, Holly Nicolas, and David Yih. Roslyn, N.Y.: Ellipsis Arts, CD 4120, 1997.

————. *Bouyon Rasin: First International Haitian Roots Music Festival*. Notes by Claus Schreiner and Gage Averill. Global Beat Records 9601, 1996. Live recording.

————. *Caribbean Island Music: Songs and Dances of Haiti, the Dominican Republic, and Jamaica*. Recording and notes by John Storm Roberts. New York: Nonesuch Explorer Series H-72047, 1998.

————. *Caribbean Revels: Haitian Rara and Dominican Gaga*. Recorded by Verna Gillis. Notes by Gage Averill and Verna Gillis. Washington, D.C.: Smithsonian Folkways FE 40402, 1991.

————. *Divine Horsemen*. Recorded by Maya Deren between 1947 and 1953. New York: Lyrichord LLST 7341, 1978. Vodou field recordings.

————. *Fond des Negres, Fond des Blanc: Musiques Paysannes d'Haiti*. France: Musique Du Monde, 1997.

————. *Haiti Rap and Ragga: Match la Red*. France: Declic Communications 319-2, 1994. Features "Master Dji" Georges Lys Herard.

————. *Konbit: Burning Rhythms of Haiti*. A&M 75021-5281-2, 1989.

————. *Music in Latin American Culture: Regional Traditions*. CD is companion to book of same title. New York: Schirmer Books, 1999. Features one recording of Rara and two recordings of Vodou.

————. *Music of Haiti*. Vol. 1, *Drums of Haiti*. Washington, D.C.: Folkways Records F-4403, 1950. Vol. 2, *Folk Music of Haiti*. Washington, D.C.: Folkways Records F-4407, 1951. Vol. 3, *Songs and Dances of Haiti*. Washington, D.C.: Folkways Records F-4432, 1952. Recorded and with notes by Harold Courlander.

————. *Rhythms of Rapture: Sacred Musics of Haitian Vodou*. Produced by Elizabeth McAlister. Notes by Elizabeth McAlister, Gage Averill, Gerdes Fleurant, and others. Washington, D.C.: Smithsonian Folkways, SFCD 40464, 1995.

————. *Vodun-Rada Rite for Erzulie*. Recorded in Haiti by Verna Gillis. Washington, D.C.: Smithsonian Folkways 044911. Vodou field recording

Atis Endepandan. "*Ki Sa Pou-N Fe?*" Paredon Records P-1027, 1975.

Augustin, Frisner. *Drums of Vodou*. Tempe, Ariz.: White Cliffs, 1994.

Beauvoir, Mathilda. *Le Vaudou: Chants et Danses d'Haiti: Ceremonie Vaudou*. France: CBS, Inc., 1973.

Bigga Haitian. *I Am Back*. A Royal Productions/Jomino/Roots International, 1997. Ragga style music with Kreyòl and English toasts.

Black Leaders. *Tout Moun Jwen*. Krazy Staff Productions/Cross Over Records, KS-BL001, 1997. Haitian Ragga music.

Boukan Ginen. *Jou A Rive*. Danbury, Conn.: Xenophile 4024, 1995.

Boukman Eksperyans. *Kalfou Danjere*. New York: Mango 162-539 927-2, 1992.

————. *Kanaval Rasin-Vodou Adjae*. Converge Ent/Sumthing Distribution, 2000. A compilation of Carnival songs.

————. *Libète Pran Pou Pran'l/Freedom Let's Grab It*. New York: Mango 162-539946-2, 1995.

————. *Revolution*. Tuff Gong Records, 1998. Track 7, "Peye Loa Yo," uses Rara rhythm and *vaksin*. Track 5, "Tipa Tipa," is a Carnival song critical of the "big eaters" in the government.

————. *Vodou Adjae*. New York: Mango 16253 9899-2, 1991.

Cheriza, Pierre. *Haiti: Musique du Vaudou*. France: Musique du Monde 92731-2, 1999. Excerpts of a field recording of a seven-day service from a village in Plaine du Cul-De-Sac, Haiti.

Foula. "Sovè." Track on *Global Celebration,* Vol. 4: *Authentic Music from Joyous Festivals around the World.* Roslyn, N.Y.: Ellipsis Arts, CD3234, 1994.

Hill, Richard, and Morton Marks. *Voodoo Trance Music: Ritual Drums of Haiti.* Lyrichord, LLST 7279.

Jazz des Jeunes. *Super Jazz des Jeunes.* Ibo Records ILP 113, n.d.

Jean, Wyclef. *The Eclectic: 2 Sides II a Book.* New York: Sony Columbia, 2000.

———. *Wyclef Jean Presents the Carnival.* Sony Columbia, 1997.

Kanpèch. *Pale Yo.* The Coconut Grove Recording Co., Inc., CGRC 8196–2, 1996.

King Posse. *I Like It.* Crossover Records, n.d.

———. "Retounen." Track on *Putomayo Presents: Carnival 2001.* New York: Putomayo Recordings, 2001.

Koudjay Banbou Nwa. *Sanba M'Dogwe.* CDP&P-113, n.d. Includes song "Maman Poul La Troillot."

Martely, Michel (Sweet Mickey). *Pa Manyen.* Canada: Josy Record and Video Club, CDJR 031, n.d.

Mini All Stars. *Raraman.* Mini Records MRS 1191, 1986.

Original Rap Staff. *Kè Pò Pòz.* France: Declic AMCD 77120, 1996.

RAM. *Aibobo.* Cave Wall Records, 1995. Includes "Fey" and "Anbago."

Rara Grap Plezi. *Roots of Haiti.* Vol. 5. Mini Records, n.d.

Rara Machine. *Break the Chain: Kase Chenn.* Shanachie Records 64038, 1989.

———. *Vodou Nou.* Shanachie Records 64054, 1994.

Wawa (Jacques Fortere). *Haitian Voodoo.* Sounds of the World SOW 90171, 1977. A reissue of an out-of-print Wawa album.

———. *Roots of Haiti.* 5 vols. on Mini Records 1978 and 1979. Volume 5 is Rara music, *Rara Grap Plezi.*

Wawa and Azor. *Wawa and Azor Collections 8 and 3 and 9 and 1.* Geronimo Records, GR 0014–79.

Wawa and His Group. *Le Vaudou Haitien.* Vols. 1–6. Michga Records, n.d.

Zobop. *Vodoo Red.* Port-au-Prince: Cine Disc CD 12192, 1994.

VIDEOGRAPHY

Divine Horsemen. Produced by Maya Deren. Mystic Fire Video, 1951. 60 minutes.

Killing the Dream. New York: Crowing Rooster Productions, 1992. Documentary film.

Rara. Produced by Verna Gillis, Gail Pellett, and Original Music (Firm). Tivoli, N.Y.: Original Music, 1985. 1 videocassette, 15 minutes.

Rara 1991. Produced by Gage Averill, with assistance by Elizabeth McAlister. 1991. Assorted unpublished footage.

Rara 1993. Produced by Chantal Regnault. 1993. Assorted unpublished footage.

Rara in Léogâne. Port-au-Prince: Arc-en-Ciel Video, 1993.

Index

Page numbers in italics refer to illustrations.

Aboudja (Ronald Derencourt), 233n.12
Abraham, General, 39
Abrahams, Roger, 31–32, 33, 56, 89, 151, 219n.7
Accaau, Jean-Jacques, 141
adultery, theme of, 64, 66, 67–68
African nationalism, 205
Africans, 119, 120–21
Afro-Creole vs. European cultural forms, 55–56, 122–23. *See also* Catholic Church
Afro-Haitian religion. *See* Bizango societies; Petwo; Rada; Vodou
ago (Vodou exclamation word), 66, 222n.14
AIDS, 63, 64, 75; Haitians perceived as transmitters of, 201, 235n.44; and "the Jew," 130; theme of, 77–78
Aiyzan (Harry Sanon), 233n.12
Alexis, Gerson, 31
Amnesty International, 13
angaje (under contract), 34, 213
anti-Semitism. *See* Jews
antisuperstition campaigns, 171–72
apiye pa frape (leaning not hitting), 50
"*Apre bal la tanbou lou*" ("After the dance, the drum is heavy"), 168
Arawak people, 225n.19
Aristide, Jean-Bertrand: army replaced with police force by, 142; corruption/politics of, 12, 13–14, 201; election of, 5, 12, 160, 209; familial images used by, 171; Governor's Island Agreement signed by, 211; Krèyol promoted by, 160; Lafontant attempts coup against, 172, 186, 209; in New York City, 205–6, 209, 210; ousting of, 2, 5, 12, 140, 160, 205–6, 210; *pwen* used by, 168; return of, 5, 160, 212; support for, 2, 3, 14, 169–70, 174, 186, 205–6, 212; and Ertha Pascal Trouillot, 39; vulgar songs about, 80–81
Asefi, 42–43
atache (auxiliary military guards), 213
audience, 5–6, 44
Augustin, Frisner, 17–18
avan gad (front guard), 137, 138, 213
Averill, Gage, 47, 50, 140, 173, 199
Avril, Prosper, 165
Azaka, Kouzen, 98, 139, 225n.25
Azouke (Gregory Sanon), 233n.12

Babylon, 169
Bakhtin, Mikhail, 15, 78
Bakongo people, 226n.38
balanse Rara (playing without walking), 143
banbou (an instrument), *38, 45,* 46–47, 213, 220n.30
Banda (religious rite), 88–89, 110
banda (rhythm and dance), 29, 73, 88–89, 213
bann a pye (band on foot), 46, 213

Bann Bourgeois de la Lwa, 145
bann dangajman (bands "under con-
tract" with the *lwa*), 34, 35, 36
"Bann Sanpwel-la nan Lari-a" (The
Chanpwèl Band Is in the Streets;
track 20), 145
Barber, Karin, 142, 154
Barth, Fredrik, 199
Basch, Linda, 187
bas drum, 45, 213
Basquiat, Jean-Michel, 194
baton twirling, American, 54, 221n.47
Bawon, 91, 92, 213
Bazin, Marc, 210
Beaubrun, Mimerose (Manze), 233n.12
Beauvoir, Rachel, 49, 139, 156
Bel Air (Haiti), 150
Bèl Krèk de Janine, La (Janine's Beau-
tiful Clitoris), 74
Belle Fraîcheur de d'Anglade, La (The
Beautiful Fresh Air of the Glade), 27–
30, 37, 39, 144–45, 152, 155
Bennett, Michelle, 79
benyen (protective baths), 44, 213
betiz, 59–67, 68–69, 74, 77, 78, 80,
82–83, 213
Bettelheim, Judith, 72–73
Biamby, Phillipe, 165
Bigga Haitian (Charles Dorismond),
194, 234n.27
big man. See *gwo nèg*
bigup (a dance), 49
Bizango societies, 33, 75, 87, 88–89,
97, 107, 110, 213
Black Atlantic, 4, 7
Black Indians, 7, 151
blackness, definitions of, 202–4,
236n.48
Black popular culture, 195–98
Black Power movement, 188
blan (white; foreigner), 213
blues, 7
boat people, 200
bòkò (sorcerer), 33, 213
Bonga (Gaston), 233n.12
bòt pipol (boat people), 200
Boukan Ginen, 209, 226n.46
Boukman Eksperyans: "Bawon," 212;
female vocalists in, 73; "Gran Bwa
Kriminel," 209; "Jou Malè," 210;
"Kalfou Danjere," 93, 210; "Nanm
Nan Boutèy," 107; "Ogou Feray,

Oh! I was at war, they put me on
watch," 2, 217n.2; "Peye Pou Peye,"
211; *Revolution,* 234n.29; "Sanba,
sa fè'm mal O," 48; "*Woy, men
moun yo,*" 166
Boukman, 204
bounda (butt), 213
bouzen (prostitute), 64, 68, 213
Boyer, Jean-Pierre, 141
Brijit, 91
brooms, ritual use of, 100
Brown, David H., 54, 56, 101, 122,
196, 229n.48, 236n.48
Brown, Karen McCarthy, 68, 167
buffets, 79–80, 224n.48
Buju Banton, 75
Bush, George, 210
bwa (wood; slang term for "penis"),
69, 70
bwile Jwif (burning the Jew in effigy),
114, *115,* 116–21, 213

cabildos, 137
Cacos du Nord, 141
calypso, 7, 61–62
campagne des rejetés (antisuperstition
campaigns), 171
capoeira, 7, 9
Carnival, 7, 33, 49–50, 63, 155;
bands, 138. *See also* vulgarity and
the politics of the small man
Carnival of Fraternity, 2
Carter, Jimmy, 212
Catholic Church: anti-Semitism of, 120;
antisuperstition campaigns of, 171–
72; Easter's importance in, 123–24,
132; on marriage, 67–68; satirization of, 63; slave-owning by, 120;
and Vodou, 110, 121–24, 126
Cedras, Raoul, 12–13, 82, 160, 175,
209, 211, 212, 224n.48
Celestin, Andres, 156
"Cemetery at Bizoton" (track 14), 71–
72
cemetery/crossroads, spiritual work at,
91–111; capturing *zonbi,* 98–102,
225n.22, 225n.26; crossroads-
cemetery relationship, 92–93,
225n.13; Petwo-Bizango protection
ceremony, 93, 94, 95–97; Protestant
zonbi, 109–10; skulls, use of, 104,
105, 106, 226n.36; spirits as popu-

lating, 91; tombs, breaking open, 104; *vèvè* (cornmeal drawings) in, 93, 95, 97, 225n.18; *zonbi* in Afro-Haitian religious complex, 102–9, 225n.29, 226n.50
center-periphery relationships, 196, 198, 235n.34
Chanpwèl societies, 88, 92, 98, 106, 107, 138, 139, 213
chante pwen (to sing "points" or messages), 213. See also *pwen*
Charlemagne, Manno, 212
Charles, Carolle, 202–3
charyio-pye (band without instruments), 45, 145, 213, 220n.27
chawonj (something smelly or nasty; someone who will have indiscriminate sex), 213
Chen Mechan (Angry Dog), 36
cheve Simbi (Simbi's hair), 191, 193
Chiko (Yves Boyer), 233n.12
children as wealth ("*Pitit se beyen*"), 43
Christ, in Vodou, 128–29
Christianity. *See* Catholic Church
Christophe, Henri, king of Haiti, 136–37
CIA, 165, 232n.8
circum-Atlantic interculture, 4
Citè Jérémie (Port-au-Prince), 155
Civil Rights movement, 178, 188
class: and consumption, 78–82, 224n.48; Lucifer as symbolic of inequality in, 129; and political insecurity, 161, 165–66, 177–80; and work, 90
Claude, Sylvio, 210
Clinton, Bill, 3, 210, 211, 212
cocaine trafficking, 13–14, 165, 232n.8
Code Noir, 120
code switching, 55–56, 63, 77
Colastin, Phenel, 18
colonels. See *kolonèl*
Columbus, Christopher, 4, 10, 118, 217n.4
competition, 148, 151, 153, 231n.36
conversos (converted Jews), 119, 131. *See also* Jews
Cooper, Carolyn, 64, 67, 68, 69
Cosentino, Donald, 81–82
costumes, 52, 54, *148*, 228n.40
counterclockwise rituals, 97

Courlander, Harold, 31
Courtain, M., 153
Creole history, 4, 217n.5
crime, 176–77
cross-dressers, 75, 223n.37
crossroads. *See* cemetery/crossroads, spiritual work at

Dahomey, 87
dance, 48–56, 219n.13; carnivalesque, 49–51; couples/courtship dances, 48; of *majò jon*, 52, *53*, 54, 55; *mazoun*, 55; rhythms, 48; ritual dances, 49, 221n.39; spiritual work via, 51
dance-hall tradition, 7, 61–62, 63–64, 67, 75, 185, 194
dans (dance), 219n.13. *See also* dance
dans Bizango (secret society ceremony), 44
dans Petwo (religious ceremony), 44
Davis, Wade, 156
Dayan, Joan, 120–21
death, as preordained, 106
decolonization, 196
Delen, 144–45
Demme, Jonathan, 234n.13
Democratic Party, 199
demons, 36, 220n.21
Depestre, Rene, 108
Deren, Maya, 103
Desir, Wilson, 206
Dessalines, Jean-Jacques, 204
dezòd (unruly), 213
Diallo, Amadou, 186
diaspora. *See* New York City, Rara in
Dieubon, Papa, 135–36
Dieupè, Papa, 124–25, 145
Dieuvè, 144
disko (a dance), 49
disoso (an instrument), 46
djab (demons), 36, 220n.21
djakout (straw shoulder-bag), 213
Djames, 205
DJ Frankie, 194
Dominique, Didier, 49, 139, 156
Dorismond, André, 234n.27
Dorismond, Patrick, 186, 234n.27
dreadlocks, 191, 193
drug trafficking, 13–14, 165, 232n.8
drums, 45
Dunham, Katherine, 18, 220n.30
du Plexis, Jerry, 234n.29

Duvalier, François ("Papa Doc"), 11, 13, 35, 61, 80, 82
Duvalier, Jean-Claude ("Baby Doc"), 5; burning Jew in effigy banned by, 114; consumption by, 79–80; crime/corruption under, 176; demonstrations against, 184, 233n.3; fall of, 142, 160; homosexuality under rule of, 75–76; leaves Haiti, 209; pop music promoted by, 61; repression by/totalitarian rule of, 160, 163, 164, 165–66

ekzèsis (exercises), 213
elite, 78–82, 224n.48. *See also* class
Engagés (indentured servants), 34
èskwad (work brigades), 46
Ethiopia, 192
ethnicity, 199
European models of culture, 196
European vs. Afro-Creole cultural forms, 55–56, 122–23. *See also* Catholic Church
Exume, Jean Joseph, 176

fanatik (dancers in the crowd; fans), 90–91, 143, 213
Farmer, Paul, 19
FDA (Food and Drug Administration), 201
feasting, 79–80, 224n.48
fèt (party), 219n.13
fèt chanpèt (village patron saint's feasts), 33
fete (to party), 213
fetish, 226n.38
fighting, physical, 148, 151–52, 155–56
Fleur de Rose, La, 148
Food and Drug Administration (FDA), 201
Ford Foundation, 199
foul (big crowd), 50, 213
Foula, 188, 189, 190, 234n.13
François, Michel ("Sweet Mickey"), 80, 165
Fraph, 165, 173, 211, 213, 232n.8
"Fre Dieuvè Pa'p Mande Prete" (Brother Dieuvè Will Not Be Asking to Borrow This Year; track 8), 144
"Fre Dieuvè Pa'p Mande Prete" (orchestral version; track 9), 144

French culture, 77
Fugees, The, 194, 234n.29
fwomaj (cheese; slang term for symptoms of sexually transmitted disease), 72, 213

Gaga festival (Dominican Republic), 220n.20
gagann (a physical competition), 50, 155
Gates, Henry Louis, Jr., 167
gay men, 75, 76–77, 214
Gede, Papa, 60–61, 119
Gede spirits, 29, 60–61, 73, 91, 213
Geffrard, Nicolas, 141
gender: and *ti nèg*, 67–70; and work, 33, 89–91, 224n.6
Gerard, General/President, 108, 147, 153–55
Gillis, Verna, 31, 55; *Rara* (film), 21
Gilman, Sander, 118
Gilroy, Paul, 4, 205
Ginen, 87–88, 106, 128, 213
Glick Schiller, Nina, 187, 199–200
Godo (Patrick Pascale), 233n.12
gogo (a dance), 49
Goman, 141
gouyad (a dance), 26, 73, 88–89, 213
Governor's Island Agreement (1993), 211
graj (an instrument), 47, 213
Gran Mèt (God), 213
Grann Seli, 91
Gray, William, III, 211
green cards, 189
"Grenn zaboka sevi zòriye anba l'acha'w—aswè-a m'p'ap dòmi—Yas!—yas Maman!" (An avocado seed will be your pillow tonight—I won't be sleeping—Hey—Hey Mama!), 194–95
grotesque body, 15
"Guantanamo M'Rive" (I Ended Up in Guantanamo; track 17), 41–42
Guantanamo refugee camps, 166–67, 211
gwo bon anj (good big angel), 103–4, 214
gwo nèg (big man), 15–16, 67, 142–43, 214
Gwoup Sa, 188

Haile Selassie I, emperor of Ethiopia, 192
hairstyles, 191, 192–93
Haiti: democracy in, 5; history of, 10–14; independence/militarism of, 11, 140, *158*, 175, 201–2; literacy in, 11; names of, 4, 217n.4; politics of brutality in, 19; slave revolution in, 204
Haitian nationalism, 204–6
Halaou, 141
Hall, Stuart, 187, 195–96
Hannerz, Ulf, 196, 235n.34
Hardin, Kris, 143
Hendrix, Jimi, 188
"Here are the people" slogan, 166
high vs. low culture, 15, 123, 127, 130
hip-hop, 7, 67, 73, 185, 191; and *rasin* culture, 194–95, 234n.29
Hobsbawm, E. J., 196
homosexuality, 64, 75, 76–77, 214, 223n.37
house, concept of, 29
Human Rights Watch/Americas, 12, 13
Hurbon, Laënnec, 127

Ile (house), 29
Inquisition, 118, 119, 131
insecurity. *See* political insecurity
"Instrumental Isolations" (track 4), 20
instruments, *38*, 44, 45, 46–47
invented tradition, 196
Israel, 132
Izmery, Antoine, 13, 211

Jamaica, 192, 193
Jamerican and Sha, 194
jazz, 7
Jazz des Jeunes, 166
Jean, Wyclef, 194–95, 234n.29
je'm ap gade (my eyes are watching), 172
Jérémain migrants, 40–41
Jesuits, 120. *See also* Catholic Church
Jesus, in Vodou, 128–29
Jew(s), 113–33; African ancestry of, 132; burning in effigy, 114, *115*, 116–21; conversion/expulsion of, 118–19, 131–32, 227n.12; demonization of, European tradition of, 113–14, 116–18, 126, 132, 226n.1, 227n.9, 227n.18; Haitian images of, 130–31; historical presence in Haiti, 131–32; Rara's identification with, 113, 124–30, 228nn.39–40; and Vodou as Satanic cult, in Catholic imaginary, 121–24, 126
Jonkonnu, 7
Judas, 116–18, 126, 227n.9
Judensau, 119
jwif (Jew). *See* Jews
Jwif, Papa, 130

kaka (shit), 80
"Kalfou" (track 18), 231n.36
"Kalfou Danjere" (Dangerous Crossroads), 93, 210
kalinda (a dance), 49
Kanep, General, 27–28, 37, 39, 152
Kanpesh, 212
Kapitèn La Kwa, 91
Kapitèn Zonbi, 91
kasik (legendary Haitian Indian king), 55
Kassav, 195
kata drum, 45
Kat Sèkèy (Four Coffins), 39
kay (house), 29, 214
"Kay Ile" (The House of Ile; track 3), 29
Kenskoff (Haiti), 27
Kertzer, David, 177–78
kès drum, 45, 214
KiKongo language, 87, 224n.4
kilòt (underpants), 62, 214
kilti libète (freedom culture), 188
King Posse, 194
kings *(wa)*, 29–30, 45, 84
Kingston (Jamaica), 198
klere bouk sentiwon (a dance), 49
kleren (cane liquor), 30, 214
klewon (an instrument), 214
koko (vagina), 74, 214
kole (slow dancing), 49
kolonèl (colonels), 30, 138, 141–42, 153, *197*, 214
konbit (work brigades), 46, 49, 214
konè (an instrument), *38*, 46, 214
Kongo, 87, 97, 100–102, 104, 110, 224n.4
konpa dirèk (pop music), 48–49, 61–62, 195, 214
kontra-a (a contract), 220n.20
kontredans (a dance), 49

kote moun yo (where are the people),
172
"Kote Moun Yo? Mwen Pa Wè Moun
Yo" (Where are the people? I haven't
seen the people), 166–67
Koudjay, 81, 209, 212
kou'd le ("hit of bad air"), 214
kou'd poud ("hit of powder"), 214
kraze Rara (crash the Rara), 148, 153–
54, 214
krèk (clitoris), 74, 214
Kreyòl (Haitian Creole), 22–23, 160,
180, 194, 235n.39
"Kwiy Nan Men, M'ap . . . al Roule
Tete" (track 6), 62, 69–70, 223n.26

Lafontant, Roger, 81, 172, 186, 209,
210
lage kò-w (let go of yourself), 50
Laguerre, Michel, 139–40
Lakay, Konbit, 156
lakou (extended family compound),
89, 214, 224n.6
Lakou Souvenance (central Haiti), 2
lanbi (an instrument), 46, 214
land ownership, 138
langèt (clitoris), 74, 214
language, 169–70. *See also* Kreyòl
Lavalas (the Flood), 169, 206, 214
Legba, 92, 97
Lenten *ekzèsis* (exercises), 39–43
Léogâne (Haiti), 148, 231n.36
lesbians. *See madivin*
lese frape (let hit), 50, 214
literacy, 66–67
Loker, Zvi, 131
Lòlò (Theodore Beaubrun, Jr.),
233n.12
lòt bò dlo (the other side of the water), 214
loud-talking, 167–68
Louima, Abner, 186
Louis XIV, king of France, 120
low vs. high culture. *See* high vs. low
culture
Lucifer, 129
Lukumi, 229n.47
lwa (deities or spirits), 214; associated
with Rara bands, 88; engaging of, in
spiritual work, 33, 35–36, 86, 87,
98; and militarism/organization, 139–
40, 230n.13; ranks/militarization of,

91; Raras' contracts with, 35–37,
220n.20; *sèvi lwa,* 11
lwa pwen (spirit that is purchased, not
inherited), 214

Maccoby, Hyam, 227n.9
machann (market women), 138, 214
Madiou, Thomas, 141
madivin (lesbian), 64, 68, 75, 76–77,
214
magic: vs. Ginen, 87–88, 106, 128;
travay maji, 8; *wanga,* 44, 90, 215,
225n.19; in warfare, 152–55. See
also *pwen;* sorcery
maji (magic), 214. *See also* magic
majò jon (baton majors), 45, 214;
dance of, 52, 53, 54, 55; order of
appearance of, 138
Makandal, 121, 153, 204
makoutes. See tonton makoutes
Malval, Robert, 211
manbo (priestess), 90, 104, 105, 214,
225n.19
manbo asogwe (priestess holding the
rattle), 92
Mande Gran Moun (Ask the Elders),
139, 144, 146
Manley, Michael, 193
manman (mother), 214
manman drum, 45, 214
mapou tree, 2
Mardi Gras, 214
mare lapli (tie up the rain), 37
marenn (godmother), 214
mariaj Rara (Rara marriage), 153, 214
Market Day for Ti André, 217n.9
Marley, Bob, 33, 169, 188, 193–94
marriage, 67–68, 222n.18
Martely, Michel ("Sweet Mickey"),
80
masisi (gay men), 75, 76–77, 214
Maskawon rhythm, 45, 47
Masonic ceremonies, 33
mayomberos (Kongo-Cuban priests),
100–102, 214
mazoun (a dance), 30
Mbembe, Achille, 60, 78–79, 80, 162
"*Men anpil chay pa lou*" ("With many
hands, the burden is not heavy"),
168
merengue (dance music), 61–62
mèt (owner), 214

mete nanm nan boutèy (putting the soul in a bottle), 104

Mèt Kalfou (Master Crossroads), 88, 92–93, 97

Mèt Minwi, 91

militarism/organization, 51–52, 135–57; "big man-ism," 142–43; and financing, 143–44; grassroots peasant organizations, 136, 141–42, 157, 229n.2, 230n.22; and Haitian independence, 140; hierarchies/titles of, 137–38, 139–40, 144, 156–57, 230n.11; and *lwa*, 139–40, 230n.13; and magical warfare, 152–55; and mistrust/plots, themes of, 150–51; and musical competition, 148, 151, 153, 231n.36; and naming of bands, 139; and origins of Rara, 141; and patronage, 136, 144–48, 156–57; and physical fighting, 148, 151–52, 155–56; president of a Rara, 143–44, 150; Raras' relation to other military hierarchies, 138–40, 229n.8, 230n.11; and regimental music corps, 140; vs. royal imagery, 136–37; and rules/regulations, 147–48; and U.S. occupation of Haiti, 141–42, 230n.22

Mirville, Ernst, 155

mistrust/plots, themes of, 150–51

mizik rasin movement. See *rasin* culture

Modèl, 75, 150

Moral, Paul, 139

Moriset, Moris, 92

Morse, Richard, 167, 171

Moses, 131, 132

Moun Ife, 188

moun sa yo (those people), 171, 172–73

mouvman Rara (Rara movement), 214

Mouvman Rasta Faray Ayisyen (Haitian Rastafari Movement), 193–94

"M'Pap Mache a Tè" (I Don't Walk on the Ground; track 15), 28, 66

M.P.P. (Peasant Movement of Papay), 229n.2

music, 44–48; hocketing, 19, 46; instruments, 38, 44, 45, 46–47; and *lwa*'s presence, 45; military ethos in, 51–52 (*see also* militarism/organization); orchestras, 44–45; *rasin*, 188–91, 212, 233n.12; regional styles, 45–46; rhythms, 45, 47; *sanba*, 47–48, 64; sexual (see *betiz;* vulgarity and the politics of the small man); *simidò*, 47; singers/performers, 45, 47; tonalities, 47. *See also* songs

mwen pa moun isit (I'm not from around here), 172

Mystere de la Passion, Le, 118–19

Mystery Plays. See Passion Plays

mystical work. See spiritual work

Nago (Yoruba nation in Vodou), 214

Namphi, Henri, 165

nanm (soul), 103–4

"Nanm Nan Boutèy" (Soul in a bottle), 107

National Coalition for Haitian Refugees, 13

nationalism, 204–6

Native Americans, colonial domination of, 119

Nazon rhythm, 45, 47

nèg (black man), 214

Neptune, The (ship), 40–41

New Orleans parades, 7

New York City, Haitian presence in, 184, 194, 199–200, 233n.1, 235n.39

New York City, Rara in, *182, 183*–207; emergence of, 4–5, 184–85; and Haitian women, status of, 189; as invented tradition, 196; men's/women's roles in, 185; and roots identity, 198–202; secularism of, 185, 188–92; and transnationalism, 187–95. See also *rasin* culture

nkisi (a container of spirit), 104–5, 226n.38

non pwen (nickname), 214

Nunn, Sam, 212

OAS (Organization of American States), 210

ochan (a musical salute), 43, 44, 45, 51–52, 140–41, 214

ogan (an instrument), 47, 214

Ogou (god of war), 175–76, 214, 230n.13

Oloffson Hotel (Haiti), 224n.48

"Oman an hood never quarrel" ("Woman and wood never quarrel"), 69 organization. *See* militarism/organization

Organization of American States (OAS), 210

Original Raps Stars, 194

"*Ou al nan Rara, se Jwif ou ye*" ("If you go in the Rara, you are a Jew"), 125–26

ounfò (religious house), 214

oungan (priest), 33, 90, 104, 105, 214, 225n.19

oungan asogwe (priest holding the rattle), 92

ounsi (religious society members), 47, 214

"Pa Gen Fanm Konfyans" (There Are No Trustworthy Women; track 12), 64–65, 145–46, 220n.27

palaso (a dance), 49

Palo Monte, 229n.48

parenn (godfather), 214

Paris, 197–98

Passion Plays (Mystery Plays), 118–19, 123–24, 126

patronage, 136, 144–48, 156–57

"Pa Vle Zenglendo" (We Don't Want Criminals; track 13), 176–77, 190, 209

peasant movement, 136, 141–42, 157, 162, 229n.2, 230n.22

peristil (religious dance space), 49, 51, 214

Petwo, 75, 87, 88–89, 97, 110, 214

Petwo-Bizango protection ceremony, 93, 94, 95–97

peye sòti ("pay to go"), 214

Pike La Kwa, 91

pilgrimages, 36–37

Piquets du Sud, 141

play. *See* work: vs. play

plays, 32–33

Plaza Hotel (Haiti), 224n.48

ploge (slow dancing), 49

poisons, 153

political events, chronology of, 209–12

political insecurity, 159–81; causes of, 161; and class/poverty, 161, 165–66, 177–80; cultural setting of, 163, 164, 165–67; and metaphoric speech, 161–62, 180 (see also *pwen*);

and Rara armies perceived as mobs, 177–80

politics. *See* vulgarity and the politics of the small man

Port-au-Prince (Haiti), 197–98

pòt drapo (flag bearer), 137, 138, 214

poto mitan (ritual centerpost), 214

poud (powders), 153–55

pou plezi (a dance), 49, 56–57, 214

poverty, and political insecurity, 161, 165–66

powders, 153–55

Powell, Colin, 212

pran ason (taking the sacred rattle), 92

pran yon roulib (take a ride in), 6, 217n.9

prenda (a vessel for spirit of recently dead person), 101

priestesses. See *manbo*

priests. See *oungan*

processions, 3, 5–6

promesa (private deal made with Catholic saints), 220n.20

prostitution, 213; and public singing, 90–91, 224n.11; theme of, 64, 67, 68–69, 72

Protestantism and Vodou, 109–10

pwazon (poisons), 153

pwèl (pubic hair), 62, 214

pwen (points), 167–77; "becoming" of, 174–77; *chante pwen,* 213; engaging of, in spiritual work, 33, 35–36, 86, 87, 98; as magic/communication, 167–68, 180; meaning of, 121, 167, 214; as passwords, 169–70, 176; Rara use of, 170–74; *voye pwen,* 42–43, 48, 168, 215

queens *(renn),* 24, 29, 30, 33, 45; *banda* danced by, 89; spiritual work of, 33, 84, 90, 91; vulgar singing/ dancing by, 58, 62

Raboday rhythm, 45, 47

racializations/racisms, 188, 233n.10

Rada, 87, 97

RAM, 166–67, 173–74, 210–11, 212

Ranger, T. O., 196

rap music, 73

Rara (film; Gillis), 21

Rara Djakout (New York City), 190, 198, 209

Rara festivals/bands, 3–10, *112;* all-night quality of, 33; as anti-Christian, 129–30, 229n.47; carnivalesque/play aspects of, 31–33, 43–44, 56–57 (*see also* vulgarity and the politics of the small man); cast of characters in, 3; contributions to bands, 42, 44; historical content of, 3–4; histories/songs/stories of, 39; in mass demonstrations, 185–86, 233n.3; media coverage of, 5, 6; in New York City, 4–5 (*see also* New York City, Rara in); as ongoing, 21–22; as peasant festival, 3, 4, 110; performative orality of, 7–8; *pran yon roulib,* 6, 217n.9; religious aspects of, 7–8, 31, 88, 110 (*see also* cemetery/crossroads, spiritual work at; spiritual work); religious/political tensions during, 4; repression of/violence toward, 9, 12–13, 175–76 (*see also* political insecurity); sources of, 55; starting a band, 34–37, 220n.20; as transitional Black Atlantic culture, 16
Rara Inorab Kapab (Cité Soleil), 210
Rara La Fleur Ginen, 93, *94,* 95–97, 105
Rara La Reine (The Queen's Rara), 155
Rara Nèg Gran Bwa (New York City), 202, 205, 206, 209
Rara Nou Vodoule (Port-au-Prince), 176–77, 190, 198, 209, 212
Rara Rosalie, 156
Rara Rosignol, 156
Rara Saint Rose, 156
Rara Ya Sezi (Rara They Will Be Surprised), 124, 125, 145
rasin culture, 214; and African nationalism, 205; blackness in, definitions of, 202–4, 236n.48; as a creolization, 195–98; and Haitian nationalism, 204–6; and hip-hop, 194–95, 234n.29; music, 188–91, 212, 233n.12; and Rastafari, 192–95, 198; style, 191–92; and zouk, 195, 198
Rastafari, 169, 192–95, 198
Rasta Sanba Ginen, 193
Reagon, Bernice Johnson, 19–20, 178
recordings, 14, 19–21, 38
reggae, 7, 192, 194, 195

regimental music corps, 140
regleman (rule), 92, 214
Regnault, Chantal, 18
rehearsals, 39–43, 214
Reisman, Karl, 56
reklamasyon (individual people serving the spirits), 35, 214
religious ritual, 43, 44
renn (queen), 214. *See also* queens
repetisyon (rehearsal), 39–43, 214
repression, 82
reputation, 15–16, 32, 34
Revolution (Boukman Eksperyans), 234n.29
Richman, Karen, 108, 168
Roach, Joseph, 4
Robinson, Randall, 211
Romain, Pierre Isnard, 34–35
roots (a style of dress), 191
roots identity, 198–202
Rose, Tricia, 73
Rosenberg, June, 220n.20
Roumer, Thérèse, 116

Saint-Domingue, 120–21, 131, 140
Salnave, Sylvain, 141
salsa (dance music), 61–62
salt, use of, 193
Sam, Vilbrun Guillaume, 141, 179
sanba (musical leader), 47–48, 64, 191, 214
Sanbaje, 233n.12
"Sanba, sa fè'm mal O" (Sanba, that hurt me, Oh), 48
Sanba-Yo, 188, 189, 190, 234n.13
Sansone, Livio, 235n.34
Santana, Carlos, 188
scatological humor, 80–82
Scott, James C., 16, 61, 79, 161, 162, 166, 177
Seabrook, William, 116–17, 179
Seaga, Edward, 193
segon drum, 45, 214
sèvi lwa (serve the spirit), 11
sexual explicitness. *See* vulgarity and the politics of the small man
sexual unions, 67–68, 222n.18
Sicot, Weber, 82
signifying, 42, 167–68
Simbi an Dezo (Simbi of the Two Waters), 37, 39, 43
Simbi Ganga, 224n.4

Simbi Makaya, 88
simidò (songwriter), 47, 214
Siryen ("Syrian" Jews), 132
skulls, use of, 104, 105, 106, 226n.36
slackness, 63–64, 193
slavery, 104; and forced conversion by
  French Catholics, 10; Haitian slave
  revolution, 204; memory/reenact-
  ment of, 86–87, 91, 103, 107, 108–
  9; slave-owning by the Church, 120;
  on sugar/coffee plantations, 10
slums, 150
small man *(ti nèg)*. *See* vulgarity and
  the politics of the small man
Sò An (Annette August), 233n.12
soca (dance music), 61–62
Sodo (a national event), 214–15
"Sodo m'prale" (I'm going to the Vodou pilgrimage), 175
Soley Leve (The Sun is Rising), 229n.2
songs: events addressed in, 40–42; as
  historical/social texts, 14–15; obscene, carnivalesque, 7, 9; for Ogou,
  175–76; phrases/themes in, 171–72;
  sexual (see *betiz;* vulgarity and the
  politics of the small man); Vodou, 7,
  8; *voye pwen* style, 42–43, 48
sorcery, 33, 90, 106, 120–21, 213. *See
  also* magic
sosyete (a religious society), 215
sosyete travay (work cooperatives),
  138–39, 229n.8, 230n.11
sòti (nightly outing), 40, 215
soul, 103–4
Soulouque, Emperor, 233n.27
spirit possession, 225n.34
spiritual work: Afro-Haitian religious
  foundations of, 86–89, 97, 110; engaging *lwa, zonbi,* and *pwen,* 33, 35–
  36, 86, 87, 98; of kings and queens
  dancing at a tomb, *84;* ritual sweeping, 100, 102; and slavery, memory/
  reenactment of, 86–87, 91, 103,
  107, 108–9 (see also *zonbi);* supernatural energy, infusing group with,
  86–87; types of, 90; warfare/espio-
  nage, spiritual, 100–102; work/
  gender, 33, 89–91, 224n.6. *See also*
  cemetery/crossroads, spiritual work
  at
Stallybrass, Peter, 15, 123
St. Surin, Lyonel, 55

superstition, campaigns against, 171–
  72
sweeping, ritual, 100, 102
Szanton Blanc, Cristina, 187
Szwed, John, 31–32, 33, 56, 219n.7

Taino people, 96, 225n.19
tanbou a liy (an instrument), 95, 215
tchancy (an instrument), 47
tcha-tcha (an instrument), 47, 215
teledjòl (word of mouth), 215
tèt kole (cheek-to-cheek dancing), 49
Tèt Kole (Heads Together), 229n.2
theory/methodology, 14–19
Thompson, Robert Farris, 46, 105
Ti Aiyti (Little Haiti), 18
ti bon anj (good little angel), 103, 215
Tido (Wilfred Laveaud), 233n.12
Ti-Jan Dantò, 37, 39
Ti-Jan Petwo, 88
Ti-Malis, 23, 148
timbale drum, 215
ti nèg (small man), 215. *See also* vulgarity and the politics of the small
  man
ti Rara naïf (little naive Rara), 34
Ti-Simone, 82
tonton makoutes, 12, 13, 163, 165,
  175, 176, 215, 225n.22
Toulabor, C., 169
Trachtenberg, Joshua, 118, 126
transmigrants/transnationalism, 16, 18,
  185, 186, 187–95. *See also* New
  York City, Rara in
transvestitism, 75, 223n.37
travay (work), 215, 219n.13. *See also*
  work: vs. play
travay maji (magical work), 8
Trinidad Carnival Devil Band, 151
Trouillot, Ertha Pascal, 39, 81, 209
Trouillot, Michel-Rolph, 11, 79, 140,
  142, 163
Troupe Makandal, La, 17–18
Tsing, Anna Lowenhaupt, 22

unemployment, 187
United States: as cultural center, 196;
  occupation of Haiti by, 141–42,
  160, 179, 230n.22
United States Information Service, 179–
  80

vagina, as beautiful, 74
vakabondaj (vagabondage), 215
vaksin (an instrument), *38,* 45, 46, 47, 213, 215, 220n.30
"Vaksinen" (Vaccinate), 189, 234n.13
Vapeur Vin Pou Wè, 147
vèvè (cornmeal drawings), 93, 95, 97, 215, 225n.18
Victor, Saint, 91
Vivien, Fito, 189–90
Vodou: and Catholicism, 110; Christ in, 128–29; definition of, 215; and Ginen vs. magic, 87–88, 106; Gran Mètla (God) of, 10; hypersexualization of, 60 (*see also* vulgarity and the politics of the small man); initiation into priesthood of, 92; Lucifer in, 129; Moses in, 131; and Protestantism, 109–10; as Satanic cult, in Catholic imaginary, 121–24, 126; sources of, 10; spirit work of, 11–12
Vodouisant (Vodou practitioner), 215
Voodoo Jazz, 188
voye pwen (sending a point) style, 42–43, 48, 168, 215
VSN (Volontaire de la Securité Nationale). See *tonton makoutes*
vulgarity and the politics of the small man, 15–16, 59–83; and adultery, theme of, 64, 66, 67–68; and AIDS, theme of, 77–78; *betiz* and absurd vulgarity, 59–67, 68–69, 74, 77, 78, 80, 82–83; and class/elite consumption, 78–82, 224n.48; and clitoris/beautiful vagina, 74; and domestic/national politics, 63–67; gender and *ti nèg,* 67–70; and homosexuality, theme of, 75–77, 223n.37; and prostitution, theme of, 64, 67, 68–69, 72; and repression, 82; and *sanba,* 64; and satirization of Catholicism, 63; and slackness, 63–64; and women's voices, 71–73

wa (king), 215. *See also* kings
wakes, 33
Wallerstein, Immanuel, 187
wanga (magical works), 44, 90, 215, 225n.19

warfare/espionage, spiritual, 100–102
War of Haitian Independence, 201–2
Washington Accord (1992), 210
whips, use of, 108
White, Allon, 15, 123
"whores" (Kreyòl meaning of), 66–67
Wilcken, Lois, 18
women: domestic rule by, 67, 89; genitalia of, as beautiful, 74; Haitian, in New York City, 185, 189; voices of, 71–73; work by, 224n.6. *See also* queens
work: and class, 90; and gender, 33, 89–91, 224n.6; and *lakou,* 89, 224n.6; vs. play, 31–32, 43–44, 56–57, 219n.7, 219n.13
World Bank, 13
world systems, 187
wozèt (strangling), 50, 155

Yanba Ye, 190–91
Yih, David, 51, 140, 150, 171–72
Yonker, Dolores, 137, 147, 220n.27
Yoruba people, 142, 143, 154, 214

zam kongo (Kongo weapons), 153, 215
Zawo, Sanba, 233n.12
zemi stone (a Taino sacred object), 96, 225n.19
zenglendo (type of criminal), 176–77, 215, 233n.27
Zenglens, 233n.27
zing (person who wears locked hair from birth), 193
zombies, 226n.50
zonbi (the recently dead), 91; in Afro-Haitian religious complex, 102–9, 225n.29, 226n.50; capturing of, 98–102, 225n.22, 225n.26; Christ as, 128, 129; definition of, 215; engaging of, in spiritual work, 33, 35–36, 86, 87, 98; Protestant, 109–10; ranks of, 139; salt eschewed by, 193
zopope (a dance), 212
zouk (dance music), 61–62, 195, 198, 215
zozo (penis), 215

Text:	10/13 Sabon
Display:	Truth
Designer:	Sandy Drooker
Compositor:	Binghamton Valley Composition
Printer and binder:	Edwards Brothers
Indexer:	Carol Roberts